Judy.

Christmas 1992 Barbados

love S.

PROVENCE
and the Côte d'Azur

Other books by James Bentley

Albert Schweitzer
Alsace
Bavaria
Between Marx and Christ
The Blue Guide to West Germany and Berlin
A Calendar of Saints
Castile
A Children's Bible
Dare to be wise: A History of the Manchester Grammar School
The Gateway to France
A Guide to the Dordogne
A Guide to Tuscany
Italy: the Hilltowns
Languedoc
Life and Food in the Dordogne
The Loire
Martin Niemöller
Normandy
Oberammergau and the Passion Play
The Rhine
Ritualism and Politics in Victorian Britain
Rome
Secrets of Mount Sinai
Umbria
Weekend Cities

PROVENCE
and the Côte d'Azur

James Bentley

AURUM PRESS

For Emma-Jane

First published 1992 by Aurum Press Limited,
10 Museum Street, London WC1A 1JS
Copyright © 1992 by James Bentley

Map by Chartwell
Decorative illustration by Joy FitzSimmons

British Library Cataloguing in Publication Data

Bentley, James *1937* –
Provence and the Côte d'Azur.
1. France. Côte d'Azur & Provence –
Visitors' guides
I. Title
914.4904838

ISBN 1 85410 190 0

1 3 5 7 9 10 8 6 4 2
1993 1995 1996 1994 1992

Typeset by Action Typesetting Limited, Gloucester
Printed in Great Britain by Hartnolls Ltd, Bodmin

Contents

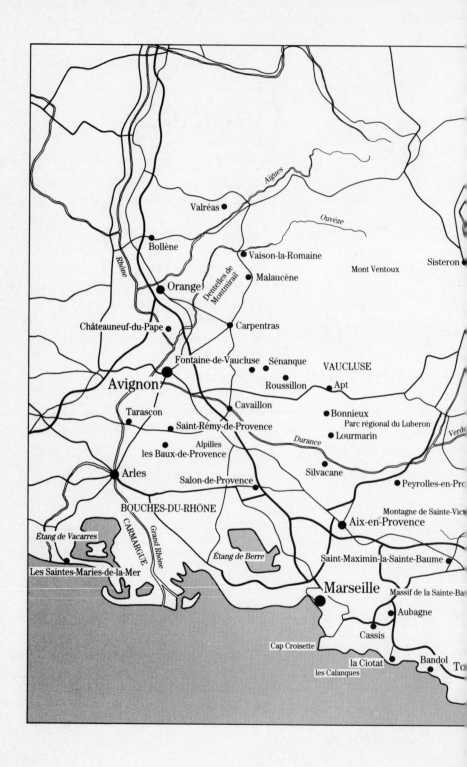

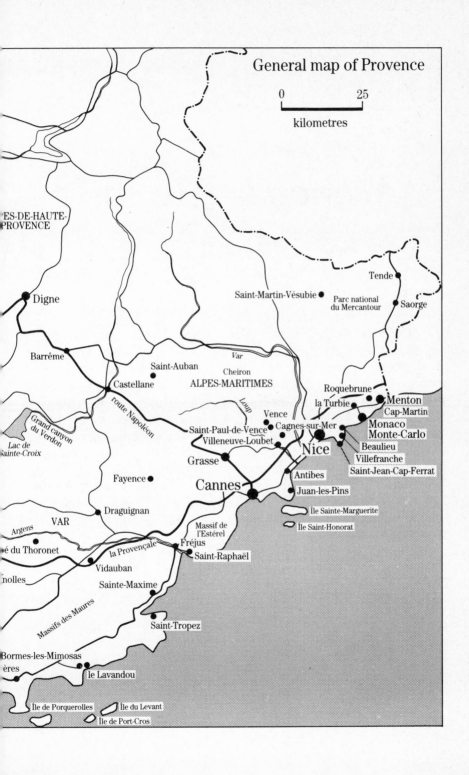

General map of Provence

0   25
kilometres

ES-DE-HAUTE-
PROVENCE

Digne

Tende

Saint-Martin-Vésubie   Parc national   Saorge
                         du Mercantour

Barrême

Saint-Auban   Cheiron
                 ALPES-MARITIMES

Castellane   Var   Roquebrune
                                                                la Turbie   Menton
route Napoléon   Cap-Martin
Grand canyon   Loup   Vence   Monaco
du Verdon   Monte-Carlo
Lac de   Saint-Paul-de-Vence Cagnes-sur-Mer   Beaulieu
Sainte-Croix   Villeneuve-Loubet   Villefranche
                                               Nice   Saint-Jean-Cap-Ferrat
                    Grasse
        Fayence
                                               Antibes
                    Cannes   Juan-les-Pins

                                               Île Sainte-Marguerite
        Draguignan   Île Saint-Honorat
Argens   VAR   Massif de
é du Thoronet   l'Estérel
nolles   la Provençale Fréjus
            Vidauban   Saint-Raphaël

            Sainte-Maxime

                    Saint-Tropez

Bormes-les-Mimosas
ères   le Lavandou

    Île de Porquerolles   Île du Levant
                    Île de Port-Cros

Acknowledgments

There are many people to whom I am deeply grateful. They include M. Pierre Gouriand and M. Claude Suard of the Hotel Westminster-Concorde, Nice; Mme Armelle Ganancia, Manager of the Hotel Univers, Cannes; Mme Michèle Bosq, Director of Promotion, Direction Générale du Tourisme et des Congrès, Cannes; her colleague Mme Martine van Damme; Mme Véronique Seban, Chef de Marché of the Comité régional du tourisme, Nice; Mme Colette d'Haenne and M. Contorson of the Hotel Cavendish, Cannes; and Mrs Pauline Hallam, Public Relations Director of the French Government Tourist Board, London. I am also grateful to David Oliver, Sales Manager of Dan-Air, and for the regular scheduled flights which his airline makes to Nice.

Above all, I must thank my daughter Emma-Jane, who researched the whole book with me, did half the work and doubled the fun.

Preface

Provence is unique, strange and enticing. Trying to define exactly why, the novelist Alphonse Daudet essayed that 'The south is homely and traditional, with something of the east in its clannish and tribal faithfulness, its taste for sweet dishes and its incurable contempt for women – which does not, however, prevent passion and voluptuousness from being carried to a frenzy.' The south, he continued, 'superstitious and idolatrous, yet ever-ready to forget the gods, at the first threat of illness or misfortune remembers the prayers of its childhood'.

Among all his works his own favourite was the long-forgotten novel *Numa Roumestan*, in which Numa's native town, Aps in Provence, Daudet revealed that he had:

constructed with bits of Arles, Nîmes, Saint-Rémy-de-Provence and Cavaillon, borrowing from one its arenas, from another its ancient Italian side-streets, narrow and pebbled like the dry beds of torrents, from a third its Monday markets held under the huge plane trees of the ramparts: the whole taking hither and thither those white Provençal roads, bordered by lofty reeds, white as snow and crackling with hot dust, over which I would run at the age of twenty wrapped in my great woollen cape.

This was a powerful mixture.

Paul Cézanne was another whose testimony to the superlative

beauty of Provence cannot be ignored. Out of ill-health, and also to please his wife, he had spent some time on the exquisite shores of the lake of Annecy in Haute-Savoie; but from there he wrote to one of his Provençal friends, 'Of course it is all right, but in no way can it compare with our own part of the country. If you have been born *there*, there is nothing else, simply no other place for you.'

Provence is where you cross the thrilling Grand Rhône and spot the Petit Rhône gliding between its green banks. Feudal châteaux rise amid olives. The ramparts of medieval villages speak of past battles and terrors. Churches dedicated to St Roch remain from plague years when recourse to this saint was the sole hope of survival. Poplars lean at the side of straight Roman roads. The *belle époque* lives on at Cannes and Nice. Mountains and restaurants seem strangely familiar, caught by the brushes of Paul Cézanne, Raoul Dufy and Vincent Van Gogh.

Provence is also a prodigiously varied region. It comprises five *départements:* the Var, the Alpes-Maritimes, the Alpes-de-Haute-Provence, the Bouches-du-Rhône and the Vaucluse. The Var is a region of oak and pine forests, bordered to the north-east by the pre-Alps. Olives grow on sunny slopes, and two great massifs, the Estérel and the Maures, add to its convoluted geology. In addition its coastline, which includes Saint-Tropez and the naval town of Toulon, is the warmest in the whole of France.

The aspect of the Alpes-Maritimes is similarly diverse, the Mercantour massif with its enthralling natural park rising to 3,000 metres, while other parts of the *département* are fissured with deep gorges. Alongside these sometimes remotely savage regions is a littoral that includes such delicious confections as Nice and Cannes, as well as the principality of Monaco.

In the Alpes-de-Haute-Provence one explores mountainous border country, with Sisteron the gateway to the Dauphiné. Here at Seyne and Entrevaux the military engineer Vauban was commanded to build defensive fortresses for his master Louis XIV. For centuries roads were sparse and ill-constructed, and communications difficult. Only in the twentieth century have towns such as Castellane taken on new roles as the hub of tourism and winter sports. Only today have visitors from the outside world at last come to relish at Castellane its ruined château, its twelfth-century priory, its Romanesque-Gothic parish church and the early eighteenth-century chapel, which seems ever likely to plunge from the rock on which it perches.

By contrast the Bouches-du-Rhône is blessed with three urban centres that are the envy of France. Arles is a quintessential Roman foundation that has adapted to the modern world without losing any of its ancient character. Aix-en-Provence is an irresistible seventeenth-century and eighteenth-century city, while Marseille has become a fantastic blend of the past and a teeming, rollicking modern port.

Save for stupendous Avignon, for Carpentras, Vaison-la-Romaine and Orange, the Vaucluse is the least-known, most secretive of the five *départements*, and for that reason possibly the most rewarding. Its natural glory is the sometimes charming, sometimes savage Mont Ventoux.

These varied qualities are mirrored again and again in Provence, sometimes in miniature, sometimes in breathtaking arrogance. At Fréjus, for example, the Roman remains, though stupendous for such an unassuming city, are matched by a complex of ecclesiastical buildings virtually unrivalled in their sober Romanesque beauty and historical fascination. The vallée des Merveilles, in the Alpes-Maritimes some twelve kilometres outside Tende, has over 100,000 rock engravings, which were etched between 2,500 and 1,500 BC. A reminder of the rich history of Provence, they visibly take the visitor back in time beyond the Romans and their predecessors – the Ligurians, Celts and Greeks – who inhabited these villages, towns, pastures and mountain ranges.

Yet some of the most attractive towns and cities of Provence and the Côte d'Azur achieved their present luscious selves a good 4,000 years later. Cannes transformed itself from a tiny village into a haven of sophisticated decadence only in the nineteenth century. Monte-Carlo was created even later. The casinos that are today a central feature of the Côte d'Azur are another nineteenth-century invention, established for the beau monde who had just begun to flock to Provence. Today we can choose to visit those parts that were once the haunt of kings, or the regions that are still the haunt of eagles.

The convolutions of the land also mean that even a few metres inland villages perch perilously on crags and the crests of hills, their walls sometimes overlooking a sheer drop to the sea. Often fortified in the past, many have now been beautifully restored.

Traditional crafts have been revived, but the boutiques lining labyrinthine streets have not destroyed the ancient beauty of these spots. The heroine of F. Scott Fitzgerald's *Tender is the Night* (a novel published in 1934) evinced the same delight in these hill villages and towns as we do today. 'Along the walls on the village side all was dusty, the wriggling vines, the lemon and eucalyptus trees, the casual wheel-barrow, left only a moment since, but already grown into the patch, atrophied and faintly rotten,' wrote Fitzgerald. 'Nicole was invariably somewhat surprised that by turning in the other direction past a bed of peonies she walked into an area so green and cool that the leaves and petals were curled with tender damp.' In these villages and towns, fountains tinkle and the bowls of the *pétanque* pitches clink.

The peonies and vines evoked by Fitzgerald scarcely do justice to the extraordinarily rich flora of this region. Tobias Smollett, who introduced the British to the Côte d'Azur in the late eighteenth century, looked on Nice from its rampart and observed that it was cultivated like a garden. 'Indeed the plain presents nothing but gardens, full of green trees, loaded with oranges, lemons, citrons, and bergamots, which make a delightful appearance,' he wrote in 1766. 'If you examine them more nearly, you will find plantations of green pease ready to gather; all sorts of sallading, and pot herbs in perfection; and plats of roses, carnations, ranunculas, anemonies, and daffodils, blowing in full glory, with such beauty, vigour and perfume, as no flower in England ever exhibited.' What he described is today matched by a host of exotic plants in this most southerly region of France.

Such charm, as well as the clear light of Provence, has attracted countless artists to the region, so that now innumerable museums are crammed with sublime reproductions, filtered through artists' eyes, of what we ourselves are enjoying there. And in its gardens, as in its architecture and food, the influence of Italy is never far away. For the English author and journalist Cyril Connolly the white sand of la Garoupe, the pale translucent water, the cicadas jigging away at their perpetual rumba, the smell of rosemary and cistus, the corrugations of sunshine on the bright Aleppo pines held the whole classic essence of the Mediterranean.

Yet ultimately the essence of Provence is neither Italian nor French. Provence cherishes its own culture and its own language. Both manifest themselves in its food and the singular lore of its food. *Aigo boulido*, for instance, which is a richly spiced sage soup, has given us the Provençal proverb 'L'aigo boulido sauvo la vido' (which means 'sage soup preserves your life'). Richly varied, garlic-garnished meals inevitably proliferate in this book. Small wonder that a village in Provence was the birthplace of the famous chef Auguste Escoffier.

By means of tours – tours of great cities, of mountain ranges, of small towns, of hill villages and of the superb littoral – my book attempts to encompass the glamour, the culture, the history and the sometimes coquettish, sometimes austere beauty of this region. I have tried to evoke the essence of Provence and the Côte d'Azur as it appears to me today. And into these tours I have also inserted the stories of the men and women of the past – travellers, artists, soldiers, statesmen, clerics, courtesans, knaves and writers – who, like me, have relished this unique part of France.

James Bentley
JULY 1991

Papal splendour
and Roman grandeur

In a celebratedly malicious portrait of Avignon, Lawrence Durrell observed in 1974 that 'Its shabby lights and sneaking cats were the same as ever', adding – for good measure – a further description of 'overturned dustbins, the glitter of fish scales, olive oil, broken glass, a dead scorpion'. Incredibly, he was describing a medieval city ringed with 4,300 metres of fourteenth-century walls with projecting turrets and battlements and, to my mind, one of the finest sights in the whole of Provence. These walls date from the fourteenth century, because an earlier ring had been demolished by the victorious Catholic King Louis VIII in the early thirteenth century, after the city had sided with the Albigensian heretics during the religious controversies which cast their bloody shadow over medieval Languedoc.

In the nineteenth century some of the citizens of Avignon were minded to tear them down again, as an incumbrance to the easy flow of traffic into their rapidly expanding city, but wiser counsels prevailed, and instead of destroying the venerable walls in 1860 they commissioned Viollet-le-duc to restore them. Today their golden walls gleam in the sun, powerfully buttressed and machicolated. When Charles Dickens first saw Avignon, one afternoon in the mid-nineteenth century, all the city was baking in the sun, yet to him the walls seemed, as they do now, like an underdone pie-crust that will never be brown, though it bake for centuries.

Even more famous than the walls is Avignon's truncated bridge, where, the nursery rhyme proclaims, 'On y danse tous en rond'. These dances took place not on the bridge (which is too narrow for anyone to dance *en rond*) but underneath it, on the Île de la Barthelasse, where the cock-fighting pits have been replaced by an Olympic-sized swimming pool. Jutting out into the River Rhône, this pont Saint-Bénézet stops abruptly in mid-stream, only four arches remaining from its original twenty-two. Built (or perhaps rebuilt) between 1177 and 1188 by the shepherd-saint Bénézet and his followers, destroyed in 1226 and then rebuilt, the bridge's second pier supports a curious Romanesque chapel dedicated to the patron of sailors, St Nicolas, which is well worth visiting. The bones of St Bénézet lay here until 1674. In the thirteenth century the chapel was given a second storey, and in 1513 was extended in the Gothic style. The powerful river swept the rest of the bridge away and, enfeebled by the ravages of the Black Death, the citizens did not have the heart to rebuild it. To cross the river nowadays you must use the suspension bridge further downstream.

East of this bridge rises the rocher des Doms, a rocky eminence which in its time supported Stone Age families and a Roman temple and today is cooled by the trees of a park. Drive through the porte du Rocher and you can park your car beneath the pedestrianized place du Palais. And in the square itself, on its 59-metre-high rock, rises the eight-towered Palace of the Popes.

The papacy transferred itself here from Rome in 1309. Clement V's predecessors had bought part of the Vaucluse known as the Comtat-Venaissin in 1274. As a Frenchman, Clement, a former Archbishop of Bordeaux, feared the power of his Italian rivals, was oppressed by the factionalism of Rome, threatened by the new Luxemburg Emperor Henry VII and felt infinitely safer at Avignon, which lies on the eastern bank of the Rhône close to Comtat. (Its name derives from the Roman *Avenio*, meaning city which dominates the river.) Clement also wished to be within easy reach of Vienne, where he had called a council to consider the accusations of corruption that had been made against the Knights Templar. He brought to Avignon his cardinals and his court. So this provincial town became the centre of Catholic Christendom.

This era is often dubbed the papal captivity, with the successors of St Peter in thrall to the Kings of France. Yet in spite of the pressures of the French monarchy (and the fact that all seven Avignon Popes were Frenchmen, as well as 111 of the 134 cardinals created during this time), the period of the Avignon papacy was a time of great creativity. Missionaries sent out from Avignon reached as far as China. The college of cardinals found a greater role for itself in governing the Catholic Church.

Although many cardinals detested the smells of the city and some of them found it far too debauched for their tastes, the Popes and their entourage built sumptuously, and next to the papal palace, on the north side of the square close to the porte du Rocher, stands an art gallery that once was the palace of Cardinal Béranger Frédol, built in 1317 and much restored in the fifteenth century. Cardinal Giuliano della Rovere, who was Archbishop of Avignon and later became Pope Julius II, transformed it in the 1480s into its present exotic state – an entrancing mix of stern medieval architecture softened by the Renaissance. In 1680 the architect François Royers de la Valfrenière enlarged it with two additional wings.

Known as the Petit Palais, since 1976 it has served as an exquisite centre of medieval and Renaissance art. Some of the earlier works are delicious (and the primitives here constitute the finest collection outside Italy), yet I find I prefer its later Italian masterpieces – especially works by Ghirlandaio and Carpaccio. The proximity of Provence to Italy is emphasized by the succession of Tuscan, Venetian and Roman works of art crammed into its rooms. And the crowds rightly press around Botticelli's 'Virgin and Child' – a portrait of a young mother sitting at a window, holding her chubby infant's head with one hand, while delicately pressing her breast with the other.

The Pope was content to live in the huge monastery of the Dominicans at Avignon. Soon his health deteriorated, and in the spring of 1314 he decided to seek solace in the clear air of his native Gascony. His train had scarcely crossed the Rhône when he died, at Roquemaure, on 6 April. A conclave met at nearby Carpentras to elect a new Pope. Factions developed, and only in 1316 did the conclave, by now transferred to Lyons, manage to agree on a new name, that of the aged Jacques Duèse, whom the cardinals hoped would soon die. He took the name of John XXII and lived for another eighteen years.

Pope John XXII had been Bishop of Avignon, and he began expanding the former palace in which he had lived. His ambitious plans were far exceeded by those of his successors. In the eight years following 1334 Pope Benedict XII (elected by a conclave that met at Avignon and made up its mind in a mere seven days) demolished the old palace and commissioned an architect named Pierre Poisson to begin building the half-citadel, half-palace in which he and his successors lived. Its chapel was consecrated in 1336. The vast palace embodied four towers, that of Saint-Jean (finished in 1338), of la Glacière (finished a year later), of la Campane (completed in 1340) and what remains one of the most impressive in Provence, the tour de Trouillas, begun in 1341 and finished six years later.

In the following decade Pope Clement VI (unquestionably the most glittering of all seven Avignon Popes, and who is reported to have said, 'My predecessors did not know how to be Popes') commissioned Jean de Louvres (or Jean de Loubières), a man of Provence, to build another palace next to that of Benedict XII. It included the tower of the Garde-Robe and the tour des Anges, and was in part decorated by the fresco-master Matteo Giovanetti, who came from Viterbo. The fourteenth-century chronicler Jean Froissart judged the whole ensemble to be the most beautiful and strongest home in the world. By contrast, Prosper Mérimée in the nineteenth century observed that it resembled more closely the citadel of an Asiatic tyrant than the residence of the vicar of Christ. Machicolated and crenellated, its outside walls four metres thick, some of its towers reaching fifty metres high, the palace was in fact from the start intended as a fortress, to protect the Popes themselves and also the treasure of the Holy See.

The papal exodus from Italy had by no means achieved escape from their enemies. During the reign of John XXII in particular, Italian cardinals continually conspired against him in the hope of bringing the papal court back to Italy; the Franciscans hated him; bishop Hugues Géraud even plotted to kill him. Clement VI made the celebrated Cola di Rienzi a papal notary, only to find that Rienzi was stirring up the people of Rome against him. Rienzi was no match for Clement, though. The Pope incited the Italian nobility against Rienzi, and after his defeat imprisoned the tribune at Avignon for many years. Clement's successor, Innocent VI, pardoned Rienzi and allowed him to return to Rome, where he was soon murdered by a mob.

Paradoxically, while Innocent's ally Cardinal Albornoz was restoring papal authority in Italy, his own reign in Avignon remained precarious. The Treaty of Brétigny, which in 1361 suspended the war between England and France, released hordes of mercenaries with nothing to do but menace the countryside, and the Pope was repeatedly forced to pay ransom to them to secure his city.

To my mind the exterior of this double palace (the *palais vieux*, which surrounds a vast courtyard of honour, and the more luxurious *palais nouveau*) is infinitely more entrancing than its interior, save for its chapels, the lovely papal bedroom in the tour des Anges and the occasional frescos. These include some luscious hunting and fishing scenes in the study of Pope Clement VI (the so-called 'chambre du Cerf' on the third floor of the tower of the Garde-Robe), frescos that you come across in otherwise bare rooms. Even the splendid pontifical chapel of the new palace has lost the tapestries that once adorned its walls, and though its sheer size is impressive, it seems strangely austere. Since Clement VI came from Limoges, part of the old palace is frescoed with scenes from the life of St Martial, the apostle of the Limousin. Other frescos depict the lives of St John the Evangelist and St John the Baptist, while still more in the new palace are devoted to portraits of twenty prophets and the Erythrean sybil.

May one see in the older palace something of the austerity of Pope Benedict XII (a Cistercian monk whose parents were bakers) and in the newer one the arrogance of Clement VI (who had been Chancellor of France)? Clement VI was responsible for the sumptuous audience chamber, modelled on the Palais de Justice, which he had known in Paris. Yet the two buildings merge splendidly. 'I know of no human work which more impresses the mind with a sensation of towering heights than does this same Palace of the Popes overhanging the very deep, narrow lane which skirts the southern side of the building,' wrote the brilliantly imaginative Hilaire Belloc. He asked himself what made it seem so high? 'Beauvais [cathedral], from the inside, looks so high that it seems a creation beyond human power,' he mused, 'but the Eiffel Tower does not look high. And so this unbroken wall above that Avignon valley, which is but a tenth of the height of the Eiffel Tower, tells you as you pass that it is the highest wall in the world.' Today it is a working palace again, serving in part as a conference centre and as the heart of the annual summer festival of theatre, dance and music, which brings more visitors to Avignon than the city can conveniently take.

When Charles Dickens visited Avignon the palace was still partly a common jail and partly a noisy barracks. Many of the state apartments had been shut up, and he found heaps of rubbish in the courtyards. He was also taken round by a shrieking 70-year-old concierge so swarthy and with such flashing black eyes that he conceived the idea that the Devil must have possessed her. The dungeons, the *oubliette* where Cola di Rienzi was chained, and the rooms that once housed prisoners of the Inquisition, often confined for forty-eight hours without food and drink in order to weaken their resolve, made his blood run cold. Yet as he later walked around the papal palace, its impressiveness overwhelmed him.

The immense thickness and giddy height of the walls, the enormous strength of the massive towers, the great extent of the building, its gigantic proportions, frowning aspect and barbarous irregularity, awaken awe and wonder. The recollection of its opposite old uses: an impregnable fortress, a luxurious palace, a horrible prison, a place of torture, the court of the Inquisition: at one and the same time, a house of feasting, fighting, religion and blood: gives to every stone in its huge form a fearful interest, and imparts new meaning to its incongruities.

In 1367, under Innocent VI's successor, Urban V (the saintliest of the Avignon Popes), the papacy felt strong enough to escape the protection of the French monarchy and return to Rome. Three troubled years there were enough for Urban, however, and in 1370 he returned to Avignon to die. Finally in 1376, Pope Gregory XI took his entourage back to Rome, where they stayed. But the troubles of the papacy did not end. After Gregory's death in 1378 thirteen French cardinals proceeded to elect a rival Pope, the 36-year-old Robert de Genève, who took the name Clement VII and chose to remain in Avignon. This 'anti-Pope' was succeeded by another in 1394, the Catalan Benedict XIII. Two more Avignon anti-Popes were elected, and the schism in the Catholic Church was not resolved until 1417.

In the meantime the city of Avignon had become a crossroads of European culture and art. Italian, Flemish and French painters flocked to Avignon and left their mark, their descendants remaining long after the Popes had gone. Fifteenth-century masters such as Nicolas Froment, Enguerrand Charonton and Simon de Chalons would never have settled at Avignon had not the papal exile made it a centre of great art. One of Charonton's most entrancing works, a 'Coronation of the Virgin' painted in the mid-1450s, can still be seen in the Musée Condé across the river at Villeneuve-lès-Avignon; and in the cathedral of Saint-Sauveur at Aix-en-Provence is an entrancing painting of the 'Virgin Mary in the Burning Bush', done by Froment in 1476.

In 1348 Pope Clement VI had paid 80,000 golden florins to buy the city from Jeanne, Countess of Provence and Queen of Naples. The price was derisory, but the beautiful Jeanne, then aged only twenty, was reputed to have arranged the murder of her husband and perhaps several others, and part of the price included a papal pardon. She rode into Avignon on a white charger, wearing a blue mantle, and was readily pardoned. After the sale, the papacy held on to Avignon until 1790, after which the city was annexed by the French National Assembly, an annexation that occasioned bloodshed and the ruin of much of the interior of the papal palace. This devastation was aggravated between 1801 and 1809 when the palace served as a barracks.

Until then, as a quasi-independent state in France, Avignon became a refuge for free-thinkers and Jews, whose nineteenth-century synagogue is still in use here. This was the city chosen by Petrarch's father as a place of exile after he was thrown out of Florence in 1313 when his son was eight years old. Petrarch regarded the city, whose thirteenth-century population of 6,000 had expanded by his time to some 40,000, as 'a sewer collecting all the ordure of the world', yet the place offered him his muse. Educated at nearby Carpentras, he was living in the city in 1327 when on 6 April he saw for the first time, outside the monastery of Sainte-Claire (a spot now identified only by a plaque in the rue du Roi-René), the love of his life, Laura, to whom he poured out a series of superb poems, lamenting the fact that he could not marry her (presumably because she was already married). Laura died in the plague year of 1348, thus providing the poet (who already had two children by another woman) with a romantic image that no longer bore any resemblance to inconvenient reality. In consequence of her timely disappearance, the poet was able to continue writing deathless poetry that made the world enamoured of his woe.

Opposite the papal palace is a splendid baroque building, the seventeenth-century city mint (or Hôtel des Monnaies), its façade lavishly decorated in 1619 by the Florentine Simone Bartolacci and incorporating the dragon of the coat of arms of Cardinal Borghese and the eagle of that of his nephew, Jean-François. This is, I think, the most Italianate building in the whole city, the swags on its façade and the rough-hewn stones of its bottom storey exactly what you would expect to see on turning a corner of Florence. Eagles and dragons not only sit proudly on the balustrade of the roof, but also glare at each other while perching on the swags. And from the papal palace a flight of steps leads up to the Romanesque cathedral of Notre-Dame-des-Doms, in which lie two of the Avignon Popes. John XXII rests in a flamboyant tomb of 1345, sculpted by an Englishman named Hugues Wilfred, which the Revolutionaries wickedly mutilated; and Benedict XII lies in another partially mutilated tomb. The name 'des-Doms' derives perhaps from *domnis*, a title of ecclesiastical dignitaries, or else from *domo episcopalis*, that is, the seat of bishops. Inside the church is a twelfth-century marble throne which once was, literally, the seat of Popes.

The magnificent lantern-tower of this church has no match in Provence or the Côte d'Azur, though it is sadly topped by an incongruously massive, gilded statue of the Virgin Mary added during the Second Empire in 1859. Look out, too, for a beautiful circular chapel, added to the south side in 1680, and for Nicolas Mignard's 'Annunciation', painted in 1637. The church porch was frescoed by the Siennese genius Simone Martini, who worked at Avignon between 1335 and 1340. He and his Italian successor Matteo di Giovanetti da Viterbo established in this city a genre of painting whose solidly modelled figures and monumental classicism spread throughout Provence.

Walk south past the papal palace and you reach the place de l'Horloge, built on the site of the Roman forum and dominated by a massive square keep of 1354 (with a nineteenth-century mannequin). Here in summer the crowds can be oppressive, in spite of the shady plane trees and the cool restaurants and cafés. In compensation the square is transformed into a street theatre, with mime artists sporting red noses and bowler hats jockeying for a place alongside bizarre madmen on stilts. Both major buildings in this square, namely the city theatre and the town hall, date from the middle of the nineteenth century, the former bearing statues of Molière and Corneille on its façade.

Beyond the town hall, the rue Saint-Agricol runs west. Take a moment to admire to the south of this street the resplendent Gothic Palace du Roure, a fifteenth-century building which was commissioned by a Florentine merchant named Pietro Barincelli and today houses a library of Provençal history and folklore. This is where, between 1881 and 1889, the Provençal patriots Frédéric Mistral and Folco de Baroncelli produced the journal *L'Aïoli*, written entirely in the patois of the region in a determined and successful attempt to revive the ancient culture and language of Provence. Rue Saint-Agricol is shaded by a fifteenth-century church dedicated to the same saint and rising from a fine flight of steps. Over its doorway is a carving of the Annunciation, and the massive square belfry is part sixteenth-century and part seventeenth-century, save for the fourth storey, which was added only in 1746. Agricol is patron saint of Avignon, a reward due to his efficacy, in the seventh century, in summoning all the storks of the region to exterminate a swarm of snakes that was infesting the town.

If you walk south along the rue Joseph Vernet from just beyond the church of Saint-Agricol you reach a mid-eighteenth-century building designed by the brothers Jean-Baptiste and François Franque, which now houses the Musée Calvet. Esprit Calvet was a professor of medicine at Avignon University and on his death in 1810 left to the city a remarkable collection, which, subsequently enriched, ranges from prehistoric finds in the region to the delightfully busy scenes of French harbours and ports depicted by the Avignon-born painter Joseph Vernet (1714–89). I looked out at its central courtyard and saw a peacock strutting proudly across the grass.

Further north, in the place Crillon, stands the classical former theatre, with its exquisite façade of 1734, and Avignon's most celebrated hotel, the sixteenth-century Hôtel de l'Europe. Napoleon Bonaparte lodged here in 1798 and was so delighted with his fare that he instructed the landlady to double what she charged his quartermaster, knowing that the mean officer would bargain down the price. Another guest was Stendhal in 1837, who was enraptured by a city that he felt was really Italian rather than French. Here too in 1858 died a remarkable woman named Harriet Taylor, whose influence on her stern husband, the philosopher John Stuart Mill, had greatly mitigated the unfeeling rationality of his utilitarian philosophy. Here Mill wrote his celebrated essay *On Liberty*. Harriet lies buried in the cemetery of Saint-Véran, and when Mill himself died in 1873 he was buried beside her. I was touched to discover that the road leading to the cemetery has been named the avénue Stuart-Mill.

Apart from the rue Jean-Jaurès and the rue de la République, which slashed the city in two in the mid-nineteenth century, Avignon remains a city of twisting narrow streets, which occasionally open out on to the River Sorgue or expand into amiable squares shaded by plane trees. Strolling through these streets, Charles Dickens was entranced to discover that 'The grapes were hanging in clusters in the streets, and the brilliant Oleander was in full bloom everywhere.' Although the alleyways of Avignon were old and narrow, Dickens found them tolerably clean, shaded by awnings stretched from house to house. 'Bright stuffs and handkerchiefs, curiosities, ancient frames of carved wood, old chairs, ghostly tables, saints, virgins, angels, and staring daubs of portraits being exposed for sale beneath, it was very quaint and lively,' he commented. 'All this was much set off, too, by the glimpses one caught, through a rusty gate standing ajar, of quiet sleepy courtyards, having stately old houses within, as silent as tombs.'

Eighteenth-century palaces mingle with tourist shops, restaurants and sixteenth- and seventeenth-century houses. The city's numerous inviting churches include the classical church of the Grey Penitents (a religious order founded here in 1226 and surviving to this day). On 30 November 1440, legend has it, the Rhône flooded this church, but the waters parted of their own accord so as not to swamp the Sacred Host on the high altar (for this church has the rare privilege of perpetually displaying the Host). Whatever the truth of this tale, the Rhône, swollen by the waters of its tributary the Durance, certainly does flood here, a fact attested by a plaque outside the church declaring the level that the waters reached on 4 November 1840, which almost equalled the inundation of 1755, which flooded three-quarters of the city.

Other fine Avignon churches are the fifteenth-century Gothic Carmelite church which dominates the quiet place des Carmes. This church is filled with medieval and Renaissance statues, as well as a sixteenth-century font and paintings that include a fine seventeenth-century portrait of St Éloi by Nicolas Mignard. In the place Carnot rises the Gothic church of Saint-Pierre, which was begun in 1358 and finished in 1525. It boasts a lovely late-fourteenth-century belfry, with an octagonal top and spire added a century later. The splendid façade of 1512 (designed by a painter named Philippe Garcin, who was clearly inspired by a rich doorway of Carpentras cathedral) and the magical doorways whose images of St Jerome, the Annunciation and the Archangel Michael were carved in 1551 by Antoine Vollard, beckon you inside to find a riot of statues and paintings (including an 'Immaculate Conception' by Mignard), as well as a choir embellished by seventeenth-century carved panelling.

Another chapel, discovered by walking north-east from the papal palace along the rue Banasterie, once belonged to the fourteenth-century Black Penitents, who would walk through the streets hooded and barefoot, flagellating themselves. A rather more charitable purpose of the foundation was to comfort prisoners and those condemned to death, and every year on the feast of the beheading of St John the Baptist they were privileged to secure the release of one prisoner. In 1739 they began rebuilding their church, to designs by one of their members named Thomas Lainée. On its baroque façade is sculpted the severed head of the Baptist. Rue Banasterie itself revives one's spirits. Its name derives from the *banastes*, that is to say the makers of willow baskets and furniture, and it is flanked by some sweet seventeenth- and eighteenth-century houses.

In its square a few paces south-west of the place de l'Horloge, the church of Saint-Didier is another gem, built in the late 1350s, the choir housing the tomb of its founder, Cardinal de Déaux. It also displays a superb painting of 1478 by Francesco Laurana depicting Jesus carrying his cross on the way to Golgotha. Known as 'Notre Dame du Spasme', because of the contorted face of the mother of Jesus as she sees her son's anguish, this little-regarded masterpiece constitutes one of the earliest Renaissance paintings

of France. The fine marble altar is by J.-B. Péru, sculpted in 1750.
From the church square the rue du Roi-René winds east, bordered
by two of the finest houses in Avignon: on the north side the Hôtel
de Crillon, built in 1648 by the architect and painter Domenico
Borboni for the colonel-general of the papal artillery, Louis III de
Berton, Baron de Crillon, with a sculpted façade by Jean-André
Borde; and on the south side the Hôtel de Fortia Montréal, built
by Valfrenière ten years earlier.

As for the rocher des Doms itself, as Belloc put it, 'Standing on
a platform of that height you can survey the valley in one sweep as
from nowhere else between Lyons and the sea, or at least as from
no other urban vantage point. Thence also you may see that great
wave-like lift of the Ventoux which is the guardian of everything
around.' Belloc deplored the fact that in his own day a motor
road had been built thousands of feet up to the summit of Mont
Ventoux. I must say that, finding it easier to drive, I do not.

No one visiting Avignon should fail to step for a moment out
of the *département* of Vaucluse into that of the Gard for a visit
to Villeneuve-lès-Avignon. Leave Avignon by the porte de l'Oulle
and drive over the suspension bridge, which leads you by way of
the camp sites, swimming pool and market gardens of the Île de la
Barthelasse. Crossing the second branch of the Rhône, the route
runs alongside the great river until you see ahead, on its rock
overlooking by sixty metres the broken bridge of Saint-Bénézet,
the square tower which is all that remains of a fortified château of
King Philippe le Bel. It was built in 1302, save for the later watchtower, a late-fourteenth-century addition. The price of entry is
well worth paying, to see the three-storeyed vaulted interior with
some fifteenth-century frescos, and above all the superb view –
of the Rhône, of the white walls and red-tiled roofs of Avignon
('like a pie-crust fresh from the oven', as Lawrence Durrell put it)
and of Fort Saint-André at Villeneuve-lès-Avignon.

The town is dominated by a huge rock, known as Mont
Andaon. Once the Rhône flowed on both sides of this rock,
making it virtually impregnable and therefore a welcome refuge
for prehistoric men and women. For the Gauls and the Romans
it was a holy site, bearing a pagan altar which Christian hermits,
living in caves here, soon adopted for their own use. According
to an inscription in the church at Villeneuve-lès-Avignon, St

Casarie, whoever she was, died in a cave on the mount in 587. Four centuries later the Benedictines founded a monastery here, dedicated to St Andrew. Their monastery church was consecrated by Pope Gelasius II in 1118, and the whole abbey survived until the French Revolution.

The monks soon began to resent the burgeoning arrogance of Avignon, and thus afforded King Philippe le Bel the opportunity to found here a new town, the Villeneuve, which would bolster his own authority against that of the papacy. Philippe ambitiously intended to tax the citizens of Avignon itself. Offering an unusually attractive number of freedoms and rights to any man or woman who was willing to inhabit his new town, he soon attracted numerous citizens.

Notwithstanding the frequent antagonism between the king and the papacy, the cardinals of Avignon also relished his newly founded town, building there their summer palaces. One of them was Cardinal Étienne Aubert. And in 1356, having become Pope Innocent VI, he founded a Charterhouse here, as a thank-offering to a Carthusian monk who had been elected Pope but refused the triple tiara – thereby enabling Aubert to be elected to the throne of St Peter. Here Innocent would eventually be buried.

Today the Chartreuse du Val-de-Bénédiction, with its farms, stables, workshops, bakery, kitchen, mills, hospital and hospice, is a reminder of the fact that in the Middle Ages such convents were entirely self-sufficient communities. It remains the largest Carthusian monastery in France. Its fourteenth-century abbey church is graced with a forged iron belfry and entered via a seventeenth-century porch. Innocent lies buried at the east end of the southernmost of the two arched naves. On the north side of the church is the little cloister, with some well-restored monks' cells. People still live in parts of this monastery, but I was sorry to read that when the historical monuments' commission set about restoring it, a number of peasant families were slowly prised out. An English visitor in the 1920s came upon some of them, sitting out among their tubs and pots, and she reported that 'their placid and smiling faces reveal that here is that peace and rest, that consolation which heals tired and weary souls'.

The north-west corner of the Charterhouse still shelters the lavabo, where the monks would wash before entering the still-extant (though partly ruined) refectory. Beyond the refectory is Étienne Aubert's chapel, decorated with frescos by Matteo Giovanetti of Viterbo. This abbey boasts two more cloisters, one of them housing a fourteenth-century well and a fountain sheltered by an exquisite eighteenth-century rotunda.

The rest of Villeneuve-lès-Avignon is equally delightful. A nephew of Pope John XXII, Cardinal Arnaud de Via, founded the collegiate church of Notre-Dame in 1333, a building which some claim to be the first Gothic building in Provence. The fortified belfry was obviously designed as a place of refuge. The founder sleeps in a chapel inside his church, depicted in marble. Walking through Villeneuve-lès-Avignon is a treat partly because of its sometimes arcaded streets, and partly because of the houses and little palaces, which date from the fourteenth to the seventeenth centuries. The former town hospice, one of the later buildings, is now the home of the town museum and has taken from the church of the Carthusians Innocent VI's tomb, which Barthélemy Cavalier sculpted out of marble and stone. It also houses a celebrated fourteenth-century statue of the Virgin Mary, carved out of ivory, as well as Enguerrand Charonton's 'Coronation of the Virgin', whose background depicts not only Mont Ventoux but also the Castel Sant'Angelo and St Peter's, Rome.

But the most imposing building in Villeneuve-lès-Avignon is undoubtedly Fort Saint-André, built between 1362 and 1368 on the orders of King Jean le Bon, surrounded by imposing walls and defended by powerful towers. Its fortified gateway is flanked by a couple of cylindrical and machicolated towers. Inside these walls you come upon a simple, harmonious twelfth-century chapel, in the Romanesque style, the tumbledown ruins of the village of Saint-André and the remains of the former Benedictine abbey.

From Avignon the N7 follows the right bank of the Rhône north-east by way of le Pontet to the industrial town of Sorgues, which lies at the confluence of the Rivers Sorgue and Ouvèze. The Avignon Popes had a pride of lions among their pets, but they made so much noise at night that Pope Innocent VI had them brought here. So far we have been travelling through a remarkably fertile countryside producing fruit and vegetables, but Sorgues lies at the southernmost tip of a large stretch of countryside dedicated to producing the celebrated *appellation Côtes du Rhône* wines, of which the most celebrated of all is discovered by leaving the N7 some 300 metres north of the town and turning left along the D17 to drive sixteeen kilometres to Châteauneuf-du-Pape. On the other hand, it would be a pity to miss the Romanesque bridge over the Ouvèze at Bédarrides, four and a half kilometres north-east of Sorgues, and you can just as readily then reach Châteauneuf-du-Pape from there.

Overlooking the town are the ruins of the early fourteenth-century château which the Avignon Pope John XXII built both as his summer retreat and as a defensive fortress. The Calvinist leader, the vicious Baron des Adrets, demolished part of it during the Wars of Religion, and the retreating Germans blew up more of it as they evacuated the city in August 1944. The Beaux-Arts authorities have magnificently restored the papal cellars, and from the site there are extensive views of the Rhône valley as far as Avignon and across the Comtat plain to Mont Ventoux, but the machicolations now seem to me to have a forlorn look.

Châteauneuf-du-Pape itself is a picturesque little town of arches, courtyards, narrow streets and churches. The latter include the twelfth-century cemetery chapel of Saint-Théodoric, with its ancient frescos, and the eighteenth-century church of Saint-Pierre. The cultural and other needs of visitors are well catered for, with exhibitions, an annual festival of music, clean camp sites, a congress hall, sixteen kilometres of marked footpaths and, of course, a celebrated wine fair.

Though the wine of the region was already renowned by the reign of Pope John XXII (and indeed a Gallo-Roman bas-relief in the Musée Calvet at Avignon depicts barrels of wine being transported in a barge down the Rhône), the first written records of it date only from his time. His enthusiasm helped to develop the wine, and today the papal coat of arms is stamped on each bottle. As well as the museum of wine tools connected with the Caves du Père Anselme, you can visit the cellars and châteaux of the producers and taste before buying. Some of their châteaux are pseudo-medieval follies of considerable charm. In particular, the château des Fines Roches, three kilometres south of Châteauneuf-du-Pape, seems like something out of a novel by Walter Scott. It now serves as a hotel.

Altogether there are 3,200 hectares of vineyards pro-ducing Châteauneuf-du-Pape, spreading into the communes of Couthezon, Orange, Sorgues and Bédarrides, but the quality is strictly controlled. No one vigneron is allowed to produce more than 3,500 litres. As for the grapes, there are thirteen permitted varieties – *syrah, grenache, cinsault, picardan, mourvèdre, muscardin, counoise, picpoul, clairette, terret noir, roussane, vaccarèse* and *bourboulenc* – though a vigneron will usually employ no more than seven or so. One passing regretted by oenologists is the disappearance of the oak barrels in which until recently the wine would be stored before bottling. Above all other factors in producing this world-renowned wine, the large round stones in the vineyards add to the distinct taste of Châteauneuf-du-Pape, gathering heat during the sunny days and releasing it throughout the hours of darkness, so that the grapes become exceptionally mature. Yet, having written all this, when I see those shrivelled vines sprouting from that seemingly inhospitable land, I still marvel that they produce such a rarity.

In our own century Châteauneuf-du-Pape was also in the forefront of a minor revolution in the French wine trade, for in 1923 on the initiative of Baron le Roy de Boiseaumarié the local vintners formed an association of the *appellation d'origine Châteauneuf-du-Pape* – some twelve years before the French introduced a national system of *appellation contrôlée* wines, whose rules were to a large part based on those of this region. To my shame, until I visited this little town, I knew the wine only in its powerful, beautifully fragrant, purplish-red variety. I can now report that some 350,000 bottles of white (out of a total of 13 million) are also produced here annually, as well as a pungent *eau-de-vie* made from the grapes of Châteauneuf-du-Pape. The white is, in truth, a greeny-yellow in colour and, they say, is best drunk within two years of bottling. The reds can keep for up to ten years (by which time their purple hue has become a clearer red), though the vignerons recommend keeping most vintages for three years and drinking them after five years at the most. Naturally, they tell you to drink them *chambré*, by which they mean at around 17°C (63°F).

As you drive further along the D17, on a rock overlooking the left bank of the Rhône appears the round tower surmounting the ruined twelfth-century Château de l'Hers. It rises near where Hannibal is said to have ferried his thirty-seven elephants across the River Rhône in 218 BC, along with 10,000 horses and 50,000 troops, and is followed by the Château of Roquemaure on the right bank of the river. Roquemaure's parish church dates from the fourteenth century but houses a statue of St Peter which is a century older. After Roquemaure, the road shortly leaves the riverside, and then turns sharply left to rejoin it at Caderousse, a village which suffered so much from the flooding Rhône that in 1856 the exasperated citizens built a dyke between themselves and the river. The various floods are recalled by plaques on the town hall. Caderousse boasts a much rebuilt Romanesque church, whose south side is blessed with a flamboyant Gothic seigneurial chapel. It contrasts vividly with the simplicity of the older building, whose belfry is a humble affair, pierced by six arches but carrying only two bells.

From here the D17 runs directly north-east for six kilometres to the Roman city of Orange, which lies at the foot of an isolated hill on a bend of the River Meyne. Famed for its Roman triumphal arch and its arena, this had been the capital of a federation of Celtic tribes, who gave it the name Aurasio, from which Orange derives. Colonized during the reign of Augustus Caesar by veterans of the second Gallic legion and laid out in the traditional grid pattern of Roman camps, Orange has preserved the plan to this day, with the two main axes, the *cardo* and *decumanus*, still clearly visible in the present-day rue de la République and the rue Victor-Hugo. The Visigoths devastated the town in 412, but failed to destroy the essential pattern of its streets.

The fortunes of Orange soon revived, especially after Charlemagne made it the seat of a count. A bishopric since the fourth century, Orange received its franchise as a city in 1247. In 1559, by the Treaty of Câteau-Cambrésis, Henri II of France ceded the city to the *stadtholders* of Holland (who then took the name Orange), and although Louis XIV took it for himself, in 1697 he was forced to give it back to the Dutchman who had become King William III of England. Only in 1713, by the Treaty of Utrecht, did Orange become irrevocably French. The ruined château on the Saint-Eutrope hill at Orange is the architectural legacy of the Orange-Nassau line, its origins dating from the era of Tiburge d'Orange in the twelfth century.

The massive Roman amphitheatre is set against a hillside at the south side of the city and dates back to the time of Augustus. No other ancient theatre is so well preserved. Three doorways on the ground floor of this magnificent building, whose stones seem to drip antiquity, were reserved for the actors. Beyond is a massive backdrop, once again a unique survivor in being perfectly preserved, decorated with columns, marble, sculptures, mosaics and a frieze of centaurs. Dominating everything is a splendid statue of Augustus himself, majestic and martial. The façade of the theatre rises to over thirty-seven metres and is more than 103 metres wide. The various devices for changing scenery can be made out, and staircases lead up to the ramps, which could seat no fewer than 11,000 spectators. This is the annual venue of a July music festival.

To add to the Roman splendour of Orange, to the west of the amphitheatre has been excavated the base of the largest Roman temple yet discovered in Gaul, a building probably dating from the second century AD, built under the Emperor Hadrian and measuring some twenty-four metres by forty. Fittingly, opposite stands the municipal museum, which displays a remarkable map of the region of Orange, drafted around AD 77 during the reign of the Emperor Vespasian, carved on three marble fragments and giving detailed information about land-ownership at the time – including such matters as which landowners were exempt from paying tribute, which land belonged to descendants of the former veterans and which still belonged to the Roman state. As a complete contrast, the museum also displays a collection of drawings by the Belgian artist Frank Brangwyn, who after taking up residence in England became a disciple of the arts and crafts leader William Morris. So fashionable did he become in the Edwardian era that Brangwyn was eventually knighted. His paintings were given to the museum in 1939 by his admirer William de Belleroche, some of whose own works are also exhibited here. Finally, the museum has a room devoted to the souvenirs and portraits of members of the House of Orange.

Before you reach the climax of Roman Orange, there are treats to be seen from later centuries. The town hall was rebuilt in 1888, but its belfry dates from 1671 and is embellished with a forged iron spire. Beyond it rises the former cathedral of Orange, a huge twelfth-century Romanesque building dedicated to Notre-Dame-de-Nazareth and so mutilated during the Wars of Religion that much was rebuilt, in particular the belfry and the apse, which today date from 1600. The best-preserved Romanesque elements are in the south porch, and over the crossing rises a fine octagonal cupola. The statue of Christ on the high altar was sculpted in 1608. The whole church rises on the site of a pagan temple dedicated to the cult of Diana. Of the other churches of Orange that of Saint-Florent, built in the fourteenth and fifteenth centuries, once belonged to a convent of the Cordeliers, and twentieth-century Protestants now worship in a sixteenth-century church built by Dominican monks.

The rue Notre-Dame runs from the west end of this church to meet the rue Victor-Hugo (which, not surprisingly, used to be called simply the rue Droite or straight street), where you turn right. The street is prolonged by the equally straight avenue de l'Arc de Triomphe. It leads directly to the third Roman marvel of Orange, the triumphal arch set up by the warriors of the second legion to commemorate their victories in Gaul under Julius Caesar in AD 49. A dozen Corinthian columns support the arch, which is decorated with sculptures, trophies, armour, sirens and ships (a reference, perhaps, to the naval victory of Augustus at the Battle of Actium in 31 BC), as well as with captive Gauls, some of whom are even named. War steeds, armed soldiers and battles are also sculpted on the arch. An inscription, which includes the name of the Emperor Tiberius, long led scholars to believe that the arch was built around the year AD 25, but nowadays experts believe that later generations of Romans re-dedicated it to him and that in truth the monumental construction was erected during the reign of Augustus.

The N7 winds its way northwards from Orange through more stretches of fertile country by way of Mornas, a village set among rocks and boasting a Romanesque church and a massive ruined thirteenth-century château, with double fortifications, which was enlarged 200 years later. The remains include a Romanesque keep, a couple of square towers and a little chapel. Here during the Wars of Religion the Huguenots began the habit of throwing vanquished Catholics off the cliff on to rows of halberds, a practice soon imitated by the Catholics themselves. Today Mornas seems peaceful enough, its ancient heart embellished with Renaissance and Gothic houses, its cemetery sheltering a twelfth-century chapel. The route continues as far as Mondragon, with more Renaissance houses and again a ruined château (sacked in 1562 during the Wars of Religion) looking down on the village from a spur. Nearby is an ornithological reserve covering some 2,000 hectares.

From here I recommend taking the picturesque D26 as far as Bollène, which shades the left bank of the River Lez. This is now a land of shepherds and truffle-hunters, though Bollène is celebrated for its almonds as well as for its mutton and truffles. Although its ramparts have almost entirely disappeared, apart from a thirteenth-century gateway, plane trees surround the ancient town, following the original boundaries. The nineteenth-century sculptor F. Charpentier was born at Bollène, so the pretty town has more of his statues than one really needs to see, the best being the curious 'Improvisateur' and 'la Pensée' inside the town hall (which was built in 1887) and 'les Lutteurs' outside it.

Oddly enough, the statue of the brilliant chemist Louis Pasteur near the bridge over the River Lez is not by Charpentier but by A. Martial. Pasteur was here in 1882. Studying the diseases prevalent in the region, he discovered a vaccine, derived from pigs, which could conquer swine fever. In consequence, Bollène is blessed with a Pasteur museum. For my part I prefer to visit the Picassos and Chagalls in the town museum. Bollène is otherwise notable for sixteen Ursuline nuns who refused to renounce their old ways at the time of the Revolution and were guillotined at Orange in 1793. Pope Pius XI beatified them all. Their former convent is now the Hôtel-Dieu, and you can admire a seventeenth-century retable in its chapel. The main church of the town dates mostly from the sixteenth century. Dedicated to St Martin, it is flanked by a cool garden.

Drive east from Bollène through Suze-la-Rousse, with its isolated château set amid trees, to turn north along the D576 and reach the olive town of Visan. Here are the remains of the fourteenth-century fortifications built by the Pope of Avignon and a ruined twelfth-century château, as well as a partly Romanesque church dedicated to Notre-Dame des Sept-Douleurs. It houses a painting by Nicolas Mignard.

You are now in a curiously isolated part of the Vaucluse, a region entirely surrounded by the *département* of the Drôme. The centre of this canton, Valréas, lies nine kilometres north-east of Visan and stands on a hill which is dominated by the rectangular keep of a fourteenth-century château and washed by the waters of the River Coronne. The boulevards surrounding old Valréas mark out the lines of its former fortifications, and its town hall is a splendid, partly Gothic, partly eighteenth-century building.

The parish church of Valréas is a complex affair, with Gothic side aisles, a Romanesque belfry with two simple arches and an octagonal tower over the crossing. On its south porch is carved Christ in glory, surrounded by saints. Some of the bas-reliefs inside the church are deftly sculpted, particularly those representing the work of the summer solstice. Not content with this lovely parish church (which is dedicated to Notre-Dame-de-Nazareth), Valréas also has a chapel of the White Penitents, built in the late sixteenth century and filled with fine woodwork and *trompe-l'oeil* paintings. More chapels dot the Grand'Rue, a street that also contains some superb sixteenth-, seventeenth- and eighteenth-century houses. On the evening of 23 June the citizens dress up in medieval costumes and celebrate the feast of the little St John, with a 4-year-old boy as its hero.

The Valréas enclave is composed of fortified towns on the northern edge of the Comtat, papal possessions which only in 1791 decided to join France, becoming part of the Drôme. When the Vaucluse was created in 1793, the citizens voted to leave the Drôme and join the new *département*. This is a region of excellent camp sites and invigorating walks. Côtes du Rhône wines, truffles and lavender are staple products of the countryside. Valréas also enjoys an annual lavender festival on the first weekend of August, as well as filling its regular Wednesday market with truffle stalls from November to February. Sheep and dairy cows graze in the meadows in the shade of cypresses.

West along the D941 you reach Grillon, its medieval heart set on a hill and surrounded by twelfth-century ramparts. South along the D20 lies a yet more powerfully fortified village. The walls of Richerenches are defended by four fourteenth-century towers. Remnants of the Templars' commandery, as well as thirteenth-century houses, enliven the spot, which – like Valréas – sells truffles on its market stalls (on Saturday mornings) from November to February.

By way of Visan to the south-east and then further along the winding D20 you can reach the superb town of Vaison-la-Romaine, one of the best spots from which to begin an exploration of Mont Ventoux. Vaison is divided by the River Ouvèze, the modern town lying on the right bank and occupying

a site which the Romans made one of their richest foundations
in Provence. Every Tuesday it hosts one of the most important
markets in the Vaucluse, a right granted by Pope Sixtus II in
1483. Here too archaeologists have uncovered opulent Roman
remains, including the villa known as the Maison des Messii,
with baths, kitchens, mosaic floors and lavatories. The Romans'
public park is today called the portique de Pompée because of its
colonnaded Roman gateway, whose statues include the Emperor
Hadrian and his wife Sabina. Beyond, along the rue du Théâtre,
you reach the remains of a Roman theatre (site of a midsummer
festival of theatre and music). And in between the villa and this
theatre the town museum is crammed to overflowing with Roman
pots, urns, statues, herms, altars and a majestic silver bust, all
discovered in this region. Nearby is the tourist office (rendered
delightful by its museum to the wines of the Rhône valley, with
special tastings on Wednesday mornings).

To the west of the Maison des Messii is yet another excavated
Roman site, the Vilasse quarter of the city, from which came
a silver bust, now in the museum, representing a stern Roman
who lived some two centuries after the birth of Jesus. This series
of excavations astounded me, first by being yet more elaborate
than anything else I had seen in Vaison and, second, by nestling
quite happily between the houses and walls of a decent provincial
French town.

Beyond it to the west is the centre of Vaison, the place de
Montfort, with its fountain and plane trees, and beyond that
rises a majestic Romanesque monument, the former cathedral
of Notre-Dame-de-Nazareth. Its white square tower is as blank
as could be, save for the diminutive upper storey. As one might
expect here, this Christian church rises on the site of a Roman
temple, and part of its wall dates back to Merovingian times.
Its apse is held up by Roman columns and the church shelters
a sarcophagus bearing the remains of St Quentin, Bishop of
Vaison in the mid-sixth century. The pattern of the apse is that
of the sixth century (and its altar seems to be genuinely of the
same period), though most of the building you see today was
renewed from the twelfth to the thirteenth centuries. The cloister
is a quiet Romanesque gallery, filled with a diverse collection of
ancient carved stones. Its triple-arched openings look out on to
a fairly parched square with tall pine trees. Naturally the church

boasts some fine statues, especially a couple of eighteenth-century depictions of St Mary Magdalene and St Jerome. An octagonal dome decorated with the symbols of the four evangelists rises over a pseudo-crossing and leads you to expect transepts, but there are none. Some 300 metres north of the cathedral is a twelfth-century chapel dedicated to St Quentin.

In spite of these antiquities, Vaison insists that its 'old' town (or what is known as *le Vieux Bourg*) lies south of the river. From the town hall the Grand'Rue leads to a Roman bridge that spans the Ouvèze with a single arch of nearly eighteen metres. The envy displayed by the Counts of Toulouse towards the Bishops of Vaison was responsible for the building of this separate upper town, for in the twelfth century Count Raymond of Toulouse constructed here a château to keep the bishops sufficiently respectful. Marauders, and especially the religious troubles of the sixteenth century, persuaded nearly all the citizens of Vaison to take refuge under the shadow of this château. They returned to the lower town only in the nineteenth century. After the papacy had wrested control of Vaison from the counts, papal legates reinforced the walls of the upper town and set up here aristocratic houses as well as a new cathedral.

Built for the most part in the thirteenth, fourteenth and fifteenth centuries on an escarpment rising swiftly above the waters, the old town is threaded with twisting streets and dotted with picturesque squares. You enter by a fortified double gate in the fourteenth-century walls, defended by a medieval tower, which is surmounted by a cast-iron eighteenth-century belfry. The former cathedral of the old city was built by Bishop Pons de Sade in 1464, though a couple of chapels were added in 1601 and the gallery and façade date from 1776, scarcely two decades before the revolution suppressed the bishopric. From its square is a splendid view of Mont Ventoux, though a yet better one is gained by twisting your way up to the ruins of the château at the furthermost part of the cliff.

Before leaving Vaison it is worth seeking out its former Jewish quarter. But we have temporarily travelled far enough, and it is time to sit in the shade of the plane trees of the pretty place du Vieux-Marché, slaking our thirst while listening to the water dripping from an eighteenth-century fountain.

Mont Ventoux
and the intimate charms
of the Vaucluse

The rocks of the Vaucluse, declared Henry Crabb Robinson in 1837, are sublime. Mountains do not change their character overnight. In the Vaucluse you can still exult in their sublimity, and I begin this chapter with a tour of them.

Running south-east from Vaison-la-Romaine, the D938 skirts the River Ouvèze and then continues through the gap carved between Mont Ventoux on the left and the Dentelles de Montmirail on the right. To the left appear the grandiose ruins of the tenth-century château of Entrechaux and to the right the picturesque village of le Crestet. As its name indicates, le Crestet perches on the crest of a hill, and here the bishops of Vaison would escape both from their daily cares and from their secular enemies, the Counts of Toulouse. At le Crestet the bishops did not neglect their spiritual duties, and a church, dedicated to Saint-Sauveur, was built here in the eleventh century and rebuilt in the sixteenth.

Next appears the fortress of Entrechaux, built on top of a peak to dominate the entrance to the Toulourenc valley. Beside it stands a twelfth-century Romanesque chapel with lovely capitals, and the village also possesses another Romanesque chapel, dedicated to Notre-Dame-de-Nazareth. Soon the road reaches the town of Malaucène. No fewer than four gates remain from the medieval ramparts, which today are marked out by the plane-shaded boulevards that surround the town. Its narrow twisting streets, ancient plane trees, elegant houses and eighteenth-century hospital are guarded by the remains of a fortress, which became a stronghold of the Huguenots during the Wars of Religion and was partly demolished in the early nineteenth century. In 1539 the clock tower of Malaucène was built, just in time to serve as a watchtower during the same Wars of Religion. Its upper storey dates from 1761. Malaucène also has a fortified church of Saint-Michel-et-Saint-Pierre, built at the behest of Pope Clement V in the fourteenth century, yet for the most part retaining the style of Provençal Romanesque. It seems readier to repel invaders than to welcome worshippers. Its porch is protected by an unusual *bretèche*. But once you enter it becomes a church again, with a splendid organ console of 1638. Though the nave remains Romanesque, many of the chapels have ogival vaults, and the apse was rebuilt in the eighteenth century.

Lying on the northern slopes of Mont Ventoux, Malaucène is an excellent spot from which to begin a tour of the rest of this mountain. By the nineteenth century the trees that once covered its lower slopes had almost all been cut down. In 1860 the decision was made to replant, and cedars, limes and pines slowly restored the ecology of the chalky white mountain. They provide shelter for over a hundred different types of birds, including the only kind of eagle to feed off snakes. Narcissi, wild flax and iris, wild strawberries, box-wood and juniper trees now find nourishment on the lower slopes of the mountain. Hidden among the trees are wild boar, doe, red and brown squirrels, badgers, stags and fawns.

Hikers on Mont Ventoux are here extremely adequately served by the tracks known as *Grandes Randonnées*, which are usually well-marked and also set out virtually step-by-step in booklets. Even so, parts of the climb to the 1,912-metre-high peak of this austerely attractive mountain are strenuous. To reach the summit of Mont Ventoux by the *Grande Randonnée 4* from Malaucène, allow a good five hours. This route passes through oaks by Beaumont-du-Ventoux, with its twelfth-century chapel of Saint-Sépulcre, and then by Sainte-Marguerite, whose fourteenth-century church has a pre-Romanesque altar, before climbing through more oak trees interspersed with apricot, cherry and almond trees.

By car the road to take is the D974, which pauses at the chapel of Notre-Dame-du-Groseau. Since Roman times this spot has been a place of worship. The Romans built an aqueduct from here to Vaison-la-Romaine to carry the waters that rise from the splendid spring, which bubbles out at the foot of a vertical cliff here. They built a temple nearby, and then the Christians set up a monastery in the seventh century. The Saracens demolished most of it in 683, but its church was spared, to be rebuilt and fortified in the eleventh century by the Benedictines. Today what remains is the twelfth-century sanctuary, with its octagonal cupola, an apse and a Romanesque belfry. The Avignon Pope Clement V used to spend part of his summers here, and in consequence his coat of arms appears in the frescos inside the church.

Some halfway up the mountain the road reaches the foresters' Maison des Ramayettes, where in the midst of boxwood and pines there is a belvedere with superb views of mountain peaks, of valleys and of Beaumont-du-Ventoux. The road climbs on, with a view to the north of the 1,445-metre-high Mont Serein, with its ski-slopes and chalets, and then twists its way through larches, pines and rocks to the summit. Here in the fifteenth century Bishop Pierre de Valeriis of Carpentras founded the church of Sainte-Croix. The nineteenth century added an observatory, the twentieth century a meteorological station, radar masts for the military, and a hotel. The views can be superb, though Mont Ventoux is a law unto itself and can irritate the traveller by summer haze and winter clouds.

From here the road winds down to the col des Tempettes, aptly named, for the winds on Mont Ventoux, which itself means windy mountain (unless, as some allege, it means white mountain), can be ferocious. From this 1,829-metre spot you can look down on to the village of Brantes, its seventeenth-century church and ruined château perched some 569 metres above the Toulourenc valley, its potters and cast-iron workers producing their traditional wares. Further on is the ski-station of le Chalet Reynard, after which the road turns right to run along the south face of the mountain as far as Saint-Estève, Sainte-Colombe and Bédouin. These slopes foster olive groves and the grapes – *syrah, grenache, cinsault* and *carignan* – that are used to make the *appellation Côtes du Ventoux contrôlée.* I sipped a deep-red glass of it at Bédouin, meditating on the grim revenge taken on the town in 1794 after some unknown person had ripped up the recently planted tree of liberty. The Committee of Public Safety ordered sixty-three citizens to be publicly executed. They are commemorated by an obelisk outside the town. Then, before taking the D19 back towards Malaucène, I went into the early eighteenth-century church to admire the medallions painted for it by Nicolas Mignard, depicting rather too sumptuously for my taste scenes from the life of the Virgin Mary and the passion of her son.

Equally rewarding is an exploration of the villages along the extraordinary range of lace-like rocks known as les Dentelles de Montmirail. Winding swiftly upwards of Malaucène, the D938 runs south-west towards Carpentras. After fifteen kilometres a little road takes you right to le Barroux, its warren of narrow streets guarded by a half-fortress, half-château built in the Italian style by Henri de Rovigliasc between 1539 and 1548. Its chapel was frescoed in the eighteenth century, and today the fortress is a major study centre for the archaeology and history of this region of Provence. A little further on, the next turning left (the D13) takes you on a short detour to Caromb, whose church is a thirteenth-century Romanesque gem, its apse built a century later, with an additional fifteenth-century chapel on the north side housing a retable of the same date. The other furnishings of the church, including its organ console and pulpit, were carved in the seventeenth century. A square machicolated tower is a melancholy reminder of the once formidable medieval fortifications of the village. The local wine merchants have installed in their cave a museum of agricultural implements, which I failed to visit, preferring to imbibe.

Return west from Caromb by the D21, cross the main road south and you find yourself running along the southern edge of les Dentelles de Montmirail as far as Beaumes-de-Venise, which is situated on the River Salette beside a cliff pierced with caves. The village has an eighteenth-century fountain and is dominated by a ruined château. The vineyards surrounding the village produce a particularly valued muscat grape, from which is derived a gentle, though decidedly sweet, wine.

Nine kilometres to the west of Beaumes-de-Venise stands the

Romanesque chapel of Notre-Dame-d'Aubune, close to a plateau
known locally as the cemetery of the Saracens, ever since the
Frankish king Charles Martel defeated them in 732. The tower of
this soberly beautiful church is remarkably elongated, with one
blind storey and then two more pierced by twinned, slender
openings.

From here a good road runs north-west to Vacqueyras, two
kilometres east of which is situated Montmirail itself. The name
almost certainly means marvellous mountain (or *mons mirabilis*),
and the view of the Dentelles is magnificent from here. Montmirail is also the source of a saline spring long reputed to have
therapeutic powers. The twelfth-century tower which guards the
spring is called the tower of the Saracens, for no good reason, so
far as I could discover.

Three other extremely picturesque spots lie north of Vacqueyras
on the western side of les Dentelles de Montmirail. Gigondas is
noted as much for its wines as for its site. The powerful red wine
of Gigondas was known as long ago as the fourteenth century,
but received its *appellation contrôlée* status only in 1971. It now
ranks second only to Châteauneuf-du-Pape in repute.

This village is an excellent spot in which to muse on the Côtes du
Rhône wines in general, for the excellent cellars in Gigondas offer
the tourist ample opportunity for tasting. Côtes du Rhône wines are
produced in some 100,000 acres of vineyard, spread along either
side of the River Rhône and stretching north out of Provence as
far as Vienne. These northern vineyards are almost all situated on
granite soil and grow only two varieties of grape, namely *syrah* and
viognier. Those further south add many more varieties, particularly
the powerful *grenache* grape, as well as *carignan*, which gives body
to the wine, *clairette*, *cinsault*, *bourboulenc* and the perfumed
mourvèdre. The appellation *Côtes du Rhône Villages* applies in
the Vaucluse to wine produced in Beaumes-de-Venise, Cairanne,
Rasteau, Roaix, Sablet, Séguret, Vacqueyras, Valréas and Visan.
As for how long you can keep these wines before drinking, the
whites and rosé wines from the Côtes du Rhône region last for no
more than two years, the reds for up to four. But great vintages
and individual vineyards suggest to the buyer that their wines
may well have a much longer shelf-life, up to eight years or
even longer. Finally there is one curious difference between the
whites of the northerly vineyards and those of Provence, for the

former can sometimes be laid down for as long as eight years but the latter never for more than three.

Gigondas has retained parts of its medieval walls and a ruined château, as well as its eleventh-century church, inside which are a couple of gilded statues of St Cosmas and St Damien. Further north are two villages which we have already noted for producing *Côtes du Rhône Villages*. Sablet, with its fourteenth-century church, perches on a 146-metre height, still in part defended by medieval walls. Finally, three kilometres away by the D23, the circular village of Séguret guards a twelfth-century church and a ruined château. Séguret is enchanting enough to attract a sufficient number of artists, amateur and professional, to host an annual summer school of painting; and in mid-August the village erupts into its wine festival. The village is enterprising enough to provide visitors with a signposted tour of its twelfth-century gateway (the porte Reynier), its eighteenth-century fountain and its fourteenth-century belfry, a tour that ends at the parish church.

Such treats delay one's arrival at Carpentras, a city noted for its *berlingots* (striped boiled sweets invented in the nineteenth century by a genius named Gustave Eysséric) and for its truffles. The latter are sold on the weekly Friday morning market between November and February, along with the usual fruits, vegetables, bric-à-brac and clothing. Today the city, set on the left bank of the Auzon in the lush Comtat plain, is the sub-prefecture of the Vaucluse. From mid-July to 15 August the city sponsors a cultural festival, known as the *festival international Offenbach*, with theatre, dance, music and special exhibitions.

To the north-east of Carpentras is an eighteenth-century aqueduct, built in the 1720s to supply the burgeoning city with water and still retaining forty-eight slender arcades. Then the bridge over the Auzon leads directly to an eighteenth-century chapel, Notre-Dame-de-Santé, built in thanks to the Virgin Mary for defending Carpentras against the plague. Nearby plays a fountain of the same era. The avenue de Notre-Dame-de-Santé runs from here into the boulevard du Nord, whence shortly appears the fourteenth-century porte d'Orange, all that remains of the fortifications built for Carpentras by the Avignon Popes. These once embodied thirty-two defensive towers, all of which matched the golden porte d'Orange, where you can still make out the lines of its portcullis. The destruction of these ramparts in 1840 simply to allow the city to expand is much to be regretted.

The rue de la Porte-d'Orange runs south from the gate to join the rue des Halles, which runs left through covered galleries and past the twelfth-century belfry, once part of a château belonging to the Counts of Toulouse. This delightful street reaches the town hall, housed in an early seventeenth-century hôtel. An earlier town hall, built in the 1470s, was destroyed in a fire on the night of 21 November 1713, though one of its towers survived, surmounted by a forged iron belfry of 1577. The new town hall was enlarged in 1891, a building worthy enough to stand alongside its neighbouring eighteenth-century houses.

These initial delights are an inadequate preparation for two remarkable survivors at Carpentras: the synagogue and the triumphal arch. In the fourteenth century the Comtat region became a refuge for Jews, simply because the Avignon Popes respected and needed their financial acumen and in return protected them against persecution. Carpentras, l'Isle-sur-Sorgue, Cavaillon and Avignon offered them trouble-free hospitality from then to the time of the Revolution. In their own quarters at the heart of these cities, the Jews governed themselves, electing their own rulers, who were known as *les Babylons*.

The first synagogue was built at Carpentras in 1367, but the present building dates from the early 1740s, when the Jews of Carpentras were at the height of their prosperity. Out of a total population of 10,000, one-fifth were Jews and their old synagogue could not house them all. The Bishop of Carpentras gave permission for a new building, on condition that its height did not exceed that of his cathedral. Today its rococo furnishings are in excellent condition. Silk brocade swathes the rolls of the Law, and three seven-branched candelabra light the pulpit. In the fourteenth-century basement can still be seen the *cabussadou*, the bath in which women would ritually wash on the eve of their weddings.

South-west of the synagogue by way of the place de l'Hôtel-de-Ville and the rue d'Inguimbert stands the triumphal arch, the sole remnant of Roman Carpentras, situated by the former episcopal palace of 1640 – an exceedingly imposing building by François de la Valfrenière, which is now the Palais de Justice. The arch was erected in the first half of the first century AD at the entrance to the Gallo-Roman town. It is sculpted with bas-reliefs of chained prisoners (identified by some as a Parthian and a German). One hangs his head in shame, and their useless weapons lie discarded.

Apart from a tiny Romanesque section, the former cathedral of Saint-Siffrein is a late-Gothic building, begun in 1405 at the behest of the Avignon Pope Benedict XIII and finished in 1519. The little towers rising from its façade are fifteenth-century, though the façade itself was given its classical features 200 years later. The lovely, flamboyant Gothic south doorway is called the *porte juive*, through which converted Jews were expected to enter for baptism. Although the interior of the church has retained its delicate Gothic lines, its furnishings are mostly seventeenth-century or later. The Comtat sculptor Jacques Bernus contributed a baroque statue of Bishop Laurent Buti, who died in 1710, as well as the sculpted angels on the high altar. And a bizarre curiosity in the chapel of the relics is said to be the bit of the Emperor Constantine's horse, which after his conversion to Christianity Constantine is alleged to have made for the steed, out of one of the nails of the cross of Jesus. This cathedral also possessed a Romanesque cloister until it was pulled down in the nineteenth century. Today the capitals from its columns can be seen in the Musée Lapidaire of Carpentras.

Two other notable buildings, both in part the legacy of Bishop Malachie d'Inguimbert, who was consecrated in 1735 and died in 1758, are to be found in Carpentras. The museum and library, in an hôtel designed by Antoine d'Allemand, stands in the old quarter of the city west of the former cathedral, and houses a collection of some 150,000 volumes, of which 2,300 are manuscripts and some 200 *incunabula*. Its basis was the personal library of the bishop, much of it bought in Italy. Malachie d'Inguimbert opened it to the people of Carpentras in 1745 and bequeathed it to the city on his death. The second notable building is the Hôtel-Dieu, built for the sick and poor at the bishop's expense between 1750 and 1760 and standing in the place Aristide-Bruant at the southern tip of the city. Its architect was again Antoine d'Allemand, and for the entrance hall of the hospice he created a splendid staircase with delicate wrought-iron balconies. The benefactor's statue stands in the place Aristide-Bruant. He himself lies in a tomb (by Étienne d'Antoine) in the baroque chapel of the Hôtel-Dieu. His foundation is still in use, and has preserved its eighteenth-century pharmacy, with pestles and mortars and a collection of ceramic jars still in their original cupboards, as well as some fine paintings by Mignard. As for the paintings in the city museum, these include a 'Martyrdom of St Catherine' by Il Guercino, some seascapes by the excellent Joseph Vernet and a flattering depiction of the Abbot of Rancé by the court portraitist Hyacinth Rigaud.

The D4 and then the D39 lead directly south-east from Carpentras, crossing the River Nesque to reach the health resort of Saint-Didier-les-Bains, where privileged sick can forget their rheumatism and recover in a Gothic château built by the Counts of Thézan in the first half of the sixteenth century, frescoed and embellished in the eighteenth century. In a wing added in the eighteenth century they say that Beaumarchais finished his *Marriage of Figaro*. The village fountain is dated 1685. A little way south is a troglodyte village, le Beaucet, with a twelfth-century church and a tumbledown château. Le Beaucet is also celebrated as the spot where the patron saint of Provençal farmers, St Gens, who was born at nearby Monteux in 1004, retired to live the life of a hermit. He could tame foxes and make them plough his fields. After his death in 1027 miracles abounded around his tomb. Even today he is reputedly the bringer of rain, and on the third Saturday in May members of the confraternity of St Gens still carry his statue from Monteux to le Beaucet to make sure that enough water will fall on the vines of Provence.

The plateau of Vaucluse now offers superb vistas as the D341 snakes its way towards the promontory on which stands Vénasque. The Celts and then the Romans settled here, and parts of their walls remain. Then, from the sixth to the tenth century, Vénasque was the seat of a bishopric. In consequence its church is a notable affair, and its baptistry incorporates ancient Corinthian columns, which may well derive from a Roman temple to Venus. The main church has an early thirteenth-century dome, a Romanesque west door, a Romanesque nave extended in the fifteenth century, a fifteenth-century apse, an eighteenth-century belfry with a spiky flèche and gargoyles peering down. On the terrace above it, a tree shades a fountain. In May and June Vénasque has a daily cherry market.

Oak trees and pines of the forest of Vénasque now flank the D4 as it twists through the plateau. The highest point is the 627-metre col de Murs, before the road starts to snake downwards through

Murs with its little Romanesque church. Sinuously the road runs south through picturesque Joucas and then on through the plain, crossing the D2 to reach Roussillon, a village – as its name indicates – of rusty-pink houses. Magically sited on a platform of rock, Roussillon has a fourteenth-century church and is surrounded by quarries and rocks of virtually every shade of ochre. Return to the D2 and drive west to Gordes, whose site on a spur of Mont Ventoux is almost as spectacular as that of Roussillon. A town surrounded by olives, almonds and fig trees, Gordes is now the home of artists who have restored its sixteenth-century houses, relish its huge classical church and continually depict its town hall, a fortified Renaissance château built by Bertrand de Siniane in the first quarter of the sixteenth century. Gordes has also preserved a couple of doorways from its twelfth-century walls. So many artists have relished this spot, led by the cubist André Lhote and then by the Hungarian-born Op-artist Victor Vasarély (who helped to restore the château and gave to Gordes the collection of his works now housed there), that the village is now celebrated and in consequence beautifully restored. The château itself seems to mellow as it rises from a stern base, and inside is a superb Renaissance chimney.

Scarcely four kilometres north-west, through a mountainous region sown with the circular stone huts that shepherds built to shelter themselves from snow, rain and the Mistral, is one of the three finest Cistercian abbeys in Provence. The abbey of Sénanque is sister to those of le Thoronet and Silvacane. Cistercian monks began building the church in 1158, though it was finished only at the end of the twelfth century. Remarkably, in view of the fact that the Waldensian Protestants sacked the abbey in 1544, each of the four chapels of the apse has conserved its original altar. The transept is huge, and the crossing is crowned with a dome topped by a little square belfry. The pale walls of the church contrast with the mauve of the lavender fields and are matched in colour by the stones that roof them, though on the roofs of the other monastic buildings these traditional *lauzes* have been replaced with browny-red tiles. Of these buildings, which date from the thirteenth century, the prettiest is undoubtedly the cloister with its twin columns and capitals; the most daring architecturally a hall rising grandly from a single centre pillar; the most peaceful the chapter house, which has graceful ogival vaulting supported by a couple of columns with simple, stylized capitals.

Sénanque abbey was commandeered by the state at the time of the Revolution and sold. An abbot bought it back in 1854 and partially restored it, and for a time the Cistercians returned. They left in 1969, returning to a monastery on the island of Lérins near Cannes. Since that time the refectory has been restored and their abbey has served as a centre for medieval studies.

A superb natural phenomenon gushes out eight or so kilometres west of the abbey, though you must drive circuitously by way of Gordes to reach it. Fontaine-de-Vaucluse owes its reputation (and tourist hotels) to the emerald-green spring which derives from a subterranean river draining the plateaux of the Vaucluse. The abyss from which it gushes is probably in the region of 90 metres deep and lies at the foot of a 230-metre-high cliff. From here the spring tumbles through the rocks and, joined by secondary springs, flows into a lake of the River Sorgue, which is surrounded by plane trees. Naturally the gastronomy here includes succulent trout and crayfish.

From this spot, an enclosed valley (or *villa clausa*), derives the name of the whole *département*. Petrarch found inspiration and solitude here, and a column in his honour has graced the central square of the town since 1804 (the 500th anniversary of his birth), not to speak of the Hotel Pétrarque et Laure, the Petrarch Gardens and the Petrarch museum on the spot where he lived. The poet himself once wrote that this place, 'already celebrated for its wonders, has become yet more famous because of the long stay I made here and because of my songs'. A little Romanesque church, dedicated to St Véran, fronts a speleological museum, containing stalactites and stalagmites which the celebrated speleologist Norbert Casteret evidently had the gall to break off from their original caves. Looking down on the town are the ruins of a fourteenth-century castle once owned by Petrarch's friend Bishop Philippe de Cabassole of Cavaillon, a castle so shattered that in the evening sunlight it seems rather to be part of the crag itself.

Five streams of the River Sorgue turn the ancient mill-wheels and water the town of l'Isle-sur-la-Sorgue, which lies five kilometres west of Fontaine-de-Vaucluse. The former collegiate church of Notre-Dame-des-Anges at l'Isle-sur-la-Sorgue is remarkable not so much for its architecture (which is fine enough, dating from the fourteenth and sixteenth centuries and richly rebuilt in the seventeenth century by François Royer de la Valfrenière) as for the fact that the building was completely and lavishly painted by baroque artists from the Comtat, including Nicolas Mignard. Angels and gilded clouds, and cherubs and gilded swags deliriously swirl. Most of the other sumptuous works of art inside the church date from the seventeenth century. The Avignon architect Jean-Baptiste Franque built a hospice for the town in the mid-eighteenth century, and here again is a lovely set of pharmaceutical jars still housed in their original cases and cupboards.

Driving further west towards Avignon you reach first the fortified town of le Thor, which lies on the left bank of the Sorgue. Its fountains, vaulted streets and little squares are surrounded by apple trees, olives and vines. Its ramparts are pierced by a fourteenth-century gateway with a belfry on top. Here is a church finished in 1202, which (save for the mid-nineteenth-century upper storey of its belfry) has not been added to since then. Exquisitely sited beside the waters of the Sorgue, Notre-Dame-du-Lac has a nave roofed with *lauzes* and a seventeenth-century statue of the Virgin Mary by Jacques Bernus. Nearby le Thor you can visit a cave (the grotte de Thouzon) with stalagmites and stalactites happily untouched by Norbert Casteret and his ilk, as well as a ruined medieval château. And four kilometres further west is Châteauneuf-de-Gadagne, with its lovely views, remains of machicolated walls and gates, and a château famous for being the spot where the Félibrige movement (see p.84 – 6) began in 1854. The oldest church dates from the thirteenth century, but the citizens of Châteauneuf-de-Gadagne survived a plague in 1720 and in consequence built another church in honour of St Roch, to whose intercessions they attributed their escape. From here the D6 runs south for six kilometres to Caumont-sur-Durance, whose Romanesque church of Saint-Symphorien (just outside the town near the cemetery) has a crypt carved out of a rock.

Follow the course of the Durance by way of the D973 south-east from Caumont-sur-Durance as far as Cavaillon, a market town famous for its melons. Irrigation of the fertile plain began in the early thirteenth century, and the succulent melons are now supplemented on the stalls of its Monday market by artichokes, onions, haricots verts. Rambling, fishing, rock-climbing, swimming and camping on the banks of the Durance are tourist treats at

Cavaillon. On Friday evenings in summer the town organizes folk concerts in its Georges Brassens open-air theatre; and on Ascension Day a traditional *corso* is held, with processions and decorated floats towed through the streets by tractors.

Though Cavaillon was inhabited by neolithic people and derives its name from that of the Roman *oppidum* of Cabellio, today its initial aspect is that of the eighteenth century, as you enter by the porte d'Avignon, built in 1740. Next to it stands the former chapel of the hospice, built in 1755 and now an archaeological museum. From here the Grand'Rue runs through the old city, passing a late seventeenth-century chapel of Saint-Benoit and reaching the former cathedral of Notre-Dame-et-Saint-Véran, which Pope Innocent IV consecrated in 1251. Alas, the interior suffered a miserable nineteenth-century restoration, but the exterior remains magnificent, and the furnishings allow one to ignore the problems inside. These furnishings include choir stalls of 1584, with an organ console of 1653 built by the Flemish master Charles le Royer. The gilded woodwork of the apse is sumptuous, the high altar sheltered by a seventeenth-century Italian baldacchino. The chapel of Saint-Véran, added in the fourteenth century, has a wooden retable sculpted by the brilliant Barthélemy Grangier, which incorporates a painting by Pierre Mignard depicting St Véran chaining the dragon of the Vaucluse. Barthélemy Grangier, helped by his son Esprit, also created the lavish woodwork in the chapel of the Sacré-Coeur. (Esprit in his turn was responsible for the design of Cavaillon's Benedictine church, built in 1684.) In this chapel the painting by Pierre Parrocel of a saint in ecstasy depicts the local hermit, César de Bus.

On the south side of Notre-Dame-et-Saint-Véran is a sweet little cloister, built in the twelfth century and restored in the eighteenth in an exemplary manner. Beyond it are the Renaissance and classical houses that characterize this handsome city. And along the rue Hébraïque you come across the ornate synagogue of Cavaillon, built between 1772 and 1774 and housing a magnificent collection of furniture drawn from the legacy of the Jewish communities of the whole Comtat region. The Hebrew inscription over the entrance declares, 'This is the gate of heaven: the just shall enter it.' As for the nineteenth-century aspect of Cavaillon, this emerges in the place du Clos (which even has a café de la Belle Époque). To the east of this square is a so-called triumphal arch, really consisting of a couple of Roman arches, crumbling but in far better condition that the triumphal arch at Carpentras. And high above the town stands the little twelfth-century chapel of Saint-Jacques. It perches on a plateau with an orientation table, from which the views over Cavaillon itself, over the Durance valley, of the Lubéron and Mont Ventoux are remarkable and extensive.

In the Vaucluse there remain to be explored two superb eastern regions: that around Apt and the Lubéron regional park. Apt is beautiful for its situation alone, an ancient city set on the left bank of a tributary of the Durance known as the Coulon, surrounded by hills covered with olives and fruit trees. For centuries its inhabitants have made *confits* and nougats, as well as exploiting the lavender which flourishes in its fields, and the ochre which turns the soil rusty-red.

In neolithic times the whole valley was inhabited. Colonized by Julius Caesar on his return from Spain in 45 BC, the city remained faithful to the Romans. Caesar named the colony Apta Julia, and its citizens displayed their loyalty by erecting a temple to the Emperor Augustus after his death. Roman baths have been excavated beneath the sub-prefecture at Apt, though the finest surviving monument of those times is the bridge eight kilometres west of the town, which throws its three arches sixty-eight metres across the River Coulon as part of the Domitian Way. Sarcophagi, statues and other remains of Celtic and Gallo-Roman times are gathered together in the city's archaeological museum. Today Apt is celebrated both for its candied fruit (especially cherries) and for its ceramics, which are on sale each Saturday at the morning market in the place des Martyrs-de-la-Résistance.

Christianized by the third century, Apt retained its bishop until the time of the Revolution, although it also sheltered Huguenots, who remained undefeated here throughout the Wars of Religion. Undoubtedly the finest monument in the city is its former cathedral of Sainte-Anne, whose dome and south aisle, incorporated in a mid-eleventh-century rebuilding, go back to Roman times. The nave was evidently extended in the twelfth century, and a north aisle was added 200 years later. In 1709 the nave was made higher, unfortunately losing some of its fine features, such as the original ogival vaulting. What you can still make out above the present windows are the lines of the former Romanesque ones.

This is the first church in Western Christendom to have been dedicated to St Anne, the mother of the Virgin Mary. Her alleged relics were apparently brought from the Holy Land by a pilgrim and given to Auspice, the first Bishop of Apt. As often happens in such legends, the saint's bones were subsequently lost. Only when Charlemagne was visiting the city on Easter Day 776 were they discovered by a deaf and dumb baron, who was instantly and miraculously healed. St Anne's remains now lie in a fine reliquary inside the first chapel on the left as you go into the church. Such bones naturally attracted many pilgrims, and to mark the visit of Anne of Austria to the shrine in 1660 François de la Valfrenière was commissioned to rebuild the chapel in its present glamorous form. For her part, Anne of Austria gave the cathedral some chalice veils, which you can still see in the treasury, alongside ecclesiastical vestments and some lovely medieval works of religious art. There too is housed an Arabic standard, brought back from the first crusade after the Battle of Ascalon in 1099. Though woven only in the eleventh century, for long it was considered to be the veil of St Anne herself.

The next chapel on the left contains an even older treasure, a sixth-century marble sarcophagus sculpted with images of Jesus and St Sixtus and St Hyppolytus. In the same chapel the fifteenth-century painting of St John the Baptist depicts him dressed in the regalia of the Knights of St John of Jerusalem. Apart from these riches, and the remains of a fourteenth-century stained-glass window in the sanctuary illustrating the return of the papacy from Avignon to Rome, the former cathedral is noted for possessing two crypts. The upper one dates from the eleventh-century rebuilding, though its altar was preserved from the earlier church. The lower, pre-Romanesque crypt is reached by a narrow corridor decorated by tiles of an interlaced pattern typical of Carolingian times. It was here, in 776, that the alleged bones of St Anne were discovered.

On the south side of the cathedral in the rue des Marchands rises the clock tower of 1568, an almost blank building with a Gothic archway and one of the elegant wrought-iron belfries that dot Provence. This shady, narrow street of hairdressers' and chocolate shops and cafés leads west as far as the place du Palais, site of the former episcopal palace. Built in 1780, only ten years before the bishopric was abolished, the palace is now occupied by the town hall, the courts of justice and the offices of the sub-prefecture. Still further west, in the avenue Philippe-de-Girard, stands the hospice of Apt, founded in the fourteenth century, whose pharmacy – like others we have seen in the Vaucluse – still displays its eighteenth-century medicinal jars. East of the former cathedral the rue Saint-Pierre runs as far as the eighteenth-century porte de Saignon, from which you can look across the river. On its right bank stand a Romanesque chapel dedicated to St Michel and the chapel of Notre-Dame-de-la-Garde, built in 1721 as a reminder of the plague of that year.

A circle of immensely picturesque towns and villages encloses Apt, all of them reached through entrancing, and occasionally spectacular, stretches of countryside. Saint-Saturnin-d'Apt, for instance, with its three windmills, lies nine kilometres north of Apt along the N543, the remains of its château perched on a rock, its homespun Romanesque chapel still intact, though the church of Saint-Étienne was fairly clumsily rebuilt in 1862. This second church houses a wooden reliquary made in the fifteenth century. The farmers here crop grapes, asparagus, olives and cherries, while their bees busily create honey. From Saint-Saturnin-d'Apt, if you care to twist your way north-west along the D943, your route crosses ravines and passes through forests of oaks, olives and chestnuts, with eventually on your left the château de Saint-Lambert in the middle of the forest. After eleven kilometres the road reaches the sixteenth-century château de Javon, which is guarded by pepperpot towers.

Rustrel, in the foothills of Mont Ventoux, lies on the D22 north-east of Apt, the same distance away as Saint-Saturnin-d'Apt. Its town hall occupies a bizarre chapel defended by a couple of round seventeenth-century towers, one of them topped by a wrought-iron belfry. As if the rustic nature of this building were not quite handsome enough for a town hall, the entrance is pompously classical. Wind a little further east to Gignac and you find an ancient château and fortifications, in ruins, since the Catholics demolished them when they were harrying the Huguenots out of the town in the sixteenth century. Another eighteenth-century château is also in ruins, but the twelfth-century church still stands here. Wind yet more tortuously further south-east to Viens and you find a Romanesque church, Romanesque and Gothic houses and another château.

There are three lovely spots on the eastern side of the region, the first of which is Saignon, four kilometres south-east of Apt on a naturally defensive site to which you rapidly climb, and thus have a fine view back over Apt and the River Coulon. The town itself boasts a Romanesque church of Notre-Dame with a sixteenth-century façade. From Saignon the D35 runs on first to Caseneuve, with its camp sites, its medieval keep and its invigorating walking country, and then on to the hilltop village of Saint-Martin-de-Castillon. The name of the village derives from a long-gone convent of Benedictine nuns dedicated to St Martin of Tours. The Romanesque church here was restored in the nineteenth century, and a kilometre or so west of the town is another of the chapels built as a thank-offering for escaping the plague of 1720.

Just south of this village the N100 will take you directly east to Céreste, a village still walled, surrounded by hills planted with vines and olives and (since we are on the old Domitian Way) preserving two Roman bridges, one over the River Aiguebelle, the other over the River Encrême. A medieval quarter surrounds the medieval château. For some more superb scenery on the northern tip of the Lubéron regional park, on the way back to Apt make a detour south along the D48 through Castellet and Auribeau, before returning by way of Saignon.

Finally, scattered about the sparkling Aiguebrun valley south-west of Apt on the way to Cavaillon lie Buoux, Bonnieux, Ménerbes and Oppède-le-Vieux. To reach them leave Apt by the D113, which swiftly climbs the slopes of the Lubéron, that 'aspre montagne' (or harsh mountain) as the Languedoc poet Frédéric Mistral dubbed it. The road then descends into Buoux, with its little chapel whose font was once a Carolingian altar. Archaeologists have discovered near here a tooth that once chewed food for a Neanderthal man or woman. Just outside the village is part of a château built by the Marquises of Buoux and displaying thirteenth-century walls and towers, a Renaissance façade and an elegant wing added in the eighteenth century. Once powerfully fortified, Buoux became a refuge for Huguenots, with the consequence that after he renounced religious toleration, Louis XIV had the walls demolished, though many vestiges remain. This is another place to leave one's car and walk, visiting one of the caves with stalactites and stalagmites that tunnel through the rocks here, as well as seeking out the abandoned villages inhabited by

Huguenots until Louis XIV began persecuting them. Then drive on by way of the spectacularly routed D36 to reach the fortified town of Bonnieux, whose cedar-shaded church dates partly from the twelfth and partly from the fifteenth centuries. The painting of St Francis of Assisi inside is said to be by Nicolas Mignard. Parts of the town walls have survived from the thirteenth century. Bonnieux also has a charming museum of bakery.

The perched village of Ménerbes lies thirteen kilometres further west. In between appears another village on a hill, Lacoste, whose ruined château once belonged to the family of the Marquis de Sade. De Sade describes the château in both *Justine* and the *120 jours de Sodom*, which makes a tour of these ruins obligatory for students of the marquis. The town also boasts a café de Sade, and a school connected with the Cleveland Art Institute. Between Lacoste and Ménerbes is the former abbey of Saint-Hilaire, its twelfth-century church and seventeenth-century cloister meticulously restored. As for Ménerbes itself, its present parish church was built in the fourteenth century, and the whole village is protected by a well-restored Renaissance château, which still seems to me half-fortress. In the 1950s this was the home of the abstract artist Nicholas de Staël and in consequence is still often referred to as the château de Staël. Over the clock tower at Ménerbes is a wrought-iron belfry far more elaborate than the one at Apt, but slightly dented and worse for wear.

Oppède-le-Vieux, another partly fortified village, is a mere six kilometres further on in the direction of Cavaillon, though the road dips and rises *en route*. Above the village lour the remains of a château built by the Count of Toulouse in 1209. In the mid-sixteenth century this château was the home of Baron Jean de Maynier, notable for his vicious persecution of the Waldensian 'heretics' even at a time when official French policy was that they should be tolerated. Maynier is said to have massacred hundreds of them, until he was finally poisoned. Today what is most delightful about Oppède is that it was dead and lives again. Abandoned by its former villagers, it was taken over by a colony of artists, who set about restoring its medieval houses and caring for its Romanesque and Gothic church, with its straightforwardly plain, massive hexagonal bell tower, from the corners of which peer eight gargoyles.

The southern part of the Lubéron is traditionally known in

Provence as the Pays d'Aigues, that is the countryside of Aix, an agricultural region cultivated by the Romans north of the River Durance. South-east of Bonnieux the D943 takes you across Mistral's 'aspre montagne' to Lourmarin, which nestles amid vineyards, olives and cedars. Lourmarin is proud of its native son, Philippe de Girard, inventor of a mechanical spinning machine which put many out of work. The seventeenth-century house in which he was born in 1775 has been turned into a museum dedicated to his memory, and displays family portraits and souvenirs as well as models of his inventions. His father lived not here but in the magnificent château de Lourmarin, which was built in part in the late-fifteenth century and then extended by Blanche de Levis in 1560, in a Renaissance style which still warily preserves some defensive aspects. Massive chimneys, an elegant circular staircase, a room today devoted to exotic musical instruments (some from Africa and the Far East) and a well-tended garden with formal ponds rightly bring tourists here. Others of a literary bent are attracted by the tombs of the existentialist novelist Albert Camus and of the Provençal writer Henri Bosco, both of whom lie in the cemetery of Lourmarin.

Camus's former home is now a museum in his memory. Born in 1913 of Breton and Algerian parents, during the Second World War Camus opted for the Resistance and edited a secret newspaper named *Combat*. He also managed to write two famous works during these troubled times, *The Outsider* and *The Myth of Sisyphus*. In 1947 appeared *The Plague*, a novel which takes a plague that affected Oran in 1940 as a symbol of the Nazi occupation of France. Camus wrote *The Fall* a year before he won the Nobel Prize for Literature in 1957. Three years later he was killed in a road accident.

I came across the writing of Henri Bosco (who was born in 1888 and died in 1976) long before encountering Camus, since someone had the wit to set his masterpiece *Le Mas Théotime* as an A-level set book as I started studying for it. Published in 1945, it is set on a Lourmarin farm, or *mas*, as the Languedoc language has it (though Bosco called the town Puyloubiers). Whereas the works of Camus at this time were obsessed with the war and the Resistance, *Le Mas Théotime* scarcely mentions the powerful events that had rocked Europe. Instead he sets about evoking the eternal countryside of the Vaucluse. The novel begins with the following description:

Evenings in August are extremely hot in our part of the country. The late-afternoon sun sets the fields glowing like braziers. The only thing to do is stay indoors in the shade and wait for dinner. The farmhouses, flayed by cold winds in winter and naked to the scorching sun in summer, were built specifically as shelters, whose massive walls offer some protection against the fury of the seasons.

The Théotime farm lies exposed in open country, where from the beginning of July the air is unbearably stifling, save in the early mornings and sometimes at night when a slight breeze blows. Then the farmer's family sits near the spring, breathing the cool air, which is full of the fragrance of the running water and the grass. The hero Pascal prunes his vines, looks after his bees, watches wild boar stampede and collects wild plants in the hills, returning to his *mas* to label them in the loft that is his private lair.

Yet the book also incorporates the feuds and violence that can erupt in the hot Provençal countryside, and Pascal's family is opposed by his malicious neighbour Clodius. Even so, the Théotime *mas* itself is a haven of calm. One of the heroines of the story, Françoise, is a big girl, daughter of Pascal's tenant-farmer and friend, lovely but entirely unselfconscious, devoted to the land from which she springs. Another heroine is Pascal's cousin Geneviève who, after a period of impulsive craving for impossible happiness and two profitless marriages, returns to the peace of the farm. Violence returns in the hot summer when her abandoned second husband murders Clodius. Pascal helps the two to escape from the police, and seeks to renew his tranquillity as he gathers the olives and grapes and ploughs his land.

Henri Bosco could not conceive that even Geneviève was without some of the traditional virtues of the Provençal farmers. She has an uncanny power over animals, at one point cowing the herd of wild boar who are about to stampede through Pascal's crops. And before she leaves the Théotime *mas* for ever she arranges for the restoration of a small chapel in the hills above the farm, bequeathing it to Pascal. As the time approaches for the celebration of Christmas, with the scene of the shepherds enacted here for the first time in half a century, Pascal realizes his love for Françoise and confesses it to her. This novel fo brooding heat and sudden violence ends idylically. 'Soon, after Christmas, we shall be able to pick the olives,' says Françoise, as she and Pascal walk together. 'The weather is dry.' She breathes an air of happiness, thinks Pascal, 'and I felt happy too, because she was tall and beautiful, and because she was walking confidently at my side with the slow steps of a real woman of the soil.'

Bosco grew so protective of his Lubéron that he wanted it to remain as isolated from the outside world as *Le Mas Théotime* was isolated from the Hitler era. Once he wrote that 'A countryside celebrated by poets is often a bait for tourists. One day they arrive, following the poets, and the poetry disappears.' This is an irritating remark from one who did so much to spread the renown of the region, as irritating to those of its poorer citizens, who need tourism more than Henri Bosco did, as it is to the tourists themselves. His is not a view shared by the people of Apt, who have installed in the place Jean-Jaurès a Maison du Parc with brochures, maps, exhibitions and wine tasting, all connected with the Lubéron, which was designated a Regional Natural Park in 1977.

Covering around 130,000 hectares, the park stretches out of the Vaucluse into the *département* of the Alpes-de-Haute-Provence. Endangered species, such as the *capoun fé* or Egyptian vulture, Bonelli's eagle (whose wingspan can reach 1.70 metres), the short-toed eagle (whose wings can stretch another 0.10 metres) and the eagle owl (known as the *dugo* in Provençal), thrive here. Wild boar roam the forests, and beavers dam the rivers. Aspic lavender, dwarf broom and the feathery stipe penna are matched by the rock rose (or cotton cistus) and the cones leuzea. Sheep graze and the farmers make goat's cheese, honey and the red, rosé and white *appellation Côtes du Lubéron* wine. At the north-east corner of the natural park black pines flourish, brought here from Austria during the nineteenth-century reafforestation. Marked paths for ramblers, horeseback riders or hikers have been laid out, as well as a 15-kilometre cycle track from Apt to Saint-Martin-de-Castillon.

Bosco's beloved Lourmarin is an excellent spot from which to begin a round tour of the park, ending at Cucuron, which is but seven kilometres away. Leaving the town, the D943 rises and, before it falls again to reach the seventeenth- and eighteenth-century houses of Cadenet, offers a lovely view back to the château of the Garard family and Mont Lubéron. To the west appear the Alpilles and the lower valley of the Durance. The hero of Cadenet is a drummer boy, André Etienne, whose bronze statue stands in the main square. The church here was built in the fourteenth century and its architecture stands at the turning point of Provençal Romanesque and Gothic. Its impressive tower dates from 1538, with a spire added in 1844.

Only six and a half kilometres south-west, the abbey of Silvacane lies on the left bank of the River Durance. Of the three Cistercian sisters, le Thoronet, Sénanque and Silvacane, this one is probably the most impressive (though I should prefer le Thoronet, save for its coating of bauxite). Monks from Marseille came here in the eleventh century, their successors accepting the Cistercian rule in 1145. Their breathtakingly simple abbey church was built between 1175 and 1225. Its subtle variations in architectural style enable us to trace how it was built, beginning with the apse, with its own four minor apses. The crossing alone has ogival arches, the rest being in a pure Romanesque style. Even the cloister, although built towards the end of the thirteenth century, remains almost entirely Romanesque. The chapter house, the monks' dormitory, their communal room, their long and narrow sacristy have all been well-restored, as has the refectory, which the monks themselves – one might imagine with their traditional nose for a good meal – rebuilt in the fifteenth century.

The road south-east from Cadenet to Pertuis flanks not the Durance but the Canal de Cadenet. Halfway there a brief diversion left, of fewer than five kilometres, will take you to Ansouis. The town itself is perched on a hill, its houses often set into walls with a round tower and wrought-iron belfry poking up from them. Above this ensemble rises the huge château of the Counts of Sabran. Built in the eighteenth century, it is surrounded by substantial remains of its medieval predecessor as well as a garden whose plants, cypress and pine-trees seem far more exotic than one expects in France. The château becomes more elegant as it rises, the upper storeys pierced with Renaissance windows. A monumental doorway has been built in the façade, yet the overall impression in no way conflicts with the essentially rustic face of Ansouis. In one of the ancient rooms of this château, so one is told, a couple named Elzéar and Delphine, forced to marry by the King of Naples in 1299, nevertheless took vows of chastity and became so renowned that after their deaths they were canonized. A superb staircase and Flemish tapestries (depicting the saga of Dido and Aeneas) enliven the later additions to the château. And at the foot of the rock on which the château rises is a Romanesque chapel housing the bones of St Elzéar and St Delphine.

Take the D56 south-east to Pertuis, whose medieval walls have left the town a fourteenth-century gateway, and whose thirteenth-century château is represented today only by the clock tower in the place Mirabeau. In a region crammed with Romanesque churches it is a change at Pertuis to come across Saint-Nicolas, for it is resolutely and flamboyantly Gothic. It also shelters an eighteenth-century statue of St Roch, who served so many persons dying of the plague that he caught it himself, and is in consequence always pointing out a pestilential bubicle on one of his legs.

Nearby at la Tour-d'Aigues, five kilometres north-east of Pertuis, stands one of the most deliciously complex ruined châteaux in Provence. The Baron of Chantal built it around 1570 in the grounds of a medieval château. It was partly burned down in 1780 and then abandoned in 1792. Today it is owned by the *département* and cared for once again. What remains in a large and desolate square is a sumptuous eighteenth-century triumphal arch, bearing Corinthian columns and a frieze, and flanked by two square pavilions. Behind them rises blankly a medieval keep. La Tour-d'Aigues also boasts a medieval bridge across the River Lèze, and a church with a Romanesque apse and a seventeenth-century choir and nave, housing an 'Entombment' of 1810 by Sollier, who was a pupil of the great David d'Angers.

The riches of this mountainous part of the Vaucluse remain astounding. The route continues directly north-east through the hilltop village of Grambois, where you find little alleyways, the remains of ancient fortifications, a church with a Romanesque nave, thirteenth-century frescos, a triptych of 1519 and a painting said to be by Nicolas Mignard. Beyond it is la Bastide-des-Jourdans, which has preserved parts of its sixteenth-century walls and several gateways, as well as the remains of a monastery founded in 1740 where once stood a commandery of the Knights Templar.

Unless the number of delightful churches has utterly overwhelmed you, on the way back to Lourmarin do not fail to visit Notre-Dame-de-Beaulieu at Cucuron, a village surrounding a medieval keep. A fourteenth-century Gothic apse, a Romanesque nave, a fourteenth-century porch with a geometrical design on its tympanum, a massive square belfry, a high altar sculpted out of marble around 1700, a sixteenth-century 'Ecce Homo' in a side hapel and an eighteenth-century pulpit are not to be despised, however sated the visitor. The high altar seems far too sumptuous for this humble, though imposing church. It was in fact initially commissioned for the Chapel of the Visitation at Aix by Cardinal Mazarin's niece, the Duchess of Modena.

Cucuron also relishes a belfry created out of a doorway of its former fourteenth-century walls. And looking down on the intimate streets is a little fourteenth-century château. Ironically, Henri Bosco, who so resented 'strangers' visiting his beloved Lubéron, made this village the scene of his second novel, *Le Trestoulas*, which was published in 1935. In truth the novelist constantly attempted to deny this – not surprisingly, for the book scarcely pays compliments to the villagers he describes. His theme is peasant vendettas, the brutal violence they engender and the long memories people of the region have for feuds of the past. One character poisons her own uncle and sets fire to hayricks. Other characters, ostracized by the village, are willing to venture out only at night. One of them, Clapu, takes revenge on the village when he discovers some ancient underground sluices and manages to cut off the supply of water, thus destroying the livelihood of the whole community.

Yet the scents as well as the savagery of the region are superbly evoked. Clapu's protégée, a 15-year-old gypsy girl named la Cherli, smells of straw and dry lavender, since she sleeps in a haystack. The odour at night of a hedge of cypresses seems to Bosco like a physical presence. And always he reminds us of the brooding presence of Mont Lubéron itself, and the sudden storms that can flare up here, so that 'beasts and humans both feel that distant and dangerous concentration of heavy electrical masses'. Bosco's novels serve as a reminder of the inscrutable power of the Lubéron. As he put it in an earlier work (*Le Sanglier*), 'This great body, swollen with darkness and bearded with holly, breathes with the scent of an animal.'

Marseille, its coastline and Marcel Pagnol

To the hero of Alphonse Daudet's novel *Tartarin de Tarascon*, Marseille seemed like one of the wondrous, fantastic cities of the Arabian Nights, and so it still seems to me. 'As far as the eye could see, appeared a jumble of masts and spars pointing in every direction,' wrote Daudet.

Every possible national flag – Russian, Greek, Swedish, Tunisian, American – flew from the tops of the masts. The ships lay beside the wharves, bowsprits pointing like rows of bayonets over the walls of the quay. Beneath them he could see, carved out of wood, nymphs, goddesses, Madonnas and other figures, images after which the boats were called, all of them weatherbeaten, rotting, stained and mildewed.

Daudet even managed to enthuse over the colours of the streams on the quay, impregnated as they were with oil and soda. The quayside was crammed with smoky hovels in which sailors cooked their meals, with tobacconists and shops selling monkeys, parrots, rope and sail-cloth, as well as curiosity shops offering spyglasses that could have served Sir Francis Drake. Squatting beside their stalls and shouting their heads off were people selling mussels and periwinkles, while other matelots hobbled by with baskets of washing, bound for the communal fountains.

Alphonse Daudet exulted in the bustling traffic of the port:

the silks, the minerals, the waggonloads of wood, ingots of
lead, cloth, sugar, and above all the great stacks of Dutch
cheese which the Genoese were staining a gleaming red. He
loved the grain shed, the loose ears of corn pouring down in
golden streams and giving off clouds of yellow dust as men in
red caps sifted it. The smell of pitch from the ships' carpenters,
the sight of men cleaning seaweed off the side of huge vessels in
the dry docks, the deafening noise of massive sheets of copper
being fixed to strengthen the hulls, the oaths and whistles, the
songs and the sound of drums and bugles, all of it topped by
the clamorous whirl of the Mistral, enormously excited him.
And he also relished the harbour entrance, 'that marvellous ships'
thoroughfare, where perhaps an English frigate, trim and spotless
with the officers in yellow gloves, would be embarking for Malta,
or a Marseille brig would be clearing her moorings, the burly
captain sporting a silk hat and frock coat while he called out his
orders in the language of Provence.'

Charles Dickens had discovered the same vivacity as he
approached the port some 150 years ago. Dickens found the road
covered with holidaymakers, sitting outside the public houses and
smoking, drinking, playing draughts and cards and occasionally
dancing. The suburbs of Marseille seemed to him disagreeably
dusty, and he found the harbour full of stagnant water befouled
by the refuse of innumerable ships. But then the liveliness of the
city captured him.

There were foreign sailors of all nations, in the streets; with red shirts,
blue shirts, buff shirts, tawny shirts, and shirts of orange colour;
with red caps, blue caps, green caps, great beards and no beards;
in Turkish turbans, glazed English hats, and Neapolitan head-dresses.
There were the townspeople sitting in clusters on the pavement, or
airing themselves on the tops of their houses, or walking up and
down the closest and least airy of the Boulevards; and there were
crowds of fierce-looking people of the lower sort, blocking up the
way, constantly.

Already Marseille was growing slightly intimidating. When
Cézanne reached the city towards the end of the nineteenth
century, he wrote to Émile Zola, 'Marseille is the oil capital
of France, just as Paris is its butter capital,' adding, 'You have

no idea of the impudence of this ferocious populace. They have but one interest: money.' Today much of the Canebière, once its most fashionable thoroughfare, is the gregarious street of a cosmopolitan city, with the useful classless shops that most of us use most of the time, as well as cinemas and banks. Maybe this is simply a return to the past: its name derives from *chanvre*, for this was the site of the former hemp market of Marseille. On 9 October 1934 it was also the venue of the assassination, by Croatian separatists, of King Alexander of Yugoslavia, who expired outside no. 12. Another loss occurred in 1943, when the Germans were occupying the city during the Second World War and destroyed some of the most picturesque alleyways of the old port on the all-too-plausible grounds that they constituted a health risk, and out of reasonable irritation that they were sheltering too many members of the Resistance.

At the beginning of our own century Hilaire Belloc decided to walk through France to Rome. Arriving at Marseille, crippled with fatigue and trying to forget his wounded feet by drinking stoup after stoup of beer, he was accosted by a commercial traveller whom he described as the Phocaean (I presume because Marseille was founded around 600 BC by Greeks from Phocaea in Asia Minor). The man talked with extreme rapidity for two hours. To Belloc it seemed that he had seen every city in the world and remembered their minutest details. 'He was extremely accurate, his taste was abominable, his patriotism large, his vitality marvellous, his wit crude but continual, and to his German friend, to the host of the inn, and to the blonde serving-girl, he was a familiar god.' This traveller apparently came but once a year and for a day would pour out the torrent of his travels like a waterfall of guide-books. Belloc observed how 'He gloried in dates, dimensions, and the points of the compass in his descriptions.' Then the man disappeared for another year, leaving his friends to feast on the memories he had given them.

What strikes me as prescient is Belloc's final judgement on the man's race. 'He was of the old race you see on vases in red and black; slight, very wiry, with a sharp, eager, but well-set face, a small, black, pointed beard, brilliant eyes like those of lizards, rapid gestures, and a vivacity that played all over his features as sheet lightning does over the glow of midnight in June.' As he listened to the Phocaean, the thought struck Belloc that the delta of the Rhône is something quite separate from the rest of France, 'a wedge of Greece and of the East thrust into the Gauls'.

Today Marseille is even more a mixture of races, save that mixture is not quite the *mot juste*, for this capital of Provence is a city of ghettos and racial unease. Its population swollen by immigration from North Africa, the city has developed a reputation for illegal drug smuggling, criminal classes and a viciousness far beyond what it deserves. None the less, certain quarters are dangerous for the stranger, especially at night – but of how many great cities is this not true?

Yet this maritime city has experienced eras of prosperity and great achievement. Siding with Pompey against Julius Caesar, Marseille incurred the latter's extreme displeasure, and after he had taken the city in 49 BC, Caesar reduced it to the status of a Roman colony. The barbarians and the Saracens reduced it still further. Only with the era of the Crusades did Marseille begin to prosper again. By the thirteenth century the lower city was virtually an independent republic. But Marseille was never secure. Louis of Anjou took the city in 1246. The Aragonese sacked the city in 1424. In 1486 Louis XI at last claimed Marseille for the French monarchy, but the imperial forces recaptured it in 1524.

In the next century Marseille resisted in vain the pretensions of Louis XIV. The extension of royal power was in fact the city's economic salvation: under Louis XIV Marseille had a monopoly of trade with the Levant, and as a result expanded at a time when French architecture was noble. As with nearly every port in the world, slums developed alongside spacious squares and fine buildings, breeding disease. A ship from Syria brought the bubonic plague to Provence when it landed here in 1720 – in consequence of which were built the numerous classical 'plague churches' in those towns and villages that were spared as the disease spread to the hinterland. Nearly half the population of Marseille itself succumbed to the plague, yet the city recovered from the setback with ease, its wealth increased by the trading skills of the East India Company. And the nineteenth century brought even more prosperity, as France developed her colonies and the digging of the Suez Canal stimulated increasing trade. Marseille became France's premier port, a position it retains to this day.

Its population was exploding, first with Greeks escaping the massacring Turks in 1822, later with Italians driven here by the agricultural crises of their own country, then with Armenians and always with Algerians, but especially so after 1962. By the 1960s what had been a city of 110,000 people in 1820 housed 670,000, including a Jewish community some 70,000 strong (with their principal synagogue, built in the nineteenth century, in the rue Breteuil). The Algerians and Moroccans, with their own quarter and their minarets a visible emblem on the urban skyline, had come to stay.

As well as fostering two of France's greatest popular stars, the singer Charles Aznavour and the actor Yves Montand, Marseille had also gained an unjust reputation for gangsterdom. Since I intend to spend much of the rest of my life savouring the extraordinary diversity of food created by the citizens of our planet, instead of cringing from this press of nationalities (most of them, of course, French citizens), I rejoice that the immigrant population of Marseille enables me to sample such Oriental confections as *rahat-loukoum*, *tahin* and *halva*.

And from this brief survey of its history and the impressions of past visitors to Marseille I conclude that its reputation for sleaze and vice is not a modern one. It seems to me that superficial visitors set their minds simply to confirming this unsavoury reputation – trawling the Vieux-Port with its call girls and dubious shops (scarcely noticing the pink stones of the twelfth-century belfry of the church of Saint-Laurent rising at the end of the port), deriving a spurious *frisson* from the fact that the city houses a recruiting office of the French Foreign Legion – rather than opening their eyes to the real charms of Marseille.

Much depends on one's personal attitude in approaching a great port. The dramatist Jean Anouilh set Act 2 of his *Eurydice* in a Marseille hotel room, with the stage direction, 'The room is large, gloomy and dirty. The ceilings are too high, lost in the shadows.' His props consisted of 'a large iron bedstead, a folding screen and a miserly light'. Henri, one of the characters in the play, describes the city as a human ant-hill, full of smutty vulgarity and squalor. Yet having insulted the city, Henri adds, 'In the alleyways of the old port they do not kill each other as much as some people say – and all the same, it's a fine city.' I entirely agree. Set in an amphitheatre, its streets steeply rising as you leave the port, some of them stepped with a dent in the middle to allow the water to flow down, Marseille is at one moment insalubrious and the next elegant, a city of enormous character and like none other in Provence.

Two sets of fortifications protect the entrance to the Vieux-Port. On the western side is Fort Saint-Jean, dating initially from the thirteenth century. This whole complex derives from a former commandery of the Knights of St John of Jerusalem, who built here a triangular bastion. The square, machicolated St John's tower was added in the fifteenth century at the behest of Roi René, and the beacon is what remains of Vauban's additions of 1679. At the other side of the harbour entrance rise the bastions of Fort Saint-Nicholas, built on the orders of King Louis XIV in 1660 after his troubles with the rebellious Frondeurs. Its cannons pointed towards the city, since Louis feared the rebellious instincts of the people of Marseille far more than the depradations of those who might wish to attack the city.

The quayside of the Vieux-Port is also the scene of the daily fish market. Fish from the Gulf of Marseilles has been renowned since Roman times. A celebrated tale recounts that a Roman exile, defended by Cicero, was delighted when his advocate lost the case. Otherwise he would have been obliged to return to Rome, leaving Marseille, where he had never been so happy as eating its mullet. On the stalls of the market red mullet vies with bearded mullet and the mullet we know as gurnard. Fresh sardines, cod, eels and conger eels, turquoise mackerel, sea-bream, pink *pageots*, whiting and rainbow wrasse weigh down the counters.

Small wonder most of us regard *bouillabaisse* as the characteristic dish of Marseille. A meal in itself, *bouillabaisse* derives its magic from the very variety of fish bubbling in the cauldron, with a hint of saffron to tempt the nose as well as the palate. A variation of *bouillabaisse* is *la bourride*, this dish made entirely of white fish and without saffron. In the traditional restaurants most of the liquid will be set aside, ready to be dunked with slices of bread. With the rest the chef makes a sauce, adding the yoke of an egg and two spoonfuls of *aïoli* per person, a pungent blend which is then poured over the bread.

Aïoli is the mayonnaise of Provence. The Provençal nationalist Frédéric Mistral once declared that 'The essence of *aïoli* is a concentration of the heat, the strength, the exhilaration of the sun of Provence, but it also possesses the further virtue of driving away flies.' (This is correct.) He added that 'Those who dislike it, finding that it scorches their throats, had better not gallivant around our district. We'll keep to our own family.' *Aïoli* is undoubtedly fairly wild, made not only from the superb olive oil of Provence, lemon juice and egg yolks, but also traditionally from a clove of garlic for every person sitting down to the meal. The variety made without egg yolks but with mashed potatoes and breadcrumbs is equally powerful. In Provence *aïoli* accompanies every fish dish, even *brandade de morue*, whose pounded cod has already been mixed with garlic.

Far from shortening one's life, it enables you to avoid illnesses and keeps death away (or so Léon Daudet insisted, and this is also correct). I think the best way of enjoying it, and the fish of Marseille, is to look for the dish known as *le grand aïoli*, a variant of *la bourride*. Red mullet, whiting, cod and bream (and no doubt many other fish too) are poached in a broth. Then the broth is thickened with bread and eaten as a soup, after which the poached fish is served with vegetables and eaten with dollops of *aïoli*.

The fish of Marseille was renowned when Julius Caesar conquered the city. Roman rule did not last. The Visigoths took Marseille in AD 480 and the Franks finally claimed it as their own in the ninth century. Till then the Church was virtually the only authority. Legend has it that Christianity was brought here by Lazarus whom, the New Testament alleges, Jesus raised from the dead. Certainly Marseille had a bishop in the third century. Monks spread the faith, and at the beginning of the fifth century one of them, St John Cassian, founded here Saint-Victor, the oldest monastery in Gaul.

The founder was a remarkable man. Having studied under the brilliant theologian and reforming Patriarch of Constantinople, St John Chrisostom, John Cassian visited Rome and then sojourned in monasteries in Bethlehem and lower Eygpt. Not only did he found the abbey of Saint-Victor (and another one for women further inland), he then set about writing a pioneering and famous treatise, *De Institutis coenobiorum*, setting out the ideals of the monastic life. Monks and nuns, he warned, should struggle against gluttony, luxury, avarice, anger, sloth, despair, vainglory and pride. They must also, he insisted, look after novices, be given to hospitality and care for the young.

Situated outside the city overlooking the port, Saint-Victor was later to be powerfully fortified by Abbot Guillaume de Grimoard (the man elected Pope Urban V at Avignon in 1362). The present harmonious church derives mainly from the twelfth century, and the far more ancient crypt houses the sarcophagi of long-dead monks and abbots. The oldest altar is Merovingian. Over the centuries many legends and traditions have attached themselves to this church. Pilgrims still visit a thirteenth-century statue of a black Virgin enshrined here; and at Candlemas the worshippers buy biscuits called *navettes*. These are baked in the form of little ships in honour of the tradition that three saintly Marys (one a sister of Jesus's mother, another St Mary Magdalene, and the third Mary Salome, mother of the Apostles James and John) had sailed together from the Holy Land to make their home in Provence.

As the centuries passed, bishops, viscounts and the abbey of Saint-Victor itself disputed possession of Marseille in the Middle Ages. In 1069 the bishop and the viscount agreed to partition the city. The bishops fortified their part of Marseille, and in the mid-twelfth century rebuilt their sixth-century cathedral of Notre-Dame-la-Majeure in the Romanesque style.

Christianity continued to flourish here, under the leadership of several heroic bishops, and also of the remarkable seventeenth-century St Vincent de Paul. Having once been a galley-slave himself, he set up a Christian ministry to the galley-slaves of Provence, and in 1643 helped to found a hospital for them at Marseille. St Vincent de Paul is honoured by a church built at the uppermost end of la Canebière between 1849 and 1890, its two spires reaching seventy-five metres.

During the plague year of 1720 the Bishop of Marseille was a converted Huguenot named Henri de Belsunce. Refusing to abandon the infected and dying, he continued to administer the Last Sacrament to them and miraculously escaped the plague himself. In the art gallery of the nineteenth-century Palais Longchamp at Marseille hang two celebrated paintings by Michel Serre depicting his heroism. Henri de Belsunce was Bishop of Marseille from 1709 to 1755, and such was his devotion to his flock that he is said never to have left his diocese.

By the time of the French Revolution the citizens of Marseille were Republican enough to steal, so to speak, the new French national anthem from the citizens of Alsace – an anthem written in 1792 by a French officer named Rouget de Lisle when he was in fact stationed in Strasbourg. On 21 June in that same year a Marseille delegate to Montpellier named François Mireur gave such a resounding speech from a *traiteur*'s shop in Marseille that the citizens begged him to speak again the following day. Next day, having nothing more to say and conscious only that he possessed a magnificent voice, instead of spouting bombastic nonsense François Mireur sang Rouget de Lisle's resounding stanzas. The Republicans from Marseille, on their way to Paris, enthusiastically took up the emotive words:

> Children of the Fatherland, let us go,
> The day of glory has come;
> The bloody flag of tyranny
> Has been raised against us,
> The bloody flag of tyranny.
> Can you hear the shouts of fierce soldiers in the countryside?
> They enter our hearths to slay our sons and friends.
> Citizens, arm yourselves!
> Form up your battalions!
> Let us march, let us march!
> Let an impure blood water our furrows!

So what began as the battle song of the Army of the Rhine was speedily transformed into the 'Marseillaise'. Happily, although I have often stood to attention as this national anthem was being played beside a local French war memorial, I have never heard any Frenchman or woman actually singing these bloodthirsty sentiments.

A visual reminder of these stirring times is the porte d'Aix, a triumphal arch which you come across in the place Jules Guesde, as you drive into the centre of the city from Aix-en-Provence. The architect Penchaud modelled it in 1825 on the arch at Orange, and David d'Angers sculpted trophies and stirring scenes recalling the battles of France during the time of the revolution and the First Empire. Ironically, Republicanism did not last long in the city, for Napoleon's continental system was ruinous for a such an important trading port. Marseille welcomed his fall from power, and her citizens became legitimist, enthusiastic supporters of the

monarchy. In reaction to the revolutionaries' cult of the Supreme
Being, Catholicism resurged. Sailors, stevedores and caulkers
formed themselves into religious brotherhoods. To this day
many working-class families in Marseille insist on their Catholic
devotion. (Few, however, actually go to church – fewer than 15
per cent even as long ago as 1953, according to an official church
survey).

None the less it is probably fitting that the dominant
monuments of Marseille are two nineteenth-century beloved
ecclesiastical monsters: the cathedral of Sainte-Marie-Majeure
overlooking the ships docked in the basin of la Grande Joliette;
and the huge basilica of Notre-Dame-de-la-Garde on its hill at
the other side of the Vieux-Port. The cathedral, which was built
between 1852 and 1893 by the architects Léon Vaudoyer and H.
Espérandieu (who designed the massive cupolas), utterly dwarfs
the Romanesque church of 1214 which stands beside it. The
largest church built in France since the Renaissance, its principal
architect, Vaudoyer, had not the slightest compunction at slicing
off part of its humble Romanesque neighbour. Monstrous maybe,
but Sainte-Marie-Majeure, with its stripes of alternating green
and white marble, has wormed its way into the affections of
the people of Marseille. Inside, 444 marble columns support the
monster. The four statues of the evangelists beneath the central
dome were added only in 1937. The heroic Bishop de Belsunce
is remembered by a statue in the cathedral square. In competition
with its powerful neighbour, the truncated former cathedral, the
Vieille Major, has been deconsecrated, yet its Romanesque dome
and the fifteenth-century sculptures of the chapel of St Lazare
inside are still worth pausing for.

By contrast Notre-Dame-de-la-Garde, set on a chalky hillock
862 metres above sea-level, seems to me a less winning affair. Its
belfry rises another forty-five metres, and on it stands a colossal
gilded statue of the Virgin Mary. She weighs 9,000 kilogrammes,
and the belfry also carried a massive bell weighing another 8,234
kilogrammes. Standing where she does, Notre-Dame-de-la-Garde
challenges the might of the Mistral and, as Hilaire Belloc
observed, 'The Mistral does not lurk or hide'; instead 'it advertises
itself most unmistakably – that piercing wind, cutting with cold
like a sword and charging at an irresistible charge down the funnel
of the Rhone valley, is something which even the chance passer-by

remembers all his life.' Belloc added, 'There is no wind which can challenge the Mistral for its quality of deathly command.' Nor any cathedral, for that matter, and in 1983 it was discovered that the wind had so eroded the base of the gilded Virgin Mary that she was in danger of falling down. The damage was speedily righted.

The creation of Espérandieu, Notre-Dame-de-la-Garde is well worth a visit. White Carrara marble, green marble from the Alps and red marble from Africa face the interior. Inside too is a romantically suffering 'Virgin of Sorrows' by the uninhibited sculptor Jean-Baptiste Carpeaux. Over the high altar is another massive statue of the Virgin Mary, this one in silver and dating from 1853. The efficacy of the Virgin as intercessor is testified by countless ex-votos in the apses of the cathedral, as well as by little models of ships and aeroplanes set here by those who have escaped danger after praying in this cathedral.

To the north-east of the cathedral, on the same side of the Vieux-Port, the Vieille-Charité stands in the rue de la Charité. Built to house vagrants, beggars and incurables, it abuts on to a complex of ancient streets whose names still evoke the medieval city: rue des Muettes (street of the dumb), rue des Cordelles (the religious order of Cordeliers, perhaps), rue and place des Moulins (of the mills), rue du Refuge (for whom?), rue de la Fonderie-Vieille (of the old smelting works), rue des Pistoles (where, I guess, moneychangers dealt in gold coins), rue du Poirier (of the pear tree) and rue des Cartiers (where apparently lived the manufacturers of the Marseille tarot cards).

One of Marseille's greatest sons, the baroque sculptor and architect Pierre Puget (who died in 1694), began building the Vieille-Charité in 1671. His oddly successful hospital chapel, with its elliptical dome, was finished by his son François in 1724. The Corinthian façade, added in 1863, scarcely prepares you for th monumental Italianate feast inside. Beautifully restored, the Vieille-Charité no longer houses vagrants but serves as a cultural centre and a gallery of changing art exhibitions.

The Hôtel-Dieu, closer to the Vieux-Port in this old quarter of Marseille, is another remarkable example of medieval, Renaissance and eighteenth-century charity. Founded in the twelfth century as the hospice of the Holy Spirit, this first hospice was demolished by the Aragonese, but the people of Marseille built another one, which they continued to enlarge. The present building, with a splendid staircase designed by a local architect named Esprit Brun, was designed by a nephew of the great architect Hardouin-Mansart and built between 1753 and 1782.

The bust in front of the entrance is that of the finest of all nineteenth-century caricaturists, Honoré Daumier, who was born in this city in 1808. Daumier was a vehement Marseille Republican, and in consequence spent six months in jail in 1832 for representing King Louis-Philippe as Gargantua gobbling up bags of gold which he had extorted from the people. Daumier also turned to sculpture, producing a celebrated effigy of a skinned rat, which he insisted represented Louis-Philippe's courtiers. In the last two decades of his life (which ended in 1879) Daumier took up painting, and of late his skills in this field have increasingly been appreciated by the salerooms, as they were in his own time only by such of his peers as Delacroix and Corot.

La Vieille-Charité is by no means the sole exhibition centre and art gallery in this quarter of Marseille. South of the Hôtel-Dieu in the rue de la Prison is la Maison Diamantée, a luscious mannerist building begun around 1570 for a merchant named Pierre Gardiolle and rebuilt by Nicola de Robbio (Marseille's director of artillery) between 1593 and 1620. Its name derives from the fretted diamond-shaped studs on the façade. Today the Maison Diamantée shelters the museum of old Marseille, with bowsprits of old ships and a fascinating model of the city as it was in 1848. A few paces south on the quai du Port rises the city's eighteenth-century town hall, while further east, at the bottom of la Canebière, the Third Empire stock exchange also serves as a maritime museum, with models of ships from the seventeenth century to the present day.

Louis-Napoleon himself laid the first stone of the stock exchange in 1852, and he opened the building eight years later. Its sumptuous marble staircase was designed by Jules Cantini, and the statues on the façade, as well as representing the usual motifs of industry and commerce, include representations of Pytheas and Euthymenes, the famous Phocaean sailors. As you approach it, you pass by what was once a superb Augustinian church, Saint-Ferréol, built between 1369 and 1588, with an eighteenth-century belfry. Alas, the church has lost four aisles and its original façade, replaced by one of 1875. As for the rue

Saint-Ferréol, it is as elegant and expensive a shopping street as one could desire.

It crosses la Canebière, leading west to a quaintly named garden, the jardin des Vestiges. The vestiges in question are all that remain of the former Greek houses, towers, streets and fortifications of old Marseille. Imaginatively the city has installed in a museum beside the garden a permanent exhibition of the history of the city from the sixth century BC to the fourth century AD.

In the rue de Grignan, a little street between the rue Saint-Ferréol and the rue de Paradis to the south, the Musée Cantini is a seventeenth-century building sheltering twentieth-century works by Max Ernst, Hans Arp, Jean Dubuffet, Francis Picabia, the Belgian Pierre Alechinsky and the Spaniard Joan Miró. But none of the museums I have so far mentioned matches the Musée des Beaux Arts in the Palais Longchamp, a monumental nineteenth-century building situated at the end of the boulevard Longchamp (which stretches north-west from the top of la Canebière and the place Jules-Thierry) and easily reached by means of the Marseille Métro. As with the stock exchange, this building of 1869 (by Espérandieu) conspicuously displays the wealth accumulated by Marseille in the second half of the nineteenth century. Two wings connected by a colonnade; two great staircases decorated by Puvis de Chavannes with symbolic representations of Marseille as a Greek colony and Marseille as the gate to the Orient; a zoological garden; and lions guarding the entrance – all this is somewhat overpowering. I have never visited the museum of natural history in the right wing. The paintings in the left wing include not only some excellent Italian works (by Perugino, Tiepolo and Annibale Carracci) but also paintings by Rubens, Ruysdael, Corot and Courbet. Anyone with only a short time to spare should hasten to the room devoted to Honoré Daumier.

Music, dancing and theatre are catered for in Marseille by its own national theatre, installed in a 1970s building where once fish were auctioned, and thus known as the theatre of the auction (la Criée); by the Italianate Gymnase-Théâtre Armand Hammer; by the Théâtre du Merlan; and by the Opéra Municipal, a building whose classical exterior of 1786 as the result of successive restorations deliciously houses an art-deco interior of 1924.

The archaeological, Egyptian and Oriental museum of Marseille is situated in the eighteenth-century Château Borély, which is surrounded by a splendid park, together with a lake, flowerbeds and rose garden. This elegant building was begun in 1766 and finished in 1778, and was built for the Borély family, who gave it their name. The Borélys enthusiastically collected archaeological remains, and what they amassed over the years forms the basis of the present exhibition (which also includes fourteen paintings by Parrocel, also bought by them to adorn the vast salon in which they still hang).

Nearby are the botanical gardens of the city. This particular park and museum is some way from the centre of Marseille, situated beside the race course and the beach, and is best reached by bus (either no. 19 or no. 44). Far more romantic is the Château d'If, built in 1524 for François I after the siege of Marseille by the troops of Emperor Charles V. You reach it by boat from the quai des Belges. The stones of its towers and walls are as white as the rock on which it rises. Beyond this little island are the two isles of Râtonneau and Pomèques, the former the site of an imposing hospital built in 1821 to isolate those suffering from yellow fever from the rest of the city.

Château d'If was transformed into a prison in 1634 and remained one until 1872. In it were incarcerated at various times Giandevès de Niozelles (who spent six years here simply because he forgot to take off his hat in the presence of Louis XIV), and Prince Casimir of Poland, not to speak of Edmond Dantès, hero of Alexandre Dumas's novel *The Count of Monte Cristo*. Here too were interned political opponents of Louis-Napoleon after the events of 1848–9 – as well as more than 3,500 Protestants, brought here between 1545 and 1750 in preparation for a lifetime as galley-slaves.

Not least among its prisoners was the mysterious Man in the Iron Mask, whose singular fate still tingles romantic hearts. As Mark Twain so vividly expressed it in *The Innocents Abroad*, the charm lies in the mystery. 'The speechless tongue, those prisoned features, that heart so frightened with unspoken troubles, that breast so oppressed with its piteous secret, had been here. These dank walls had known the man whose dolorous story is a sealed book for ever! There was fascination in the spot.'

Another celebrated prisoner was the Marquis de Mirabeau. I never cease to marvel that the British historian Thomas Carlyle so much admired Mirabeau and was so desperately cut up about describing his death in 1791 just as the Revolution seemed to be turning sour.

The People stand mute, heart-stricken; to all it seems as if a great calamity were nigh: as if the last man of France, who could have swayed these coming troubles, lay there at hand-grips with the unearthly Power ... The silence of a whole People, the wakeful toil of Cabanis, Friend and Physician, skills not: on Saturday, the second day of April, Mirabeau feels that the last of the Days has risen for him; that on this day he has to depart and be no more. His death is Titanic, as his life has been!

Certainly Mirabeau was politically skilled. Had the French royal family trusted him, the king and queen might have escaped the guillotine. But his personal life was reckless. He reached the prison of the Château d'If having seduced and married a rich heiress named Emilie de Marignane. Then he swindled her father. Once imprisoned, he promptly seduced the wife of the governor. Maybe, after all, there is something Titanic about this rogue. Even after death he created controversy. Buried in the Panthéon, he was exhumed three years later when his plans to rescue the doomed monarchy were discovered. His bones were jettisoned into an unmarked grave in the former Clamart cemetery.

But for me, in spite of this redolent spot and in spite of the striking monuments and enticing galleries of Marseille, the essence of the city remains its markets and its cosy, noisy bars. Markets set themselves up every day in one quarter or another of this city. Watching a Marseille market closing down, as the unsaleable fruit is being jettisoned, I remember particularly a tale by Victor Hugo. In his *Memoirs of Two Young Brides*, Hugo entertainingly parodied the bizarre tastes in food that pregnant women sometimes enjoy, by depicting one of his two heroines passionate not for the finest fruit of this Marseille market but for the ones that are rotting. She writes to her fellow-bride:

My husband goes to Marseille to get for me the finest oranges to be found. He has them sent over from Malta and Portugal and Corsica;

and all of them I leave untasted. I hurry off myself to Marseille, sometimes even walking there, to devour vile, half-rotted objects that sell for a sou in the little street close by the Hôtel de Ville that runs down to the port. To me they are like flowers. I notice nothing of their deathly smell, feeling only their flavour that warms my palate, their wine-like warmth and their delicious taste.

These fetid oranges, from which her husband turns aside in disgust, relieve the nausea of her pregnancy and restore her to excellent health. She, by contrast, is terrified lest there be none left for sale. 'To me they are fruits grown in paradise,' she asserts, 'and their pulp the most exquisite food.'

As for the bars, the novelist and film director Marcel Pagnol eternally endeared himself to the people of Marseille when he set his 1932 film *Marius* in one of them – so much so that he set two sequels, *Fanny* and *César*, in the same spot. And the novelist Stendhal declared in 1836 that 'If Bordeaux is the most beautiful city in France, Marseille is the prettiest.' In these boisterous little bars I cannot quite agree, but certainly I would say she is the most raffish.

The coastline around Marseille is startlingly beautiful. To the south-east the rocky coastline that stretches from Cap Croisette to Cassis sports les Calanques – sheltered creeks whose cliffs are sometimes so precipitous as to attract mountaineers wishing to find territory testing enough for training. Their white cliffs plunge down to the sea, the slopes behind them patchily green with oak and pine.

Boat trips from the port of Marseille take tourists to see them. For hikers, the *Grande Randonnée 98* reaches the most spectacular of these creeks, the Calanque d'En-Vau. And simply driving to Cassis by way of the Puget massif is thrilling. As you approach the town, the Mediterranean coast grows rustier in colour, and the ochre houses on the waterfront of Cassis match its hue.

Cassis is a fishing port which has inserted itself between high cliffs. Its Château de la Maison des Baux dates from the end of the fourteenth century, and its medieval heart was rebuilt in a militarily precise fashion in the eighteenth century, along with a mid-eighteenth-century town hall. Although Cassis attracts a mass of Marseille trippers during the weekends of summer, the port offers quiet coves as well, especially for those who hire a boat and set off with a picnic and a bottle of the fragrant white wine of the region (which Mistral declared was sweeter than any honey and shone like a limpid diamond), along perhaps with some cheese bought at the Wednesday or Friday morning market. Cassis survives the invasion of tourism, as the town that entranced such painters as Henri Matisse and Raoul Dufy, partly because vehicles have been banned from the centre.

La Ciotat – which you should reach from Cassis preferably not by way of the D559 but by the much more attractive and vertiginous D41A, the so-called *route des crêtes*, which runs as far as Cap Canaille before twisting to the top of the highest cliffs in France – derives its name from a Greek foundation on this spot called Kitharista. In spite of its shipyards, parts of la Ciotat retain a sly charm. Overlooked by the shark-like teeth of the Cap de l'Aigle and revelling in its well-restored *vieille ville*, the port competes with Cassis in attracting tourists by means of its marina and the excellent sandy beaches that stretch eastwards as far as la Ciotat-Plage and les Lecques. Traces of the ancient fortifications include a gateway of 1628. The seventeenth-century church of Notre-Dame-de-l'Assomption houses a 'Deposition' by the seventeenth-century master Louis Finson.

Dominating the hinterland is the massif of la Sainte-Baume, the white dome of the observatory peeping over the top of its gnarled white peak. To the west sits the industrialized town of Aubagne, famous as the birthplace in 1895 of the poet, novelist and film-maker Marcel Pagnol and shadowed by an impressive 715-metre-high rock known as the Garlaban. As Pagnol himself put it, he was born 'beneath the oak-covered Garlaban at the time of the last oaks', a prophecy that at last seems to be coming true as the region is ravaged by forest fires. Since his father was a school superintendent in Aubagne, the young Marcel was initially destined for a career as a teacher. His literary talents soon broke surface, however, and by the age of sixteen he had founded a literary magazine and published both poetry and a novel (*The Girl With the Dark Eyes*). Aged seventeen he wrote a four-act play. When the Théâtre-Français rejected it, Pagnol published the work in his own magazine.

The First World War inspired another play of 1925, on the subject of war profiteers. The following year Pagnol became celebrated with the production of his play *Jazz*, and in 1928 his *Topaze* ran for two consecutive years in Paris, transferred to Broadway and was made into a film. Then followed his Marseille trilogy, from which *Fanny*, like *Topaze*, was adapted as a Broadway musical. By now living permanently in Paris, Pagnol drew on his Aubagne roots for what are his two most appealing works, *Jean de Florette* and *Manon des sources*, both of them based on the theme of traditional rivalries of the Provençal peasant and the perpetual search for water. Family reunions, nostalgia for the smells not only of thyme but also of the village school and the goats, petty quarrels, summer sunlight and summer storms are evoked with an uncanny accuracy by a man who had forsaken his native Provence but retained a lifelong love-affair with her memory.

If Pagnol exploited his native Aubagne, Aubagne today exploits Pagnol. No. 16 cours Barthélemy, where he was born, has become a place of pilgrimage, and the town has worked out a Pagnol circuit taking tourists to the sites that inspired the novelist and poet, as well as to the spots where his works where filmed and where he himself shot movies. The grotto du Grosibou, which scared the young Pagnol and his cousin, has been renamed the grotto de Marcel Pagnol.

The village of la Treille, where he and his family spent their holidays, lies north-west of Aubagne, and here he is buried. Cuges-les-Pins east of Aubagne, which served as the model for Florette, is now given over to holidaymaking, with horseback riding and a picturesque annual procession on 13 June, the feast of St Anthony of Padua. The saint's connection with the village is obscure enough. In 1350 Cardinal Guy de Montfort gave to Cuges-les-Pins a bit of Anthony's skull, which is still preserved in the sixteenth-century chapel of Saint-Antoine-de-Padoue.

I find the steep streets and lush nineteenth-century houses of Aubagne itself more rewarding than this literary pilgrimage. I like its country markets. Side by side are the baroque façade of the White Penitents and the classical façade of the former chapel of the Black Penitents. The neo-Romanesque façade of the church of Saint-Sauveur opens into a genuine eleventh-century church, though successive rebuildings have transformed much of it into an early seventeenth-century, ogival-vaulted building. From its belfry of 1515 rises a pretty spire. Inside the church are some sumptuous seventeenth- and eighteenth-century furnishings.

Aubagne goes in for terracotta figurines known as *santons*, many of them today inevitably in the form of Marcel Pagnol characters. The town has also retained a fourteenth-century gateway from the seven that once guarded it. Today it rests easily under the formidable protection of the French Foreign Legion, which moved here from Sidi-bel-Abbès in 1962 when the French quitted Algeria. Some 3,000 soldiers live in a camp a kilometre west of Aubagne, which includes a theatre, a press (to publish the legion's magazine, *Képi blanc*), a swimming pool, a library and a museum that is open to visitors, whose one golden rule must be never to ask a Legionnaire why he joined up.

Aix-en-Provence and the land of Frédéric Mistral

Whereas Marseille is a rich hotch-potch of buildings, quarters and streets dating from the Roman era to the present day ('modernity' represented by Le Corbusier's hideous *Cité radieuse*, a housing development of 1962, and Auguste Perret's more successful reconstruction of the northern section of the Vieux-Port), Aix-en-Provence remains a serene, virtually seamless seventeenth- and eighteenth-century aristocratic city. Because the water supply had to be completely reconstructed after the plague of 1720, the city is also cooled by a multitude of elegant fountains. You reach it from Aubagne by driving roughly north-west along the N96 and the A52.

Set amid the splendid countryside which inspired Paul Cézanne, the city began life as a Roman thermal resort, and its very name derives from the Latin *aquae*, meaning waters. Close by at Entremont, the Celts had already established what was probably their most important settlement in Provence. When they began to threaten Marseille, the Romans turned against them. Having defeated the Celts in 123 BC, the proconsul Caius Sextius Calvinus established below Entremont the first Roman military outpost in Gaul, a staging post on the route from Italy to northern France. The proconsul decided that the city might better be dubbed *Aquae Sextiae*.

For a time Aix-en-Provence was the capital of Gaul, but the

Roman emperors increasingly preferred Arles and the city began
to decline. As elsewhere in Provence, the barbarians and Saracens
brought disaster to Aix. The Lombards devastated the spot in
AD 574. A lifeline was thrown to the city in the twelfth century
when the Counts of Provence made it their capital, and in the
fourteenth century the bishopric, which had been founded in the
fourth century, was elevated to archiepiscopal status. In 1413 the
university of Aix-en-Provence was founded. A further stroke of
good fortune was the advent of Roi René, who ruled the city from
1442 to 1480. A multi-talented man, a friend of troubadours
and a lavish patron of the Arts, René was King of Naples and
Duke of Anjou. Though expelled from Naples by Alfonso of
Aragon in 1442, he managed to hold on to his royal title. The
citizens of Aix-en-Provence are said to have adored him – not
surprisingly since, as a painter, musician, poet and patron, he
brought gaiety to the region and also the muscat grape. His most
popular decision was to extend the Corpus Christi (or *Fête Dieu*)
festivities at Aix-en-Provence for a full five days.

In 1501 King Louis XII established the parliament of Provence
at Aix. Emperor Charles V took possession of the city in 1536,
proclaiming himself King of Arles and Provence. He was driven
out two months later. The nobility, the richer clergy, the bourgeoisie and the magistrates began building themselves palaces,
town houses and hôtels, which in the next two centuries grew
increasingly opulent. Some 190 of them have survived, many
lavishly decorated with baroque façades, caryatids, atlantes,
garlands, cartouches and wrought-iron balconies. Fortunately
(for the visitor, if not for the people of Aix-en-Provence
themselves), in 1790 Marseille became the capital of Provence,
leaving the former principal city to gel as a classical masterpiece.
Magnificent pilasters, columns, sculpted doorways, sumptuous
staircases, balconies and escutcheons combine with the murmur
of fountains to give an air of dignified calm to the city.

The waters of the lusciously decorated fontaine de la Rotonde,
created in 1860, burst out in the place du Général-de-Gaulle, in
the midst of which spurts a fountain created in 1832. Sculpted
swans (bearing children), lions and dolphins sport around its
basin, while statues of justice, commerce and art rise above. Here
the roads from Marseille, Nice and Avignon meet, and this is an
excellent spot from which to set out on a round tour of the city.

Leading from the fontaine de la Rotonde, and laid out between 1651 and 1751, is the cours Mirabeau, an avenue enriched in subsequent years with elegant town houses and today shaded by four rows of massive plane trees. Its present name derives from the rascally Comte de Mirabeau, deputy to the third estate for both Marseille and Aix. Many of the mansions lining this street are richly elegant. No. 4, the Hôtel de Villars, dates from 1710, though its Doric portico was added only in 1757. In no. 10, the Hôtel d'Entrecasteaux of 1784, the Marquise d'Entrecasteaux was slain by her husband shortly after moving into their new home. No. 14, the Hôtel de Rousset Boulbon with its exquisitely carved doors, was built a few years later. The Hôtel d'Arbaud Jouque (no. 19) was built in 1730, while no. 20, the Hôtel de Forbin, is a mid-seventeenth-century town house built in 1658. In between these and the chic shops and cafés of this thoroughfare, sweet shops ply visitors with the almond and dried-melon biscuits known as *calissons*, which are the toothsome speciality of the city, while brasseries and bookshops offer their diverse charms.

Two more fountains now freshen this avenue: the fontaine des Neuf-Canons, created in 1691, and the fontaine d'Eau Chaude of 1734 (which does in fact spurt warm water, rising from a thermal spring and encrusting the fountain with its chemicals). Next at no. 38 is the Italianate Hôtel Maurel de Pontevès, built in 1650 with a façade depicting, as it rises, three different orders of architecture (Tuscan, Ionic and Doric), and incorporating a couple of groaning caryatids who hold up its wrought-iron balcony. The cours Mirabeau ends with the fontaine du Roi-René and the Hôtel du Poët of 1724. A nineteenth-century statue of King René (unsmiling for some reason, and sculpted by David d'Angers) tops his fountain, and he holds a bunch of the grapes he introduced to Provence. Medallions depict two of his faithful minsters: Matheron de Salignac and Palamède de Forbin.

South of the cours Mirabeau even the layout of the streets follows a strictly classical grid pattern. This area is known as the quartier Mazarin, named not after Cardinal Mazarin but after his brother Michel, Archbishop of Aix-en-Provence, who commissioned its creation in 1646. The music conservatory of Aix-en-Provence (dedicated to the composer Darius Milhaud, who was born in the city in 1874) occupies the Hôtel de Caumont in this quarter, a town house of 1720 standing on the corner of rue Joseph Cabassol and rue Mazarine. Rue Cardinale runs eastwards from the southern end of rue Joseph Cabassol to reach the place des Quatre-Dauphins, named after a magnificent dolphin fountain designed by Jean-Claude Rambot in 1667 and surrounded by beautiful eighteenth-century town houses.

The place des Quatre-Dauphins is crossed by the rue du Quatre-Septembre, where at no. 12 you discover the Musée Arbaud. It houses a collection made in the nineteenth century by the artist Paul Arbaud, which includes Provençal manuscripts and *incunabula*, drawings and paintings and well over 300 portraits of the revolutionary Marquis de Mirabeau. One of its curiosities is a corpse sculpted by Jean Chastel and representing a young man killed in a brawl at which the artist was fortuitously present. A masterpiece of antiquity is a Persian warrior, a sculpture of the Pergamon school dating from the second century BC.

A little further along the rue Cardinale is the Hôtel de Boisgelin of 1659, and at the end of the street rises the thirteenth-century, fortress-like church of Saint-Jean-de-Malte, a still-flourishing church founded by the Knights Hospitallers of St John of Jerusalem, which also serves as the mausoleum of the Counts of Provence. Its belfry was finished in 1376. Beside it is the former Palais de Malte, built in the 1670s and now the home of the Fine Arts museum of Aix-en-Provence (the Musée Granet). Surprisingly enough, in it hang only eight paintings by the city's native son Cézanne, along with works by another local artist, the neo-classical painter François Granet. Here too are works by Rubens and Rembrandt, by Guercino, by Jacques-Louis David and by Dominique Ingres, as well as a fine collection of local porcelain and Gaullish remains. A pleasing touch is a portrait of Granet himself, painted by Ingres in 1807 when the two artists were working in Italy.

Rue d'Italie takes you back from here to the place Forbin. And behind the Hôtel Forbin, rue Thiers runs as far as the place Verdun. A little way to the left is the gracious place d'Albertas, created in 1745 and still a mid-eighteenth-century oasis surrounded on three sides by eighteenth-century houses. Jean-Baptiste d'Albertas designed its perfectly proportioned and unpretentious fountain, and the square derives its name from the palace of his father, first president of the court of audit of Aix-en-Provence.

Abutting on to the place Verdun is the Palais de Justice of the city, a vast neo-Greek building of 1787 to 1831. Its square is the venue of a bric-à-brac market each Tuesday, Thursday and Saturday morning. And to the north in the place de Prêcheurs rises the church of Sainte-Marie-Madeleine. Laurent Vallon rebuilt most of it in the late seventeenth century, retaining however its Dominican austerity, and a Renaissance façade was added in the nineteenth century.

Its north aisle houses an unmissable masterpiece, a fifteenth-century 'Annunciation', the Blessed Virgin Mary clad in a rich golden cape, the angel in an equally vivid red cope. This enigmatic painting combines elements of Flemish, Burgundian and Provençal art, its realism that of Flanders, its architectural precision that of Burgundy, the play of its light that of Provence. Golden rays run from the fingers of God the Father towards the Virgin, speeding with them a naked baby Jesus who carries a cross over his shoulder. But then the picture becomes almost blasphemous. Why is there a malicious-looking bat carved on one side of the arch above the angel, with an obscene, grinning demon on the other side? Above the angel's wing (which happens to be the wing of an owl) is another puzzling architectural motif: two bearded heads grimacing at each other. Mysterious persons wander about the pillars. And what is the meaning of the monkey crouching on the Virgin Mary's reading desk?

Walking on by way of the right-hand side of the Palais de Justice, I came across a street with the extraordinary name of rue Rifle-Rafle. It leads towards the town hall square, by way of the rue Chabrier and then the place Richelme, site of the daily market of Aix-en-Provence. To the north the place de l'Hôtel de Ville is shaded by plane trees and cooled by a fountain designed in 1755 by an Avignon sculptor named Jean Chastel who spent most of his working life at Aix. The Roman column that surmounts it was discovered near the city in 1626. Three days a week (Tuesday, Thursday and Saturday) a flower market sets itself up in the town hall square. To the south the corn market borders the square. Built by Georges Vallon between 1759 and 1761, under the inspiration of the royal palaces at Paris, its façade was sculpted by Jean Chastel with symbolic representations of the Rivers Durance and Rhône.

Though its clock tower dates from 1505, the town hall itself was essentially built between 1655 and 1670 to the designs of Pierre Pavillon and again in the Italian style. (The old one had been burned down by the imperial troops in 1536.) Its sculpted doors lead into a courtyard from which rises a double flight of stairs. The military man sculpted here is Maréchal de Villars. Today this town hall houses both the Méjanes library and the Saint-John Perse foundation. The former was built up by a consul of the city named Jean-Baptiste Piquet, who was Marquis of Méjanes. It consists of some 1,600 manuscripts and 300,000 books, including a *Book of Hours* written and illuminated for Roi René himself. The foundation consists of the papers and literary remains of a French poet and diplomatist whose real name was Marie René Auguste Alexis Saint-Léger Léger, who escaped to America from Nazi-occupied France in 1940 to become an adviser to President Roosevelt. The Vichy government burnt his works and took away his citizenship, but after the war, in 1960, he became a Nobel prize-winner.

As for the clock tower, it rises on the site of a doorway in the ancient fortifications of the city, and it is easy enough to make out the Romanesque base rising to the flamboyant Gothic climax surrounding an eighteenth-century astrological clock, whose wooden figures represent the four seasons. The inscription 'Aux mânes des défenseurs de la Patrie' refers, I think, to those who liberated Aix-en-Provence from Nazi rule on 20 August 1944.

From here you should make your way to the cathedral of Aix-en-Provence, by following the rue Gaston-de-Saporta northwards. Massive pillars flanking no. 17 arrest one's attention to the sober splendour of the Hôtel d'Estienne de Saint-Jean, built in 1680 by the treasurer-general of France for his wife Françoise d'Estienne de Saint-Jean and now the museum of old Aix-en-Provence. Next door is another fine building, the Hôtel de Châteaurenard of 1654 by the Parisian architect Pierre Pavillon. Its stairwell is decorated with seventeenth-century *trompe-l'oeil* paintings by the Flemish artist Jean Daret, legs and clothing apparently draping themselves over the pediment. Rue Gaston-de-Saporta runs into the place des Martyrs de la Résistance, just beyond which rises the former archbishop's palace of 1715, today serving in midsummer as the venue of an annual international festival of poetry and music.

On the way to the cathedral, look out for the Hôtel Maynier d'Oppède, monumentally rebuilt in 1757 by Georges Vallon. The cathedral itself, dedicated to Saint-Sauveur, shelters some of the few ancient stones of Aix-en-Provence: a Roman wall on the right of its flamboyant Gothic, pinnacled façade (which boasts exquisite Renaissance doors, carved out of walnut in the first decade of the sixteenth century by Jean Guiramand of Toulon with reliefs of the four major prophets and twelve sybils); the baptistery, dating from the fourth and fifth centuries, with eight columns which were probably cannibalized from the temple of Apollo in the former Roman forum; the twelfth- and thirteenth-century cloister; and Brussels' tapestries of 1514 hanging in the choir, depicting scenes from the life of the Virgin Mary and the passion of Jesus.

The right aisle of the cathedral of Saint-Sauveur is a dazzling masterpiece of Romanesque architecture; but its chief glory is the triptych of the 'Burning Bush', painted by Nicholas Froment in 1474. Froment was the court painter of Roi René, and he has depicted his patron and René's consort Queen Jeanne de Laval in the left- and right-hand side panels of the triptych respectively. The theme of the central panel, that of the burning but unconsumed bush through which God spoke to Moses, has been transformed into a Christian symbol. In the midst of the burning bush sits a demure Virgin Mary, the infant Jesus in her lap – for, as the medieval allegorists mused, she bore divinity in her womb without being consumed by it. The baby's legs are chubby; he has close-cropped hair; and he holds a looking-glass reflecting his own self sitting on his mother's knee.

To the left of this cathedral is the park from which spring the thermal baths that originally made Aix-en-Provence famous. Rebuilt in 1705 and restored in 1865 and again in 1923, they gush waters enriched with bicarbonate and calcium, which reach 34°C (93°F). Efficacious at calming the nervous and (it is claimed) improving the condition of the uterus, they also soothe the arthritic and render varicose veins less noxious. A fourteenth-century fortified tower, the tour Tourreluque, rises in the park. Its quaint name means 'I spy on everyone', and this is the sole remaining tower of nineteen that once defended the city.

From the south-west corner of the thermal park the rue Célony takes us as far as the pavilion Vendôme with its sweet garden, a building created in the 1660s by Rambot and Pavillon for Louis de Mercoeur, Duke of Vendôme, who was the grandson of Henri

IV and his mistress Gabrielle d'Estrées. The duke married Laure
Mancini, Mazarin's niece, but after her death took holy orders
and became Governor of Provence. After admiring Rambot's
groaning atlantes, which support the portal of this pavilion,
their loin-cloths stuffed with fruit, walk back down the wide
cours Sextius, with yet another fountain, this one dedicated to
Pascal, and to the church of Saint-Jean Baptiste du Faubourg.
Then take the avenue Bonaparte past the municipal casino, and
you are back at la Rotonde.

No one can leave Aix-en-Provence without a cheer for the artist
who, as a plaque on the wall declares, was born here at no. 28
rue de l'Opéra in 1839. Cézanne's father made money out of the
hat trade (his former shop still stands at no. 55 cours Mirabeau),
and so the family lived in some splendour in a newly built house
outside Aix on a woodland estate called the Jas de Bouffan. After
his death (on which Paul at last married his longtime mistress
Hortense Fiquet and legitimized their own son Paul), Cézanne
senior's fortune also proved extremely useful to his son, who
would have been hard-pressed to make a living from selling the
paintings which few recognized as masterpieces in his own lifetime.

His ghost lingers on in two other spots at Aix-en-Provence: the
house he lived in after his mother's death in 1897 at no. 23 rue
Boulegon, and the studio he had built in 1900 at what is now
no. 9 avenue Paul-Cézanne. Today this has been restored to the
supposed condition the artist left it in when he died in 1906. His
hat and cloak, reproductions of some of his paintings and the still-
life objects that feature in them are on display. Aix-en-Provence
in truth possesses no major masterpiece by Cézanne, though the
city does its best to make up for this by imaginative exhibitions.
When I was last there the Musée Granet was exhibiting twenty
of his oils and twelve watercolours; the Musée des Tapisseries
was host to an exhibition on the theme of the Montagne de
Sainte-Victoire as painted by Provençal artists before Cézanne;
the Pavillon Vendôme was exhibiting Constantin de Granet's
paintings of the mountain; the Musée d'Histoire Naturelle was
mounting another exhibition on the geology and ecology of the
mountain; and the theme of the exhibition at the Musée du Vieil
Aix was popular traditions about Sainte-Victoire.

More evocative than any of these worthy efforts seem to me
simply the landscapes that inspired the artist. At Gardanne,

fourteen kilometres south of Aix-en-Provence, Paul Cézanne lived for a time with his wife and child, making some of his earliest artistic experiments. The industrialized environs of the town have not spoiled its medieval centre, with narrow streets that open out on to wider ones lined with plane trees. Once this old part of the town was surrounded by a double ring of fourteenth-century ramparts, and among the remains of these stands the porte de Trets, which the artist so often painted. Gardanne boasts ancient mills, a seventeenth-century hunting lodge at Valabre, which has been transformed into an agricultural college, a seventeenth-century chapel, a Romanesque church of Sainte-Marie and the free-standing belfry of the church of Saint-Pierre (which was demolished a year before Cézanne died). The steeple of the church forms the apex of many of his paintings, the geometrical patterns of the village merging into the olive trees and pines which he stippled on his canvases.

Along with these pastoral scenes, Cézanne relished Marseille. 'The scene is like a playing card,' he wrote to Pissarro. 'Red roofs against a blue sea, the sun so strong that everything seems silhouetted in black and white, in blue, red, brown and purple.' The melancholy abandoned quarries outside Aix also appealed to his gloomy temperament, though the way he depicted them is far from sad. But what fired him most in the final and superabundantly creative period of his life was the silvery limestone Montagne de Sainte-Victoire, which reaches 1,011 metres into the sky to the east of Aix. In 1901 when the artist built himself the studio which at that time stood just outside Aix, he woud arrive there at five o'clock in the morning, to paint his huge canvases of women bathing. Then in the afternoon he would climb the Colline des Lauves behind his studio to create in paint the mountain as it appeared to his unique vision. Sometimes he painted it blue, sometimes white, always contrasting the solid slopes with the vivid valley below.

Cézanne painted the Montagne de Sainte-Victoire at least sixty times, breaking it down in canvas after canvas into curiously geometrical segments, which together add up to such a memorable vision that, whenever I see the mountain, I truly believe I see it not as it actually is but as Cézanne depicted it. Bright greens and pale blue-pinks contrast with pale-blue skies. Sometimes the aqueduct sneaks across the canvas. The artist gave his life

for this mountain – literally, for he was painting Montagne de
Sainte-Victoire when a storm drenched the master, causing a fever
from which he never recovered.

British and American visitors to Provence must often imagine
they have seen all these paintings before. Long before my own
visits I had admired, for instance, 'Le barrage François-Zola' in
the National Museum of Wales, Cardiff, and Cézanne's 'Paysage
rocheux' of 1887, which hangs in the Tate Gallery, London. The
Metropolitan Museum of Art, New York, displays a blue-tinted
'Montagne de Sainte-Victoire', the centre of the painting auda-
ciously bisected by a single tree and lengthwise by the aqueduct.
The mountain appears again, seen through 'Chestnut trees at the
jas de Bouffan', which is today owned by the Minneapolis Institute
of Arts.

A tour of the mountain, driving from Aix by way of the
boulevard des Poilus and the D17, reaches first the village of
le Tholonet, where Bronze Age pottery has been excavated. Just
outside the little village is the nineteenth-century Château Noir,
where Cézanne longed to buy a yellow house, but was instead
simply allowed to rent one of its rooms as a studio. The parish
church of le Tholonet is engaging, a classical building of 1780,
and the village is further enhanced by the mid-seventeenth-century
Château Gallifet. Alexandre de Gallifet, president of the parliament of Aix-en-Provence, commissioned this golden building in
the mid-eighteenth century, and, as if the hills behind it were not
enough to shelter his new home from the Mistral, he surrounded
the château and its elegant park with pine trees.

This is a region of canals, lakes and rustling streams, all of it
dominated by the vast bulk of the mountain. Three kilometres
further along the D17 you reach la Ferme d'Hubac, opposite
which is an oratory dedicated to Notre Dame. This is the starting
point for a 2-hour climb by a signposted route to the Cross of
Provence, an iron cross 945 metres up the mountainside, erected
here in 1871 as a thank-offering that Provence had not been
occupied by the Prussians during the Franco-Prussian War.

The D17 continues from la Ferme d'Hubac to reach shortly the
hamlet of Saint-Antonin-sur-Bayon, with the remains of a Roman
aqueduct and its medieval enclosure and, incredibly for such a
tiny spot, an eighteenth-century château. The eighteenth-century
church, dedicated to St Antonin, contains a gilded wooden

retable. To the south is the wooded plateau du Cengle (with some none-too-strenuous marked hikes), and due east the road reaches Puyloubier. The *Grande Randonnée 9* runs from here to the peak of Montagne de Saint-Victoire, the pic des Mouches, a climb which takes around four hours. Puyloubier has picturesque narrow streets and a Romanesque church, which was much rebuilt in 1860, as well as a partly restored medieval château. Inside the church is a fifteenth-century statue of St Ser, who was beheaded near here by the Visigoths in 485.

From Puyloubier the D57 takes you precariously as far as le Puits-de-Rians, where you double back to drive around the northern slopes of the Montagne de Sainte-Victoire. Here nestles the exquisite village of Vauvenargues. Vauvenargues is protected by the majestic Château des Clapiers-Vauvenargues, flanked by round towers, its present form mostly dating from rebuilding in the seventeenth and eighteenth centuries, though the machicolated square entrance dates from the fourteenth century. In 1958 Pablo Picasso installed himself inside its fourteenth-century walls. The parish church of Saint-Sidoine is Romanesque; and 885 metres up the mountainside stands the seventeenth-century pilgrimage church of Notre-Dame-de-la-Victoire. From here the D10 runs back to Aix-en-Provence by way of tiny Saint-Marc-Jaumegarde, with its massive sixteenth-century château (which boasts one square tower and three round ones) and its mid-nineteenth-century classical church. In the vicinity stretches a 4-kilometre-long artificial lake.

In the north-eastern triangular wedge of the *département* of Bouches-du-Rhône, formed by two motorways (the A7 or *autoroute du Soleil* and the A8 or *la Provenç*ale), are a good number of fine towns and villages. A drive from Aix to the north-east corner of the *département* by way of the N96 will pass by Venelles, which is surrounded by vineyards producing the *Coteaux d'Aix-en-Provence* wines. Venelles-Haut, perched on a cliff, was ruined by an earthquake in 1909, so now the people live in Venelles-Bas, but its château remains, as well as a windmill and the church of Saint-Hippolyte. This was begun in the Middle Ages – though its present Gothic aspect is due to a nineteenth-century restoration. The village craftsmen and women weave tapestries and welcome holidaymakers. Further on we reach the valley of the Durance and Meyrargues, a village of narrow twisting streets and ancient houses dominated by the twelfth- and seventeenth-century Château de Vauclaire (which is now a hotel). The church of Saint-André at Meyrargues dates from 1737.

Peyrolles-en-Provence, still in the wine country of *Coteaux d'Aix-en-Provence*, was once a fortified village, and you can still see some of its medieval ramparts and one of its medieval towers. The parish church was once Romanesque, though it was greatly altered in the seventeenth century, but the finest ecclesiastical building in the village is the chapel of Saint-Sépulcre, a very late Romanesque building with a seventeenth-century belfry and a painting of the Entombment which, it is claimed, was painted by Roi René himself. These are not the only two churches in this little spot, whose Mairie consists of a splendid Romanesque château, extended in the seventeenth century. A seventeenth-century belfry, a watchtower and the seventeenth-century hôtel make up the ensemble at the heart of the village.

East of Peyrolles-en-Provence is Jouques, with its neolithic cave. As with Venelles, the older village, perched on its cliff, has been replaced by a newer one, which is none the less filled with ancient churches and a medieval château. Finally, at the very edge of the *département* lies Saint-Paul-lès-Durance, its Renaissance houses rising from a rocky prominence, along with the restored sixteenth-century Château de Cadarache and the eighteenth-century church of Saints-Pierre-et-Paul.

Similar treasures can be explored in this *département* on the western side of the autoroute du Soleil, where the bare and tortuous peaks of white limestone known as the Alpilles have attracted countless artists and would-be artists to such villages as Eygalières, where they paint the ruined château and clock tower of 1676 as well as the peaks. Among its numerous churches nothing could be simpler or more satisfying than the nearby tumbledown chapel of Saint-Sixte. Eygalières is surrounded by typical Provençal farmhouses (or *mas*), some of which have become hostelries, and prosperity has enabled its inhabitants to restore their homes.

The easiest way of exploring this ravishing part of the Bouches-du-Rhône from Aix-en-Provence is to drive north-west along the N7, passing through Saint-Cannat which, with its nine fountains, huddles around the fifteenth-century belfry of its neo-Gothic church and relishes its thirteenth-century house of the Knights Templar, its eighteenth-century château and its eighteenth-century town hall. Five kilometres further on the road reaches the rich town of Lambesc, with its fountains and belfry, its classical town houses and its stately eighteenth-century church. This town owes its opulence to the fact that in the seventeenth and eighteenth centuries it was the seat of the assembly general of the communities of Provence.

Now drive south-west and then west to reach Salon-de-Provence, pausing to visit and admire the powerful medieval château in the little village of la Barben, a château which Roi René sold in 1474 to Jean II de Forbin. The parish church of la Barben dates from the eleventh century. Salon-de-Provence, like Venelles-Haut, was badly damaged in the earthquake of 1909, but the thirteenth-century church of Saint-Michel (with its beautiful arcaded belfry and splendid Romanesque doorway) and the fortified Renaissance Château de l'Empéri (once the home of archbishops, now a military museum) escaped, along with numerous old houses, including the Renaissance town hall of 1665. So did the Gothic church of Saint-Laurent, built for the Dominicans in 1344. Its belfry, as it rises, transforms itself from Romanesque to Gothic. The font predates the church, probably by five centuries.

The astrologer Michel de Nostradame, better known as Nostradamus, whom we shall shortly come across again, is buried in this church, since he married a woman of the town and made his home here. The house in which he lived stands on the corner of the rue Nostradamus and houses a small museum dedicated to the genius (or possibly fraudster, though at Salon-de-Provence one would be unwise to suggest this to the Association des Amis de Nostradamus). Another museum housed in the château depicts the uniforms and history of the French Army from the time of Louis XV to the First World War.

Salon-de-Provence prospers in part from tourism, in part from olive oil, hosting an annual festival of jazz and another devoted to classical music. Here you can find an aerodrome, a hippodrome, camp sites and the opportunity to sail down the river in canoes. As for its olive oil, suffice it to repeat that the olives of Provence have long been celebrated. The playwright Racine declared that they were the finest in the world, and Mme de Sévigné described them as 'admirable'. Mistral, needless to say, wrote Provençal poetry about picking them, and avowed that he must 'óufri l'ôli vierge à l'autar dôu bon Dieu' ('offer the virgin oil at the altar of the good God'). Other refreshment is provided by the two local wines of the region: those denoted *Coteaux d'Aix-en-Provence* and *Coteaux des Baux-de-Provence* (the latter promoted from a *VDQS* wine to an *appellation contrôlée* on 11 May 1984). Nine kilometres north-west lies Eyguières, a town of classical architecture as well as the ruins of a medieval château that once belonged to Queen Jeanne. Castelas de Roquemartine, with a tenth-century chapel dedicated to Saint-Sauveur, lies two kilometres further north.

From Eyguières the D17 travels westwards through the pretty village of Mouriès, which is guarded by two châteaux, one of them (the Château de Joyeuse-Garde) the gift of Roi René to Jeanne de Laval, the other (the Château de Servones) built in the seventeenth century. The road reaches a yet smaller village, Maussane-lès-Alpilles, with its fountains, oil mills, elegant houses and the eighteenth-century Château de Montblanc.

The D5 winds north to where in the Rhône valley at the entrance to the stony, almost desert landscape of la Crau, Saint-Rémy-de-Provence still looks out on the Alpilles. On the way I can never resist a tiny excursion west to les Baux-de-Provence and, judging by the tourist-infested streets in summer and the shops selling trinkets, jewellery and souvenirs, few others can. The geographical situation of the town is almost ridiculously spectacular, rocks rising from the plateau and the Alpilles in the distance. Mistral's remark, that in such a town citizens were bound to be eagles and never vassals, is often quoted. They are now in thrall to tourists. Tourism has brought its own gifts to les Baux, including money, which has impeccably restored much of the medieval and gorgeous Renaissance architectural heritage of the town. Today visitors eat extremely well at les Baux and enjoy a rich diet of annual cultural events, including a festival of art, with musical evenings, in summer, and on the feast of St John (conveniently transferred without ecclesiastical permission to the last Saturday in June) a folklore festival. Horseback riding, especially around the nearby tortuous val d'Enfer (pausing to marvel at the Renaissance jewel known as the pavilion of Queen Jeanne, which was really built for a Protestant baroness named

Jeanne in 1581) and visits to the 200-metre-long prehistoric 'cave of the fairies' (grotte des Fées) are further delights.

In the Middle Ages the barons of les Baux ruled over seventy-two Provençal towns. Princes of Orange, they also patronized troubadours. Les Baux thus played a central part in that astonishing efflorescence of courtly love poetry which took place in twelfth-century Provence. At that moment the modern Western notion of love was there created. As Denis de Rougemont wrote, 'In the twelfth century in Provence love was regarded as a dignity. It not only imparted a titular nobility, but actually ennobled. Troubadours were raised socially to the level of the aristocracy, which treated them as equals. There are numerous instances of villeins being knighted on the score that they sang the praises of Love.'

Their songs, especially women's lyrics (the 'Chansons de Femme') and the complaints of those who had made unhappy marriages (the 'Chansons de Mal Marié'), issued in powerful, moving mini-dramas, expressed in complex rhyming verse. 'I've done my husband no wrong,' sings one ill-used wife, 'save to embrace my lover!' A love-sick girl toils at making a robe for her absent lover; he arrives and their bliss is indescribable. Others chant of lost love and being cruelly jilted. I should like to have sat in a twelfth-century Provençal court listening to such singing. Sometimes, too, I think that the twentieth-century natives of Provence carry in their hearts some of the more cynical insights of the troubadours, especially when they begin to repeat their traditional sayings. 'Gau de carriero, doulou d'oustau', they cry about a roving-eyed *flâneur*, which is Provençal for 'Cock in the street, sorrow in the home.' The feminine equivalent runs 'Fiho troutiero et fenestriero, raramen bono meinagiero', meaning 'A girl who runs around and displays herself at the window rarely makes a good housewife.'

The occasional savagery of the troubadours' lyrics could be matched in the Middle Ages by a physical savagery. One of the barons of les Baux, Viscount Raimond-Louis de Beaufort of Turenne, an enemy of both the papacy and the Counts of Provence, made condemned prisoners leap to their deaths from the walls of his château, which perched on the *baou* or sheer cliff from which the town derives its name. Arresting though these aspects of the town's history might be, his viciousness was exceptional. In

the thirteenth century, after the Holy Roman Emperor had made
its rulers Kings of Arles, les Baux also experienced a remarkable
cultural, literary and architectural flowering, of which the troubadours were merely a part.

After les Baux had become part of the kingdom of France in
1481, Louis XI demolished its château. Connétable Anne de
Montmorency, as lord of the city, built another one. Then,
during the religious controversies of the Reformation, the people
of les Baux converted to Protestantism. Still rebellious, in the early
seventeenth century they sided with the Duke of Orleans against
King Louis XIII. In consequence, the troops of Cardinal Richelieu
besieged and took the town. The people seized the opportunity
to revolt against their masters, successfully begging Richelieu
to destroy the defences of the château and sell the lordship
of les Baux to the townsfolk themselves. Although their wish
was granted, such assertiveness was not to the taste of Louis
XIII. Having taken the citizens' money, in 1642 he raised the
status of les Baux from a barony to a marquisate, and gave
the town to the Grimaldi family of Monaco, who held on to it
until the Revolution. They built yet another château which the
Revolutionaries sacked, leaving the massive romantic ruin you
see today, its keep seemingly leaning over a cliff to gaze balefully
across the surrounding countryside. This thirteenth-century keep
is the best-preserved part of the fortress, followed by some of the
towers which once guarded its ramparts, and other halls and
rooms, some of them dug into the rock itself. In the afternoon
sun it gleams a golden-yellow.

The rest of the town is delightfully set on its rocky site. Of
the surviving parts of the sixteenth-century walls of les Baux only
one gateway, the porte d'Eyguières, remains, with steps lining its
defensive walls to enable defenders to repel enemies. There are
troglodyte homes in the town as well as in its château. Some of
the houses are inscribed with their dates. Many of them, including
the Hôtel de Ville, are in immaculate condition, looking (like the
town hall) exactly as they did in the seventeenth, or in other cases
in the previous, century.

The Romanesque church of Saint-Vincent, embellished in the
seventeenth century with a new apse, is still a cool haven. Its
stern exterior with a fortified doorway makes the elegance of the
interior seem all the more entrancing. In the same place Vincent

stands the seventeenth-century Chapelle des Pénitents-Blancs. I wish I liked its modern stained glass, by Max Ingrand. In their heyday the Protestants built themselves a chapel, and parts of it can still be seen in the rue Neuve, with a legend over its 1571 doorway proclaiming in Latin that after darkness comes the light.

Responding to the influx of visitors, les Baux has created numerous museums: one of local history (in the quite forbidding Hôtel de Manville, built in 1571); a slightly better one devoted to archaeology (in the Hôtel de la Tour-de-Braue, which dates from the fourteenth and fifteenth centuries); and an interesting collection of local artists from our own era in the Hôtel des Porcelets of 1569 (which is, if anything, even more forbidding than the Hôtel de Manville). The museum of carved figures and cribs is housed in a former sixteenth-century priory which once served as the town hall. And an interesting museum of printing (the Louis-Jou foundation) occupies the early sixteenth-century Hôtel de Brion.

Returning to the D5, drive northwards to Saint-Rémy-de-Provence. On the way lies the remarkable Roman town of Glanum. The Greeks founded Glanum in the third century BC on the site of a Celtic shrine. Then the Germanic Cimbri occupied the site, until the Romans expelled them. Building on the Greek settlement, the Romans have left us Glanum's finest monuments: a triumphal arch rejoicing over the victories of Julius Caesar in Gaul and depicting some of the conquered, and the *mausolée*, a tall, arched and colonnaded cenotaph set up to commemorate two grandsons of Augustus Caesar, both of whom died young. Greek remains include a council chamber and several houses. Further excavations have revealed a sacred spring, tiled streets and a sewerage system, the opulent house of the Antes, the outlines of villas and baths, and the oldest known mosaic in Provence. And there is obviously more still to be uncovered.

Just before you enter Saint-Rémy-de-Provence you reach its finest religious building, the former priory of Saint-Paul-de-Mausole, with its many eleventh- and twelfth-century buildings. In 1807 it became an asylum and a hospital. Its two most celebrated inmates were Vincent Van Gogh and Dr Albert Schweitzer. The French had interned the saintly missionary doctor and his wife during the First World War as German citizens (since they were

born in Alsace at a time when it had been annexed to Germany).
They were moved to Saint-Rémy-de-Provence in March 1918.
The moment Schweitzer entered the huge, unadorned room on
the ground floor it struck him as strangely familiar. 'Where had
I seen that iron stove, and the fluepipe crossing the room from
end to end?' he asked himself. The answer was in a drawing by
Van Gogh, who had, as Schweitzer put it, 'immortalized with his
pencil the desolate room in which today we in our turn were sitting
about'. Schweitzer added, 'Like us, he had suffered from the cold
stone floor when the Mistral blew!'

Saint-Rémy-de-Provence is ringed by its still-intact fourteenth-
century wall, along with a seventeenth-century gateway. Inside
is a feast of ancient houses, one in the rue Hoche the birthplace
in 1503 of the astrologer Nostradamus. Initially Nostradamus
practised medicine, but in the 1550s he published the two collections of enigmatical, rhyming predictions that made him famous.
He ended his days as physician in ordinary to King Charles IX.
Other distinguished buildings at Saint-Rémy-de-Provence include
the museum of the Alpilles, formerly the sixteenth-century Hôtel
Mistral de Mondragon, the baroque Hôtel Estrine and two
eighteenth-century châteaux: the Château de Roussan (which is
now a hotel) and the Château de Lagoy, whose park contains a
twelfth-century Romanesque chapel.

Seven kilometres north-west of Saint-Rémy-de-Provence is an
apparantly humdrum village whose name resonates throughout
Provence, for on 8 September 1830, at the mas du Juge, a farm
just outside Maillane on the road from Saint-Rémy-de-Provence,
was born Frédéric Mistral. The son of a prosperous farmer,
Mistral was a graduate of Nîmes University and took a law
degree at the University of Aix-en-Provence, where he studied
under a man named Joseph Roumanille, who had already begun
writing poems in what was then dubbed the dialect of Provence.
Under his inspiration Mistral decided to devote his life to the
rehabilitation not only of Provençal as a language in its own
right – the language of the troubadours – but also of every
aspect of Provençal life. A group dedicated to this end and calling
itself the Félibrige was founded in 1854, soon taking on as its
child the whole of the Languedoc, that region of France where
the vernacular word for yes was not 'oui' but 'oc'.

As well as publishing in 1878 a two-volume dictionary of the *langue d'oc* under the title *Lou Tresor dóu Félibrige,* Mistral wrote four long narrative poems, of which two have survived in the literary pantheon of France. The first, *Mirèio,* written when Mistral was but twenty-seven years old, tells the tale of the daughter of a rich farmer who loves the son of a poor basket-maker. Her parents thwart their love, and she dies tragically in the church of les Saintes-Maries-de-la-Mer. *Mirèio* was published in twelve cantos in 1859, and by 1863 Gounod had turned it into an opera. After its first performances in Paris, Gounod rewrote the opera with a happy ending.

Mistral himself was wise enough to publish *Mirèio* in one and the same volume in both the *langue d'oc* and French, thus:

MIRÈIO
CANT PROUMIÈ
LOU MAS DI FALABREGO

MIREILLE
CHANT PREMIER
LE MAS DES MICOCOULES

*Cante uno chato de
    Prouvènco.
Dins lis amour de sa jouvènco,
A travès de la Crau, vers la mar,
    dins li bla,
Umble escoulan dóu grand
    Oumèro,
Iéu la vole segui. Coume èro
Rèn qu'uno chato de la terro,
En foro de la Crau se n'es gaire
    parla.*

*Je chante une jeune fille de
    Provence.
Dans les amours de sa jeunesse,
A travers la Crau, vers la mer,
    dans les blés,
Humble écolier du grand
    Homère,
Je veux la suivre. Comme c'était
Seulement une fille de la glèbe,
En dehors de la Crau il s'en peut
    parlé.*

This opening stanza of Canto 1 of *Mireille* (*Mirèio*) means:

THE LOTUS FARM

I sing of a maiden of Provence,
Telling the love-story of her youth,
Across the Crau, towards the sea and through the
    fields of corn,
As a humble pupil of the great Homer,
I wish to follow her. She was
Simply a daughter of the soil,
Spoken of by no one outside the Crau.

Mistral's was a mock-modesty. Almost immediately this apparent diffidence disappears. In the next stanza he avows to raise Mireille to the status of a queen, telling her story in his own 'scorned speech' ('lengo mespresado'), because he writes only for shepherds and farming folk.

Mistral's masterpiece, *Lou Pouèmo dóu Rose* or *Le Poème du Rhône*, is another tragedy. Published in 1897 it recounts a voyage along the River Rhône by a barge named *Lou Caburie*. Again a rich man, this time a youthful Prince of Holland, falls in love with a poor French girl, this time the daughter of a ferryman. When the barge is accidentally sunk by colliding with the first steamship to sail the river, though the crew is saved, the lovers drown. We are, I suppose, meant to conceive the steamship as a symbol of the crass modernity which had attempted to obliterate the ancient culture of Mistral's beloved Languedoc.

Mistral spent most of his life in the village where he was born. A tireless publicist for his cause, between 1881 and 1889 he edited a journal devoted to the culture of the Languedoc and delightfully entitled *L'Aïoli* (see pp.9 and 53). The mas du Juge where he was born can still be seen. The mas du Lézard, where he and his mother lived after the death of her husband in 1855, still stands in the centre of Maillane. Mistral married in the 1870s and built for himself and his bride a home close by his mother's. It now serves as a Mistral museum, with a stirringly noble statue of the writer, sculpted in 1929, adorning its garden. In 1904 he was awarded the Nobel Prize for his contributions to literature and philology. He died in 1914 in the house that he had built, and was buried in the village cemetery in a tomb modelled on a pavilion of Queen Jeanne at les Baux. Its ornaments include the seven-branched star which the Félibrige movement took as its emblem, and several charming faces of *belles Arlésiennes*.

The village church at Maillane, Notre-Dame-de-Bethléem, which enshrines a black statue of the Blessed Virgin known as Notre-Dame-de-Grace, is thronged for a Requiem Mass in the *langue d'oc* on the anniversary of Mistral's birth, and for another on 25 March, the anniversary of his death. The anniversary of his birth is also celebrated by a folklore festival, with Félibrige dancing in the streets. His influence is such that (at least in the part of France where I live) children today are taught at school not only French but also the *langue d'oc*.

From Maillane the D5 winds on for three kilometres through cypress-studded countryside to Graveson. Here the church of la Nativité-de-la-Vierge was rebuilt in the nineteenth century, though the Romanesque choir and apse were left untouched. The walls of a former château still stand, pierced with two gateways, one of which once hauled up a drawbridge. Today the fine houses of Graveson are guarded by the seventeenth-century Château de Breuil.

This northernmost section of the Bouches-du-Rhône is filled with other villages as pretty as Graveson, and four in particular are within easy reach. To the north of Graveson the fifteenth-century château from which Châteaurenard derives its name squats on its rock overlooking the River Durance. Open to visitors (except in December and January), it has preserved two round machicolated towers from its original four. I find these towers very quaint: stones rise two-thirds of the way and then the rest are seemingly made out of concrete blocks. I have consulted numerous books about Châteaurenard, but none explains this phenomenon. The château was once the home of the anti-Pope Benedict XIII who, like us, must have mounted these towers for an exhilarating view of Mont Ventoux and the Alpilles.

The surrounding countryside is heavy throughout spring, summer and autumn with the scent of apples, peaches, pears, strawberries, grapes and melons, and not surprisingly Châteaurenard has become the home of a massive international fruit and vegetable market. Just over six kilometres away to the east lies the village of Noves. This time it is the chapel of Notre-Dame-de-Pitié, built from the twelfth to the eighteenth centuries on the site of a Gaullish oppidum, that dominates the Durance. After the plague reached Noves in 1721, those who were spared made this chapel a centre of pilgrimage. Noves is still surrounded by part of its fourteenth-century walls, four crenellated gateways opening in its towers, one of which supports an eighteenth-century belfry. When these walls were built, they incorporated the beautiful Romanesque church of Saint-Baudile, which had stood here since the mid-twelfth century. The citizens claim that Petrarch's Laura was born here. With its camp sites, fishing and hunting, Noves welcomes tourism and celebrates the Feast of the Assumption (15 August) with bullfights *à la cocarde*.

At the end of August they have the alarming custom of letting the bulls run wild through the streets.

Barbentane lies west of Châteaurenard, by way of Rognonas, whose seventeenth-century church has a Gallo-Roman font. The château of Barbentane brings a flavour of the court of Louis XIV to Provence, with a hint of Tuscany too. Begun for Paul-François de Barbentane in 1674, it was finished only in the following century, when Joseph-Pierre Balthazar de Barbentane was Tuscan ambassador. From Tuscany he brought the marble which decorates the interior of his home. The ochre of its walls is set off by the deep green of the trees surrounding the Château de Barbentane. Although the château is classical in inspiration, the garlands and fanciful arabesques of the so-called *salon des statues* are entirely rococo. A Chinese room, a chapel, some delicate eighteenth-century wallpaper in other exquisite rooms, make a visit to this château rewarding (though I dislike the guided tours, which do not allow you to stand and stare long enough). The garden contains some 300-year-old plane trees brought here from Turkey. The rest of the village hangs together magically, the white stones of its Renaissance houses and its Romanesque-Gothic church guarded by two fortified gateways in the remains of the fourteenth-century ramparts, the whole overlooked by the keep of the former episcopal château. Anglicus Grimoard, the brother of Pope Urban V, built the château in 1365, and its 45-metre-high keep is still called the tour Anglica.

The fourth village which ought not to be missed in this corner of the Bouches-du-Rhône is Boulbon, four kilometres south-west on the way to Tarascon. Before reaching Boulbon the road crosses the D81, where an excursion left will take you to the Abbey of Saint-Michel de Frigolet. It lies in a valley full of pines, cypresses, olives and thyme (for which the Provençal word is *ferigoulo*). The trees seem to be encroaching upon the pale-yellow walls and the pink-tiled roofs of the abbey itself. Once an Augustinian priory and today the home of Premonstratensian monks, the monastery's origins go back to the twelfth century, if not earlier. When the Premonstratensians took over in 1858 they built themselves a new monastery church. The interior of their neo-Gothic basilica of the Immaculate Conception, finished in 1866, is a riot of colour, enough to convert the most prejudiced opponent of such pastiches, and it happily incorporates the Romanesque pilgrimage chapel of Notre Dame de la Bon Remède, where Anne of Austria came in 1632 to pray for the gift of a son. The result was the future Louis XIV, at which the queen presented the chapel with its sumptuous baroque panelling housing paintings by Nicolas Mignard. The monastery has also preserved a little Romanesque church dedicated to St Michael, and to the south of this building its thirteenth-century cloister.

When Mistral was young the monastery housed a school where he was educated. He later recorded these experiences in his memoirs, but what seems to have delighted him chiefly in later years was the excellent wine produced in this region, perfumed with *ferigoulo*. Canto II of *Mirèio* sings its praises, as well as that of la Crau and the muscat of the Vaucluse:

> When Bacchus leads the dance,
>   Brawny and naked as an ancient athlete,
> And the workers, their feet dyed with juice,
>   Are treading the vintage of la Crau,
> And the good wine pours out of presses filled to the brim,
> And ruddy foam rises in the vats;
>
> When the leaves of Spanish broom
>   Hold the clear silkworms,
> Each an artist in his tiny loom,
>   Weaving in a golden web
> Fine, fragile cells spun of sunlight
> Where millions of them creep and sleep,
>
> On a day like that Provence is glad,
>   For this is the time for jesting and laughter:
> The *ferigoulo* and the Muscat of Baume
>   Are quaffed, and afterwards the people sing.
> Lads and lasses in between their labour
> Dance to the tinkling of the tambourine.

Like the lovers at the end of that canto, I took a few apples, some fresh cheese and, with a glass of wine, lunched beneath the lotus-trees.

Then I returned to Boulbon. Boulbon lies on the wild, chalky slopes of the massif of la Montagnette. Like all these villages on what was once the frontier of Provence, Boulbon was fortified, and once more part of the fortifications remain, as well as the

ruins of a massive château built here in the thirteenth century
by the Counts of Provence. Boulbon boasts a seventeenth-century
church dedicated to St Anne, but its finest religious building is
the late-twelfth-century cemetery chapel of Saint-Marcellin. It is
kept locked, but a notice on the door tells you where to find the
custodian. On 1 June the menfolk of Boulbon process to this
chapel, carrying bottles of wine for a blessing. Mistral would
have approved, and so do I – though personally I would not bar
the womenfolk.

From Tarascon to Arles and les Saintes-Maries-de-la-Mer

Tarascon peers balefully across from the left bank of the Rhône at Beaucaire, with which it is connected by a 450-metre-long suspension bridge. Although Tarascon was badly damaged in the Second World War, its fortress remains intact, a moated building on a rock overlooking the river. Whenever I reach this spot I drive across the bridge to the right bank of the river for the ravishing sight of the château and church reflected in the waters.

Begun in 1401 and finished in 1499, the château is nearly 103 metres long and thirty-six metres wide and rises in parts to a height of forty-eight metres. Its predecessors included an eleventh-century feudal château built to dominate both the surrounding countryside and the river traffic. In 1291 under Charles II of Anjou the old château began to be rebuilt, and the new fortress became the administrative centre of Tarascon. Similar ups and downs ended in 1370, when 1,800 florins were spent on a further renovation of the venerable fortress. But the major reconstruction which left us the château we see today was begun in 1401 under the direction of Louis II of Anjou. By 1406 he had spent nearly 34,000 florins on the project. Louis died in 1417, but his successor Louis III continued to patronize the rebuilding. In the following half-century the work was continued under a master-mason from Tarascon named Jean Robert. Two celebrated sculptors, Simon de Beaujeau and Jacques Morel of Lyons, were engaged in the 1430s to embellish the building with sculptures that are as clean-cut now as when they were first carved.

When Louis III died in 1434, his brother and heir, René of Anjou, was the prisoner of the Duke of Burgundy, who was disputing René's claim on the duchy of Lorraine through the inheritance of his first wife, Isabelle of Lorraine. Further misfortunes befell Roi René, above all the seizure of his kingdom of Naples by Alfonso V of Aragon in 1442. Thenceforth René was obliged to devote his energies and taste as a patron of the Arts to Provence – to its great good fortune. Between 1447 and 1449 he was at Tarascon, welcoming there with exuberant festivities his nephew (the future King Louis XI) and Jeanne de Laval (soon to be his second wife). René inaugurated the completion of the château, including its chapel, which was built for him by Jean Robert. The château was almost complete, though for the rest of his life René continued to enrich it with furnishings and paintings.

The château at Tarascon escaped demolition at the Revolution by becoming a prison. During the 'White Terror' in 1795 it saw the melancholy end of twenty-three Jacobins, including a woman and a girl of fifteen, who were stabbed to death and then thrown into the Rhône. The vicissitudes of the nineteenth century saw the château falling into decay, until it was taken over by the state as an historical monument in 1840 and then judiciously restored in the 1890s by the architect Henri Revoil. Today it is enormously impressive – massive walls; crenellations and machicolations; walkways for archers around certain walls; metal grilles defending exposed windows; courtyards, including the austere *cour d'honneur*, slightly menacing, I think, in spite of its arcaded galleries and the elegance of its staircase tower; beamed ceilings; the vaulted council chamber; and a double-storeyed chapel. Some of the walls are carved with excellent graffiti, especially those of fifteenth-century ships in the *salle des galères*. The lack of furniture in the château has been remedied in part by six tapestries (lent by the French historical monuments commission), woven in Brussels between 1532 and 1535 and depicting the triumphs of Scipio, the vanquisher of Hannibal.

The busts of Roi René and Jeanne de Laval which the Revolutionaries threw out have been recovered and placed under the staircase tower. They are the worse for wear, particularly Jeanne's, half of whose head has been sliced off. One of René's most inspired innovations here was to revive the popular festivities connected with the *tarasque* of Tarascon. This mythical beast, half-dragon, half-crocodile, lived in a cave in the rock on which the château rises, terrorizing the inhabitants of the town until St Martha (the sister of Lazarus whom Jesus raised from the dead) arrived here, held a crucifix over the brute, put her girdle around its neck and led the *tarasque* about as peacefully as a child's pet. Naturally this act endeared her to the people of Tarascon, and she became the town's patron saint. Her alleged remains were discovered in 1197, and the citizens built as their shrine the collegiate church of Sainte-Marthe. A *tarasque* procession is still held annually on the last Sunday in June – I am not sure why, since the feast day of St Martha is 29 July.

The relics of St Martha still reside in the crypt of her church at Tarascon, a crypt that remains virtually the only Romanesque part of Sainte-Marthe. You can, however, trace Romanesque work at the base of the belfry and in the south porch, which is delicately sculpted with grotesques and the heads of animals. The rest of the church has been built and rebuilt. Though side chapels proliferated through the centuries (to be embellished with paintings by Mignard and Parrocel), the overall feel of Sainte-Marthe remains basically fourteenth-century Gothic.

Tarascon suffered in the Second World War, but the bombardments did not obliterate all its arcaded houses, its ancient streets, gateways, Renaissance houses, and the town hall of 1648. Inside the eighteenth-century church of Saint-Jacques is a painting by J.-B. Van Loo of Martha conquering the *tarasque*, and another by Mignard of the saint receiving Jesus in her home. The hospital of Saint-Nicolas has a fifteenth-century chapel and a pharmacy with yet another remarkable collection of eighteenth-century ceramic jars. The Palais de Justice dates from the eighteenth century, and the Dominican convent suppressed at the Revolution has been turned into a theatre and cultural centre.

And since 1872 the story of St Martha and the *tarasque* has given way as the most celebrated legend of Tarascon to that of Alphonse Daudet's character Tartarin. A house dating from 1850 on the boulevard Itam has been turned into a museum recalling Tartarin's exploits, his renown in play and film, and the life of his creator. Initially resented by the town as an insult to its self-esteem, the braggard, cowardly and lovable Tartarin of Tarascon has now become more famous than Tarascon itself. His creator, Alphonse Daudet, had been inspired with an enthusiasm for Provence by meeting Frédéric Mistral in 1860. Daudet's poverty and venereal disease enriched the background of his most celebrated novel, for they forced him to convalesce in Algeria in 1861 and 1862, after which he wrote *Chapatin le tueur des lions*, an obvious prototype for Tartarin. He published *Les Aventures prodigieuses de Tartarin de Tarascon* in 1872.

In his memoirs Daudet revealed that in a tiny green notebook he had over the years made a complete summary of the south of France, 'its accent, gestures, frenzies and the ebullitions caused by the sun, and the honest tendency to tell lies, a habit proceeding from excessive folly, gossip and good-nature'. He recorded proverbs, country songs, the street cries of hawkers and the noises of the fairs. 'Even the crimes of the south and the explosions of passion and drunken violence brought about without drink' were all recorded. From these memoranda, Daudet declared, he drew such books as *Tartarin de Tarascon*. The south which he cherished was 'pompous, classical and theatrical, loving display and resplendent costume (disregarding the occasional stain), loving oratory, plumage and military music floating in the wind'.

Tartarin of Tarascon encapsulates it all, supremely the bombast. 'Possessed as he was with a mania for adventure and a craving for excitement, an insane longing for travel and dangerous exploits, at the age of forty-five Tartarin had never left his native town, not even for Marseille,' the novelist tells us. The furthest he had journeyed was across the Rhône to Beaucaire. Why? 'Because Tartarin resembled Sancho Panza physically (short, pot-bellied, heavy, fat and bloated), though with Don Quixote in his soul.' Daudet merrily creates the double-talk between Don Quixote and Sancho Panza which wars in Tartarin's mind:

DON QUIXOTE	SANCHO PANZA
Cover yourself, Tartarin, with fame and glory;	Cover yourself with warm flannel, Tartarin.
Oh for double-barrelled shotguns!	Oh for well-knitted vests and warm knee-caps!
Oh for hunting-knives, lassos and moccasins!	Oh for cosy ear-muffs!
An axe! An axe! Won't someone give me an axe?	Jeanne, please bring me my cup of chocolate.

At which Jeanne appears with not only hot chocolate but also a well-grilled steak flavoured with aniseed.

Once Tartarin nearly went to Shanghai, and after a while came to believe that he really had done so – for, as Daudet explains, in the south the sun magnifies everything, transforming Sparta (a straggling village) and Athens (a little provincial town) into cities of enormous size. The same sun transforms a man who nearly went to Shanghai into one who has done. Then one day a circus visits Tarascon, forcing Tartarin to face up to his destiny. Standing in front of a lion's cage, he is overheard to murmur of his own skills as a lion-hunter. The would-be hero has no choice but to prove himself.

Tartarin equips himself for the hunt and, bound for Algeria, takes the train to Marseille. His dear friend Major Bravida is at the head of the townsfolk as they tearfully bid him farewell.

'The railway employees themselves were sobbing in corners, while the populace viewed the scene from outside through the railings, crying "Long live Tartarin!"' The great man cries 'Goodbye all' and kisses Major Bravida on both cheeks. 'Then, leaping on the platform he stepped into a compartment crowded with ladies from Paris, terrifying them almost to death at the appearance of this strange creature with his rifles and revolvers.'

Alas, the expedition is an utter failure. The only lion Tartarin manages to kill (by accident) is a tame, blind beast belonging to a couple of beggars, and for this he is imprisoned, forced to buy its carcase and fined 2,500 francs. He manages to obtain a camel on which to ride back to the port. Tartarin returns to Tarascon penniless, not a single wild lion killed, leading a crazed camel – and receives a hero's welcome, for he had sent the skin of the blind mangy lion back to Major Bravida. At first the hero imagines he is being mocked; but then he stiffens his back. The book ends magically. ' "This is my camel," cried Tartarin; and already, under the influence of the Tarascon sun, that splendid sun which makes one tell lies unwittingly, he added, patting the camel's hump, "It is a noble beast, and one who has seen me kill every one of my lions." '

Drive south-east from Tarascon by way of Saint-Gabriel to the ochre-coloured town of Fontvieille. At Saint-Gabriel, a spot inhabited in Gallo-Roman times, stands a twelfth-century chapel whose sober proportions contrast with the vigour of its sculpted porch. Fontvieille, with its picturesque houses, some of them troglodyte, is guarded by a watchtower of 1353. Just outside the town is the nineteenth-century Château de Montauban, once the home of Daudet, and in a rock-strewn terrain to the south of Fontvieille stands the windmill of 1814 which is said to have inspired the *Lettres de mon moulin*, which Daudet published in 1869.

The stories recounted in that volume are justly famous, though the author wrote them not here but in Paris. I envy Daudet's skill at evoking the dream of medieval Provence. Inventing an Avignon Pope named Boniface of Yvetot, he wrote:

Those who never saw Avignon at the time of this Pope have seen nothing. For gaiety, for life, for bustle and for festivals celebrated with style there was never a city like it. From dawn till dusk there were processions, pilgrimages, the scattering of flowers in the streets, fine tapestries decorating the walls, cardinals arriving by boat along the Rhône, flags flying, galleys decked out with bunting, the Pope's soldiers singing in the squares in Latin, and the mendicant friars sounding their rattles.

Pope Boniface of Yvetot is an unforgettable creation. He loved the *farandole* (the native dance of Provence) and would beat time to it with his hat, scandalizing the cardinals but making the common folk cry, 'Ah, what a fine prince of the church, what a right sort of Pope this is!' He relished yet more a deep red Châteauneuf-du-Pape. And most of all he adored his handsome mule. In the lower storey of the mill outside Fontvieille is a little museum dedicated to the author, filled with souvenirs and displaying the illustrations done by José Ray for the first edition of *Lettres de mon moulin*.

Arles lies seventeen kilometres south-west of Fontvieille. On the way the route passes the abbey of Montmajour, a Romanesque masterpiece which was to inspire the pencil of Van Gogh. Hermits came here in the early years of Provençal Christianity, guarding an ancient cemetery. The abbey itself, founded in 949 by a devout woman named Teucinde, prospered by reason of a special pardon offered to those who came here, especially on 3 May (the feast of the discovery of the true cross). In years gone by the only approach to this monastery was by boat, but the monks also drained the marshlands surrounding their abbey, again reaping financial benefits for themselves as well as enriching the lives of the surrounding farmers. As with many another monastery in this part of France, Montmajour fell on hard times after the Revolution. It is to the credit of the twentieth-century civil authorities that the whole complex has been so well restored (though parts still remain romantically in ruins). The abbey church, with its delicately sculpted capitals and a crypt dug out of the rock, was vaulted around 1200. The cloister, worthy of comparison with that of Saint-Trophime at Arles, was begun in the second half of the twelfth century. Its south gallery was finished 200 years later, while the west gallery was rebuilt in 1717. The refectory remains a majestic Romanesque hall, while the machicolated tour des Abbés turns out to be a defensive keep, built by Abbot Pons de l'Orme in 1369.

To many visitors Arles is a city made radiant and tragic by the final outburst of superb painting and mania of Vincent Van Gogh who, on 14 December 1888, here attacked his friend Paul Gauguin with a razor. Fewer than two years later he killed himself at the age of thirty-seven. Certainly the citizens of Arles, ashamed at their past neglect of Van Gogh, have perfectly reconstructed at Port-de-Bouc the bridge of Langlois which he immortalized in the first of his Provençal paintings and which they had foolishly demolished.

To others the name of this Provençal city has a musical resonance, recalling Alphonse Daudet's play *L'Arlésienne*, or rather the incidental music that Georges Bizet wrote for it – now widely performed in a couple of orchestral suites, one arranged by Bizet himself, the other by his admirer Ernest Guiraud – for the play itself was a flop.

Yet for most visitors and many locals, first and foremost Arles is the city of bullfighting, fights that usually kill the bull unless they are those *fêtes de la cocarde* in which the trainee matadors simply pluck flowers from between the besieged animals' horns. Of the numerous corridas that take place in Provence, the July *cocarde d'Or* at Arles is the most celebrated, rivalling in prestige the city's festival of music and theatre, which is mounted in the same month.

Bullfights take place on Sundays from Easter throughout the summer in the city's Roman amphitheatre, which is today known as *les arènes* and dates as far back as the time of the Emperor Hadrian. Arles owes much to the Romans. Its Celtic-Ligurian name was Arelate, which means town in the marsh, and although it is situated at what in Roman times was the innermost navigable part of the Rhône, it came properly to life only when Marius ordered the digging of a canal from the town as far as the Fos gulf. The marshy lands were drained. Arles became prosperous and in 49 BC gratefully sent ships to assist Julius Caesar when he was besieging Marseille. The Rhône was bridged and Arles became part of an important commercial thoroughfare. The reign of Augustus Caesar proved a halcyon period for the city. A bishopric established in the third century was an archbishopric less than a hundred years later. Seneca found a wife in Arles. The Emperor Constantine loved to stay here, and in 314 chose Arles as the seat of an ecclesiastical council to deal with the Donatist schismatics.

Attacked by Visigoths, Burgundians and Ostrogoths, Arles was a provincial capital in the ninth and tenth centuries and rose again in the eleventh century as an independent city much like some of the Italian republics. Three towers still survive from her medieval fortifications. Yet the city flowered most of all under the Romans.

This efflorescence is everywhere visible in the city, and especially in its bullfighting arena. In Roman times this amphitheatre could seat 26,000 spectators. In the Middle Ages it was transformed into a military bastion and later sheltered more than 200 houses and a couple of chapels. Paradoxically this misuse helped to preserve the amphitheatre (though it is in a worse state than that at Nîmes) until its excavation and restoration in the nineteenth century. An ellipse some 136 metres by 107, today it has lost its upper storey. Still standing are the two lower ones, supported by Doric and Corinthian pilasters. Preserved too are an ancient architrave, marble walls, mosaic floors, a podium and galleries covered with massive tiles.

Another vestige of the Roman era lies a few paces south-west along the rue du Jeu-de-Paume. This theatre, built in the time of Augustus Caesar, with a diameter of nearly 104 metres and its impressive twenty ranks of seats (of the original thirty-three), could once house 16,000 people – today all that you see is little more than one-third of the original construction. Two massive columns, one of African marble, the other of Carrara marble, remain from the proscenium. The tower of Roland is all that is left of the former entrance to the theatre. In the evenings during the summer season the tourist board of Arles mounts *son-et-lumière* displays in this evocative ruin.

East of the amphitheatre are two other venerable remains. The first is the church of Notre-Dame-la-Major, celebrated as the venue of the third Christian Council of Arles in AD 455 – a sign of the city's importance before Aix-en-Provence and Marseille had superseded it in the eyes of the Roman world. Notre-Dame-la-Major rises from the site of a pagan temple, and an inscription in its porch declares that the present building was consecrated in 453. In fact its oldest part today is its twelfth-century Romanesque nave. The side aisles both date from the fourteenth century, the apse and Gothic choir from the sixteenth, the façade from the seventeenth and the belfry from the nineteenth. The most ancient survivals in this church are what are popularly described as the buckle, sandals and tunic of St Césaire, who died in 542. The ivory buckle certainly might once have been his, for it is Byzantine work dating from either the sixth or the seventh century.

In the church square a modern monument recalls two pas-sionate Provençal patriots, the Marquis Folco de Baroncelli and Joseph d'Arbaud. Inspired by Mistral, the former – realizing that he was a rotten poet – quitted Avignon to spend the rest of his life as an honorary *gardian* (or herdsman) of the Camargue, attaching himself to the ranchers who herded the bulls and white horses of that marshy, desolate and romantic region. His ally d'Arbaud wrote one celebrated novel, *La Béstio d'ou Vaccarès*, which – curiously enough – retains a vital message for our own day. The Vaccarès is the largest lake in the Camargue, a haunt of wildlife so rare, and the support of an ecology so threatened, that casual visitors are now banned. In his novel, published in 1926, Joseph d'Arbaud had already foreseen the possibility of the destruction of a fragile environment by humans, conjuring up a creature with a human face which had so suffered at the hands of mankind that it had taken refuge in the remote Camargue by the Étang de Vaccarès.

Siting the monument to these wonderful fanatics in this square was an inspired decision in 1963, for the church of Notre-Dame-la-Major shelters a late-sixteenth-century statue of St George, the patron saint of the *gardians* of the Camargue. One of the most delightful annual festivals at Arles takes place on May Day, when *gardians* ride through the streets, with *belles Arlésiennes* sitting on their horses' rumps, and an open-air Mass is celebrated in front of Notre-Dame-la-Major.

Beyond the apse of the church stretches the best-preserved section of the Roman walls of Arles, running south beside the boulevard Emile-Combes, where you can make out the stones of the Roman base overlaid by Carolingian walls, the whole topped by medieval ramparts. Nearby the ancient Aurelian Way entered Arles through a gateway, the porte d'Auguste, marked today by a couple of round defensive towers.

The boulevard Emile-Combes leads south to the most animated part of modern Arles, the boulevard des Lices, flanked on both sides by civic gardens (the northern of which houses the ancient rampart known as the tower of Roland). Its cafés are shaded by plane trees. This is the scene of the Wednesday and Saturday morning market at Arles, as well as many of the yearly festivities of the city, including the April sheep fair. Even here antique Arles surfaces, for a splendid Roman mosaic has been uncovered in the basement of the Crédit Agricole Bank.

The southern garden is known as the jardin d'Hiver, the northern one as the jardin d'Eté. In the latter, Arles has made up for its neglect of Van Gogh during his lifetime by setting here a bust of the artist. Establishing himself in the place Lamartine, Vincent had dreamed of setting up an artists' colony at Arles (though when his fellow-artists came he abused them). The wild yellow paint of the café in which he lived inspired his painting now known as the 'Yellow House'. His 'Café de Nuit' was based on the restaurant Alcazar in the same square. Much else that he created here found its way back to his native Holland and to the Stedelijk Museum there: his bedroom with its yellow bed and red coverlet; 'La vieille Arlésienne', one of the first works he painted after arriving in Provence; his view of Saint-Rémy-de-Provence; the shacks he painted at les Saintes-Maries-de-la-Mer; his views of la Crau. The portrait of Vincent's loyal friend and drinking companion, the bearded postman Joseph Roulin, is today in the Rijksmuseum Kröller-Müller, Otterlo, as are 'Langlois bridge with women washing' and the blue and yellow 'Café terrace on the place du Forum' (a spot which still survives as the Restaurant Vaccarès). As for the portrait of the kindly young physician, Dr Félix Rey, who attempted to care for Van Gogh during his confinement as a madman, today it hangs in the Hermitage, Leningrad.

Not that the citizens of Arles need censuring for being put out by a man who one Sunday in December 1888 walked into a brothel, asked for a girl named Rachel and presented her with his severed ear, adding, 'Guard that carefully.' Soon thirty citizens had petitioned the mayor about Vincent's heavy drinking and behaviour with women and children. As a middle-aged seamstress who lived near the Yellow House declared, 'Everyone in the neighbourhood is frightened. The women in particular no longer feel secure because he indulges in touching them and makes obscene remarks in their presence.' She testified that the previous Monday he had taken her by the waist and lifted her into the air. Vincent's response was to describe the citizens of Arles as cannibals. The response of the superintendent of police was to have him committed to the care of Dr Rey in the Hôtel-Dieu.

From the boulevard des Lices, the rue Jean-Jaurès leads north into the sole large square in the whole of Arles, the place de la République (for apart from the boulevards, almost all the city consists of tortuous streets laid out in the Middle Ages). Since 1676 the centre of this square has been marked by an Egyptian obelisk. Rising from a fountain with four bronze lions, this obelisk once stood in the Roman circus to the west of the city (a site even now being excavated).

Three excellent buildings flank this square, the finest the former abbey church of Saint-Trophime to the right. The porch of Saint-Trophime is a magnificent relic of Romanesque sculpture. In the tympanum God appears amid the symbols of the four evangelists.

Above, a lintel is carved with the seated statues of the twelve apostles. Angels surround them, three sounding the trumpet for the Last Judgement. The souls of the saved are welcomed by angels into the bosoms of the patriarchs; the damned are dragged away to the inferno. Other scenes depict incidents from the birth of Jesus: shepherds and their flocks; the adoration of the Magi; the visit to King Herod; and the massacre of the innocents. Lions devour human beings. Rich foliage decorates pilasters. Samson takes on a lion, and Delilah takes on Samson. More huge statues depict the apostles once again, the stoning of St Stephen and of course St Trophimus, the third-century Christian sent with five others from Rome to evangelize Gaul. He became the first Bishop of Arles and is here dressed in his bishop's vestments.

The rest of Saint-Trophime lives up to this entrance. A narrow, twelfth-century Romanesque nave, vaulted like the side aisles of the same era, is crossed by an early eleventh-century transept. (Look out in the left crossing for Louis Finson's superb seventeenth-century painting of the Annunciation, his 'Martyrdom of St Stephen' in the nave and his 'Adoration of the Magi' in the flamboyant Gothic chapel of the kings, which was built on the right aisle in the 1620s.) A choir and deambulatory were added in the fifteenth century. In the seventeenth century ogival vaulting was added to the sacristy. One of several early Christian sarcophagi in this former cathedral now serves as the altar of the chapel of the Holy Sepulchre in the deambulatory. It dates from around 400 and its carvings depict Jesus between St Peter and St Paul. The chapels on the north side are also Romanesque, whereas the great chapel on the south side was added only in the seventeenth century. The 20-metre-high nave is the tallest in Provence. Here in 1178 the Holy Roman Emperor Frederick Barbarossa was crowned King of Arles, and in 1456 the cathedral saw the marriage of Roi René to his second wife, Jeanne de Laval.

Saint-Trophime has not only retained the chapter house, refectory, dormitory and kitchen of the Augustinian canons who once lived here; it also boasts a delicious, complex cloister, shaded by cypresses, its galleries supported on twin columns. Two Romanesque galleries were built in the late twelfth century; the Gothic west gallery was rebuilt in the mid-fifteenth century and the south gallery some half a century later. The carvings of the north gallery predate even those of the main entrance, dating from the third quarter of the twelfth century. The unknown Romanesque sculptors have clearly sought inspiration here from Roman models, with which the region of Arles and Nîmes abound. Like the artists who worked on the entrance, they also apparently relished depicting the stoning of St Stephen. More touching and gentle is the carving of the holy women gathering spices to perfume the body of the dead Jesus. Stephen's stoning reappears in the exquisite carvings of the capitals of the cloister, which also depict Martha driving out the *tarasque* of Tarascon. As for the nearby archbishop's palace, this eighteenth-century building with a splendid balustraded staircase is now a city library.

Opposite the church of Saint-Trophime in the place de la République stands the pagan lapidary museum, installed in the church of Sainte-Anne, which was built with money partly provided by King Louis XIII between 1621 and 1629. A rustic chimney in my own French home derives from exactly the same era and is carved in the classical style. This church, by contrast, is an architectural anachronism, a survival – as so often in Provence – of Gothic forms well into the seventeenth century.

The contents of the museum are rich. Pagan remains are legion at Arles, chiefly because as well as its amphitheatre and theatre it has two pagan cemeteries that archaeologists have ravaged. A marble statue of Mithras surrounded by serpents and the signs of the zodiac comes from the amphitheatre. A carved third-century sarcophagus hails from the cemetery of Trinquetaille. Another sarcophagus carving depicts Apollo and the Muses, while a mosaic shows Orpheus charming the animals. Unfortunately the so-called Venus of Arles, discovered in the Roman theatre, has been carted away to the Louvre in Paris, though a colossal, 3-metre-high statue of the Emperor Augustus, found in the same spot, remains. Still further west in the rue Balze is the remarkable museum of Christian lapidary art, installed in a seventeenth-century Jesuit college and chapel and probably unequalled in treasures outside the Vatican. You can climb down steps under this museum to the slightly spooky underground alleyways used by the Romans to store their corn.

If you have time, one of the two cemeteries from which many of the treasures in the lapidary museum come is well worth visiting.

For fifteen centuries both pagans and Christians have found their final resting place at les Alyscamps, a funereal Champs-Élysées to the south-east of the city. This cemetery became so renowned that bodies would be brought from afar, floated down the Rhône to Arles, their mourners putting in the coffins a burial fee for the privilege of being interred here. Even Dante had heard of the custom, though instead of regarding les Alyscamps as a blessed spot, redolent of the sanctity of St Trophimus, he included it in his *Inferno*:

> Casting my eye around as soon as I entered,
> I see on every side a vast wide space,
> Replete with bitter pain and evil torment.
> As where the Rhône stagnates on the plains of Arles . . .
> This spot is thickly spread with sepulchres.

Of this once enormous necropolis remains the half-Gothic, half-Renaissance chapel of Saint-Accurse (so named because it was built in 1520 to expiate the murder of a man named Accurse de la Tour), an alley bordered with tombs and the semi-ruined Romanesque church of Saint-Honorat, built originally in the fifth century, its octagonal belfry still guarding the dead. (Scholars suggest that it was once illuminated with a flame which guided pilgrims to the cemetery.) A plaque marks the spot where Van Gogh came to paint the graves.

Back in Arles itself, to the north of the place de la République rises the town hall of Arles, built between 1673 and 1684 to the design of Mansart. Its belfry is older, raised in 1555 and carrying a statue of Mars founded in the same year. Beyond it is the place du Forum, filled with cafés and situated, as its name implies, almost exactly on the site of the Roman forum from which survive two Corinthian columns from the façade of a former temple. In the middle of the square is a statue of 1909 by Théodor Rivière depicting Frédéric Mistral. Mistral has every right to be commemorated here, for he greatly benefacted the city. At the corner of the rue Frédéric-Mistral west of the pagan lapidary museum is the Arlatan museum, dedicated to the ethnography and history of Provence. Housed in a Gothic, sixteenth-century hôtel with an elaborate courtyard, it was founded in 1896 on the initiative of Mistral, who not only gave much of his time to cataloguing the exhibits, but also spent much of his Nobel Prize money on the project. Provençal crèches, a model of the *tarasque*, costumes of yesteryear (whose equivalents are worn in Arles during the annual celebrations for the Feast of St John on 23 June), documents relating to the kingdom of Arles, some of the lovely walnut furniture of this region, ceramics, souvenirs of the plague of 1720 and the like cram its rooms, one of which is devoted to the creation of the Félibrige movement by Mistral and six allies in 1854.

Across the handsome rue de-la-République (once the rue Royale), with its seventeenth- and eighteenth-century town houses, stands the sixteenth- and seventeenth-century Hôtel-Dieu in which Van Gogh was incarcerated. Now excellently restored, it has been renamed the Hôpital Van Gogh and serves as a cultural centre and library, displaying contemporary works of art in honour of the man who during his own lifetime failed to sell a single canvas.

One further museum in Arles ought not to be missed. It stands due north of the Arlatan museum on the left bank of the grey waters of the Rhône. The Musée Réattu was once a commandery of the Knights of Malta, founded here in the fourteenth century and subsequently much enlarged (with, among other additions, a seventeenth-century entrance and a vaulted chapel of 1503). The building was despoiled at the Revolution but then bought by an Arlesian painter named Jacques Réattu. On his death in 1833 he left the house to his daughter, who on her death in 1868 left the commandery to the city. As well as sheltering a museum dedicated to the Knights of Malta, the Musée Réattu also houses Dutch, Italian and Provençal paintings (including works by Réattu himself). Picasso gave the museum fifty-seven drawings, and latterly the archivists have concentrated on collecting an impressive number of photographs by twentieth-century masters. Close by are the baths of Constantine, one pool still sheltered by an apse.

You are now on the edge of the so-called new suburb (properly, the *Bourg-Neuf*) of Arles, which spread beyond the Roman ramparts in the Middle Ages. Two monuments remain from the past in this quarter, the church of Saint-Julien, rebuilt in 1648 but still displaying the same Gothic anachronistic style as Sainte-Anne; and beyond it to the north-east the double round towers of the seventeenth-century porte de la Cavalerie. It guards the place Lamartine, today decorated with a bust of the poet. The Yellow House where Van Gogh lived was obliterated by the allied bombs of 1944.

The D570 takes you south-west from Arles into one of the most extraordinary regions of France, la Camargue. A national park since 1928, the Camargue lies between the Petit Rhône and the Grand Rhône, still marshy despite numerous attempts at draining the region. Romans hunted here. Cistercian monks farmed salt in its soggy fields. Its 85,000 hectares include lagoons on which breed pink flamingos (some 6,000 of them), storks and cormorants. No other zoological and botanical reserve in Europe matches the parc zoologique du Pont-de-Gau. The *gardians* of the Camargue, wearing cowboy stetsons and leather breeches, ride around protecting the black bulls and white horses and also providing tourists with the romantic notion that at last they have discovered the 'real' Provence – even though there were no such *gardians* before the nineteenth century. The ecology of this national park is well set out in a museum on the D570 at Mas de Rousty.

Finally your route reaches les Saintes-Maries-de-la-Mer, close by the estuary of the Petit Rhône. The holy Marys are Mary Magdalene, who bathed Jesus's feet with her tears, Mary the mother of St James the Less, and Mary Salome, the mother of St John the Evangelist and St James the Great. According to a ninth-century tradition, after the crucifixion of Jesus their enemies in Jerusalem put them in an open boat, along with St Martha and a servant named Sara, and sent them out to sea without sails or oars. Miraculously the ship arrived at Provence. Mary Magdalene went on to la Sainte-Baume, desperate to repent of her sins. The other two Marys stayed by the coast, and after their death were buried in a chapel above which arose in the eleventh century the present fortified and crenellated church of Saint-Michel at les Saintes-Maries-de-la-Mer. Its arcaded belfry was added in the fifteenth century. The saints' ship is still in the church's crypt, along with their relics and the bones of their maid. She became the patron saint of gypsies, and in the last week of May (24 and 25 May) the gypsies of France and beyond arrive here for an exuberant festival to celebrate the feast of their holy patron. For the rest of the summer les Saintes-Maries-de-la-Mer prospers happily as a seaside resort, with a seventeenth-century château and the folklore Museum Baroncelli adding to its charm, a Monday and Friday morning market filling its streets, and bloodthirsty bullfights defiling its arena at Easter and Pentecost.

Cannes, hill villages and the Côte d'Azur

When Lord Brougham first stayed in Cannes in 1834, he detested the place. Within days he was entranced. I experienced exactly the same feelings the second time my younger daughter and I drove into the city. I was exceedingly relieved that we had booked in at the Hotel Cavendish in the boulevard Carnot. Cannes is a curious city for one so elegant, since as you approach its magnificent bay, it suddenly becomes a driver's nightmare of narrow one-way streets. I was glad to scuttle into the hotel without having to negotiate them.

Fortunately, the wide and handsome boulevard Carnot, bordered with plane trees and flanked by shops and businesses, is the first boulevard you reach after the motorway exit. The *fin de siècle* dome of the Hotel Cavendish gave us a taste of what was to come in this opulent resort, which blossomed in the nineteenth century into a city of baroque villas, pseudo-Japanese pagodas, *belle-époque* palaces, pseudo-castles and suspended rock gardens, much of it built under the exuberant eye of the architect Laurent Vianney. The Cavendish also has the virtue of serving unlimited coffee at breakfast, as well as raising one's spirits by whisking you up and down from your room in one of those cage-like lifts that seem to feature in every French film of the 1930s.

That evening we ventured towards the shore and found the

place filled with American sailors. Cannes is not short of happy-go-lucky ladies, and a couple of matelots were in an advanced stage of courtship at the café table next to ours. While one sweetly fondled his newly found girlfriend, the second sailor uttered to his own companion the time-honoured words, 'Your mom must be one hellova beautiful lady.' My daughter and I strolled on towards a restaurant which on a previous visit I had identified as being inexpensive and also serving vegetarian dishes – a rarity in this region.

The words of a poet I had never heard of (Stephen Liègeard) are frequently quoted by the hosteliers of this town: 'La cuisine cannoise est comme une tranche de soleil sur une nappe de mer bleue' ('Cuisine in Cannes is like a slice of sunshine eaten on a tablecloth of blue sea'). The sunshine provides the abundant oil, tomatoes, fennel, saffron, thyme, onions and garlic which flavour the dishes. The sea provides the eels and perch, the crab and mussels, the bream and crayfish that make up a *bouillabaisse* here. I was planning on eating red mullet, a fish which the gastronome Anthelme Brillat-Savarin rightly described in 1825 as the woodcock of the sea. In Cannes they serve it with anchovy butter. I had sworn to my vegetarian daughter that the same restaurant served *pissaladière*, a splendid onion tart, along with a *ratatouille* (for vegetarians soon tire of vegetable omelettes, too many of which can damage your health).

Before we reached our restaurant we came across a sailor who had fallen in the street and lost lots of coins from his pocket. Emma-Jane kindly picked him up while I retrieved his cash. On his lapel was pinned a badge with the words 'I like Ike', and he gave us the startling news that some 6,500 fellow sailors were docked at Cannes, serving on the aircraft carrier USS *Dwight D. Eisenhower*. He also told us that the following day the orchestra of the 6th American Fleet was playing in the town. It proved to be an excellent concert, ending with the ballad 'Be my Baby'. His last valuable information was that if we went to the landing station during the day we would be taken on a tour of his ship. I asked him how big was the USS *Dwight D. Eisenhower*, and he pointed several hundred yards along the street.

So we went on a tour of the aircraft carrier. Our guide, a sailor who told us that his father had served in the US Navy for twenty years, described Cannes as one of the two best

European liberty ports (the other being Majorca). Cannes, he declared, had virtually adopted the aircraft carrier as its mascot. The vessel was leaving the town the following Saturday but, our guide promised, 'We'll be back next year.' A month later the USS *Dwight D. Eisenhower* was sailing down the Suez Canal as part of the military build-up against the seizure of Kuwait by the Iraqi dictator Saddam Hussein.

Parasol pines, palm trees and gardens line the superb promenade along the bay of Cannes, which is known as la Croisette, a name derived from a little cross that once stood at its eastern extremity. Laid out anew in 1868 and today some three kilometres long, the promenade's boutiques encapsulate the luxurious image that Cannes likes to present to the world, with the celebrated French fashion houses off-loading their *haute couture* on to anyone with an unlimited bank account. Some of its palaces are modern: the Palais Croisette built for the film festival in 1947, the Palais des Festivals, an even later construction of 1982. The latter is, to my mind, no stunning work of architecture, but it does house the accoustically perfect Théâtre Claude Debussy, in which 1,000 persons sit and listen to concerts. Undoubtedly the symbol of Cannes at its most architecturally luxurious on la Croisette is the baroque Carlton Hotel, begun in 1902 by the architect Marcellin Mayère – a dazzling white confection whose cupolas are said to have been inspired by the breasts of la Belle Otéro, that is the gypsy dancer, prodigious gambler and *grande horizontale* Caroline Otéro, with whom that architect pleaded in vain to follow him from Nice to Cannes.

'Ever since my childhood, I have been accustomed to seeing the face of every man who passed me light with desire,' Caroline once confessed. What is wrong, she asked, with being 'the flower whose perfume people long to inhale, the fruit that they long to taste'. Among those who both inhaled her perfume and tasted the fruit were Kaiser Wilhelm II, Tsar Nicholas II of Russia, Edward Prince of Wales, the Italian poet Gabriele d'Annunzio, the French statesman Aristide Briand and the second Duke of Westminster. If she really inspired the Carlton cupolas, never were breasts so ample or so honoured. The Cannois call them *Les boîtes de lait de la Belle Otéro*.

At the eastern end of la Croisette yachts bob in the port, and the reckless gamble in the Palm Beach casino at Pointe Croisette, a casino designed by Henri Rühl in the 1920s and admired by the Cannois as a masterpiece of kitsch. The locals prefer playing *pétanque* in the nearby place de l'Étang, before sipping a cognac in one of its cafés. Along the boulevard are some of the twenty-four private beaches of the town. La Croisette is blessed with eight kilometres of gentle sand (125 square metres of it brought from elsewhere in 1963), of which five and a half constitute public beaches. (There are also fourteen more beaches alongside the boulevard du Midi, of which four and a half kilometres are public, while the boulevard Eugène-Gazagnaire runs beside another large public beach.) Sports fanatics can choose from twenty tennis courts, or else practise surf-boarding, water-skiing, yachting, ice-skating and golf.

For their own part the citizens of Cannes prefer shopping elsewhere than along la Croisette, particularly on the Forville market, which opens daily (except Mondays) from eight o'clock until midday. This is where the novelist Georges Simenon, a Belgian who made Cannes his home, could be spotted buying his daily bread and wine every morning. Here fishermen offer you live bass, bream and conger-eel, while at neighbouring stalls farmers' families from the nearby villages sell their own produce – the perfume of fruit and vegetables vying with that of dill, basil and rosemary. Traders also set up their stalls in other pedestrianized streets, such as the rue Meynadier, which climbs up to the old quarter of Cannes just south of the Forville market and is enlivened with restaurants and *pâtisseries*, as well as shops far cheaper than those along la Croisette. Here the specialities are ravioli, confits, fish terrines, cheeses and truffled pâtés, while other shops sell ceramics and olive-wood carvings. This street continues into the rue Venizélos, with its open-air market. A pace or two further south from the rue Meynadier reveals the allées de la Liberté, site of a flower and bric-à-brac market, where one can still find a genuine bargain. There are, so far as I can see, no bargains to be had in the furniture and antique shops of the rue d'Antibes, which runs east from this market, but its sweet and chocolate shops are deservedly famous.

The casino at Palm Beach is but one of three in the town. The two others are the Casino des Fleurs in the rue des Belges and the Municipal Casino, the former open all year round, the latter a sumptuous affair, open from November to May (when the

Palm Beach casino is closed). Casinos here are by no means solely devoted to gambling, but host concerts, ballets and dinner dances. Yet more extravagant entertainment is provided in the Palais des Festivals et des Congrès along la Croisette and in the numerous night clubs in the town.

Perhaps because of these diversions, the one time I spotted an obvious prostitute in Cannes (unless the ladies with the matelots were such) she seemed to find no customers. On that occasion I was staying in the rue Maréchal Foch, in the Hotel Univers. The skimpily dressed lady stood desolately at the corner of the street, walked around the corner four or five times and then gave up. What I enjoyed most about this particular hotel (which presents itself as serving 'businessmen, tourists, families, honeymooners and resort guests') is its sixth floor, with a solarium, bar, restaurant and – to the delight of a writer – a reading room. Of an evening, from here you can look across to le Suquet, where the two churches and medieval tower of the old city of Cannes appear softly lit and enticing. Cannes has mastered the use of light to enhance its glamour, and even the yachts and ships glitter as the sun goes down.

Without doubt le Suquet is the most enchanting part of Cannes. Walk along la Pantiero – another haven for lovers of *pétanque* – where fishing and pleasure boats dance on the waves, and turn right into the place de l'Hôtel de Ville. The town hall here is a glorious three-storeyed classical confection of 1874–6 by the architect Durandi, also subtly illuminated at night.

Across the square at the foot of the rue du Mont Chevalier is a bust of Donat Joseph Mero, who was mayor of Cannes between 1865 and 1876. He looks piqued at being overwhelmed by palm fronds and ferns. The road leads up to the Saracen Tower of le Suquet, Mont Chevalier. Twenty-two metres high, it offers a panorama of the whole city and bay. In spite of its name it was built not by Saracens, but for Abbot Adelbert II of Lérins, who wanted to defend his monks against Saracen pirates (Saracen being the generic term used by the Christians for any Arab, Moorish or Turkish invader). On the doorway of the twelfth-century keep is the iron mask of the Man in the Iron Mask, who sought refuge here from the Île Sainte-Marguerite. Beside the mask a plaque enunciates the words of Luke, Chapter 6, Verse 37, *Dimittite et Dimittemini* ('Forgive and you will be forgiven'), since this sad victim is said to have forgiven his torturers.

Not that the so-called Man in the Iron Mask ever wore such a barbarous piece of headgear. This political prisoner, whom we have already encountered at Château d'If, and who died in the Bastille in 1703 and was buried immediately afterwards in absolute secrecy, was condemned only to wear a mask of black velvet. No one has satisfactorily explained either who he was or why he was imprisoned and masked. Voltaire suggested that he was an elder brother of King Louis XIV, and this was the suggestion made famous by Alexandre Dumas's tale *Dix ans plus tard ou le vicomte de Bragelonne* (translated into English as *The Man in the Iron Mask*). Far more likely is the hypothesis that the unfortunate prisoner was a valet named Eustache Dauger. Dauger had served the ambitious statesman Nicolas Fouquet, whom Louis XIV had sentenced to life imprisonment. When Fouquet died in 1680, Dauger learned many of the statesman's secrets and seemed a danger to the government, with the result that the unhappy valet spent the rest of his life masked and in solitary confinement. But maybe not.

The former chapel of the château, Notre-Dame-d'Espérance, dates back to a Romanesque foundation, but by the early sixteenth century this was proving too small for the growing number of worshippers. Eighty years later this church with its nave of four bays had been rebuilt. You can still see some of the effects of dedicating its eight chapels to the various guilds of Cannes. The chapel of St Joseph, for instance, has an altar carved with the symbols of the carpenters' guild. In the second chapel on the right are busts of St Peter and St Nicholas, both patron saints of fishermen (and the latter the patron saint of Cannes). Other treasures in Notre-Dame-d'Espérance include a fifteenth-century polychrome statue of St Anne, a mid-eighteenth-century painting of St Elmo (another saint devoted to protecting seamen), an Italian organ of 1857 and, over the high altar, a seventeenth-century statue of Notre-Dame-d'Espérance herself. Gilded, the Virgin carries her child in her left hand and an anchor in her right. In front of tiered seats around the church a dais is raised in summertime for open-air concerts.

On this eminence also rises the pink-tiled chapel of St Anne, dating from the twelfth century but no longer used for worship.

It stands at the end of a terrace of lime trees and parasol pines. Nearby in the Castre Museum are relics of ancient non-European civilizations – of Iran, Syria, Turkey and China. Here too I enjoyed the works of modern artists who had been drawn to Cannes, particularly the deft colours of Dufy.

Beyond the museum is a touching relic: a marble seat given by Queen Victoria in memory of her son, Prince Leopold Duke of Albany, who died on 28 March 1886 at the Villa Nevada, Cannes. Its inscriptions include a quotation from Revelations, Chapter 14, Verse 13, 'Happy are the dead who die in the Lord', as well as a poem:

> Oft near to death, here our loved son
> Passed to God's peace. He loved to share
> And lighten life, and duty done
> His youth is deathless in thy heavenly care.

Leopold had died in his thirty-first year. The final inscription on his memorial seat runs, 'Peace which the world cannot give.' I find it hard to settle on such a reverent bench.

The charms of Cannes are not yet exhausted. The narrow and traffic-free rue du Suquet trundles down into the centre from the old town, lined with restaurants whose clients spill out on to the pavement. Cannes claims to have 125 restaurants, probably the most sumptuous and certainly the most ostentatious being the Salon des Ambassadeurs in the Palais des Festivals, which can entertain 3,000 people for cocktails, 1,200 for luncheon or dinner and 1,000 for gala dinner shows.

And if few of us can afford to live in Cannes in May during the film festival, which has been a prime attraction of the town since 1947 (though it would have opened in 1939, had not war intervened), at any time of the year we can either visit one of its twenty-two cinemas or else marvel at the imprint of film stars' and film directors' hands set in concrete amid the pools and gardens of the esplanade Président-Georges-Pompidou outside the Palais des Festivals. Some have added their signatures. Here, among many, are the impressions of the hands of Harry Belafonte, Jane Birkin, Meryl Streep, Brooke Shields and Jane Fonda (who added a couple of kisses). Anthony Quinn and Claude Chabrol imprinted both hands. Rosanne Arquette added the word 'Peace'. Mickey Mouse seems to have been here to make his mark alongside the imprints of Roman Polanski, Charlotte Rampling, Franco Zeffirelli, Michael York, Monica Vitti and Anouk Aimée. Mickey's fame will outlast all of them. Marcel Carné will be remembered almost as long as Mickey, as will (I think) Gérard Départdieu and Jean Marais. As for the most moving of the impressions, they are those of the aged hands of Arletty, planted here in 1985.

So besotted with the cinema is Cannes that the town has lovingly preserved in the old port a galleon built for Roman Polanski's film *The Pirates*. But the film festival is only one of many international festivals hosted by the town throughout the year. The latter part of May sees the annual festival of show-jumping. Mid-June is the occasion for an aviation festival, while a festival of café-theatre is somehow crammed into the final week of the same month. In July Cannes plays host to an American festival, to musical evenings in le Suquet and to an antiques fair lasting a week and a half, which is held in the Palais des Festivals. There is no respite during the winter months, for the season begins with an international festival of dance in November, followed by a festival of sacred art, the April regatta and, most surprising of all, a February festival of intellectual games.

Whatever these delights, no British visitor should fail to pay his or her respects to the square where a statue of a grumpy-looking Lord Brougham, British Lord Chancellor from 1830 to 1834, rises from a pool of water. He is grumpy, I surmise, because in 1834 he had planned to visit Italy and a cholera epidemic stopped him at the River Var, where officials of the King of Piedmont refused to let him cross. Forced to stay at Cannes, Brougham was, however, charmed by the spot – and by the *bouillabaisse* of his host Maître Pinchisi. Thereafter he made Cannes his favourite winter resort, building here a villa dedicated to his daughter Eleonor, who had also enjoyed Maître Pinchisi's *bouillabaisse*. A staunch advocate of the poor (although a lord), a founder of the University of London and of a society for providing useful reading matter for the working classes, Brougham became so enamoured of the French that during the 1848 Revolution he tried to obtain French citizenship so as to gain a seat in the National Assembly. Not that Brougham was an opponent of his

own class, to the end of his life hating the newly respectable trade
unions for exercising, as he insisted, a permanently evil effect
on both capital and labour. ('No persons are more grievously
oppressed by them than the classes of the workmen themselves.')
In 1834 Brougham was about to abandon politics. Henceforth he
spent more and more of his time at Cannes, where he died in
1868.

Brougham made Cannes fashionable. His compatriots flocked
here, many of them brought by the railway, which opened up
in 1853. Without his discovery of the resort, the town would
never have attracted the likes of the tragedienne Mme Rachel,
the dumpy playboy King Edward VII, the Creole singer Joséphine
Baker, or Rita Hayworth, Orson Welles and Ali Khan. A population of scarcely 4,000 in 1834 had risen to over 20,000 by
the end of the century. New jetties were built in 1893 and 1897.
Another jetty, built in 1904 near the present Palais des Festivals,
was named Albert Edouard, after Edward VII. At the other
side of la Croisette in the place Mérimée is a more appropriate
memorial to a distinguished lover of Cannes, a medallion in
honour of the novelist Prosper Mérimée, best known for his
Carmen, who died here in 1870, having arrived twenty-four years
earlier seeking a cure for his chronic asthma. I have yet to find a
plaque on the spot where, in 1927, the notorious dancer Isadora
Duncan died when her scarf wrapped itself around the wheel of
her open-top car and strangled her.

Cannes relished royalty, their fleeting memory perpetuated by
statues. As Prince of Wales in 1890, the future Edward VII came
out of a theatre having forgotten to fasten the bottom button
of the waistcoat that covered his ample stomach. The whole
fashionable world followed suit (and still does). Another even
grosser monarch, King Farouk of Egypt, was equally fêted in
Cannes (even after a *coup d'état* by his own countrymen forced
him to abdicate). A passionate gambler, in 1957 he took on an
English merchant named Hymans at one of the casinos. After
Hymans had taken 555,880 francs from Farouk, the ex-king rose
to congratulate his victor. Hymans himself rose, and dropped
dead of a heart attack. 'That is the first time I ever saw anyone
die from joy,' commented Farouk.

Alas, the little Hôtel de Poste where Lord Brougham stayed
was not considered grand enough to match the luxurious new

hotels of the town. Now demolished, its site is marked by a placard at the edge of le Suquet. Brougham's Villa Eléonore has also disappeared. Other opulent buildings speak of Cannes's golden age, in particular the onion-domed Orthodox church on the la Croisette peninsula (a legacy of the visits of the Empress Alexandra of Russia, who came to Nice and Cannes in an attempt to cure her neurasthenia) and the neo-Gothic Villa Vallombrosa (built for the British aristocrat Lord Woolfield in 1853).

As these rich expatriates demanded villas of a more and more extravagant kind, all set in luxurious semi-tropical gardens, a late-nineteenth-century architect named Laurent Vianney came into his own. Vianney set up his practice in Cannes in 1863. By the end of his career he had designed more than a hundred villas and twenty splendid hotels. They include the Hôtel Gonnet et de la Reine (the oldest palace on la Croisette). Further along the beach rise the sumptuous Majestic and the wondrously over-wrought Hotel Martinez.

The fashionable suburb of la Californie, north of Pointe Croisette, is worth visiting simply to admire the bewildering variety of villas in Cannes, many of them deliriously baroque, most of them absurdly pompous, as well as to rise to the top of its observatory, from which you gain a splendid panorama of the town, the islands and as far afield as Italy.

Not until I had visited Cannes several times did I realize that my initial anxiety at driving down the long boulevard Carnot, with other motorists following their customary pursuit of hooting their horns at the slightest hesitation or hint of a wrong turning by the driver in front, could have been alleviated by pausing at the northern end of the boulevard for a visit to le Cannet, an oasis surrounded by olives and pines. This is where some of the celebrated ones already mentioned chose to live when Cannes became fashionable, Prosper Mérimée and Mme Rachel among them. It was also the haunt of artists, particularly of Auguste Renoir, who came here in 1902, and of Pierre Bonnard, who first visited le Cannet in 1939 and was soon to make it his permanent home.

Although le Cannet rises to a height of 110 metres above sea-level, it is sufficiently protected from the winds to be an enchantingly flowery town, sheltered on the east side by the 270-metre-high Mont Pezou and on the south by the Estérel

mountains and the hills of Croix-des-Gardes. From the fortifications of the past it has preserved the twelfth-century tour
des Calvis in the place Bellevue and, in the rue de Cannes, the
fifteenth-century, machicolated tour des Danys. The classical
church of Sainte-Cathérine was begun in 1610, though its twin
belfries were not finished until 1713 and the furnishings are
mostly eighteenth-century. These treasures apart, what charms
me most in le Cannet is the so-called *vieille ville*, a series of
well-restored twisting streets, watered by fountains and flanked
by boutiques and shops selling locally produced craftwork.

No one visiting Cannes should fail to take a boat trip
to the islands of Saint-Honorat and Sainte-Marguerite. Sainte
Marguerite, the nearer of the two, is 960 metres wide and 3,200
metres long. To explore it all, you need to walk no more than
seven kilometres. Richelieu built its fortress, Vauban rebuilt it in
1712 and Napoleon Bonaparte restored it in 1794. During the
religious persecutions under Louis XIV the star-shaped citadel
housed Protestant prisoners, and today it attempts to atone for
this by housing a museum devoted to their persecution.

Protestants in Provence, one ought to concede, generally had
a miserable time after the king had revoked the tolerant Edict
of Nantes. Victor Hugo's *Massacres in the South* scarcely
exaggerates their woes. Hugo tells how in February 1704 the
Catholics, inflamed by a Capuchin monk from Bergerac in
Périgord, organized themselves into bands and indiscriminately
killed their fellow Christians, whom they deemed Protestant
heretics. They found Pierre and Jean Barnard, uncle and nephew
aged forty-five and ten, working in their fields, and forced the
child to fire a pistol at his uncle. When Jean's father arrived on
the scene they ordered him to kill his son. The father refused, at
which the Catholics slaughtered him with a sword and his son
with a bayonet. One motive for hastening this last execution was
furnished by the Catholics discovering three young girls from
Bagnols, who were walking to a field of mulberry trees where
they were raising silkworms. Hugo describes how the Catholics
followed them into the wood and easily overtook them, for in the
broad daylight the girls had no inkling of danger. After they had
been violated, their hands were tied and they were fixed to two
trees with their heads hanging down and their legs apart. While
they were in that position, their bodies were opened. Powder

horns were placed inside the girls, and with a touch of a match they were blown limb from limb. Hugo concludes, 'This took place in the reign of Louis the Great, for the glory of the Catholic religion.'

Inevitably at Sainte-Marguerite you are also shown yet another cell in which the Man in the Iron Mask is said to have been incarcerated. This defensive fort has been given a new role as an international centre for sailing and deep-sea diving. The woods of the Île Sainte-Marguerite are threaded with footpaths and contain rare species of flora and fauna, while to the west of the island the Batéguier lake is a haven for marine birds. And the municipality of Cannes has set up here a centre for training young people in the arts of scuba diving, sailing and wind-surfing.

Different delights are offered by the thirty-five hectares of the Île Saint-Honorat. Here in 410 St Honoratus, his friend St Caprais and a few companions decided to settle as hermits, living in caves. In those days the spot was remote enough for seclusion, yet many other men sailed out to the island, attracted by the fame of the saint, and soon an abbey was established here. In subsequent years its monks included the Augustine who was to become Archbishop of Canterbury in the year 597. The rigours of the monastic life were exacerbated by repeated attacks from Saracens, who slaughtered all the monks in the late eighth century. The invaders were not expelled until 975, when the monks returned.

In 1786 the monastery was suppressed, and five years later the buildings were sold. Monsignor Jordany, the Bishop of Fréjus, bought them back in 1859, and the religious life was revived. Saint-Honorat has been inhabited since 1869 by a community of Cistercian monks, who welcome visitors between 10.00 and noon and from 14.30 in the afternoon till dusk. They inhabit a monastery in the centre of the island, which contains a twelfth-century cloister. More remarkable is the eleventh-century monastery on the south side of the island, a building fortified to resist the Saracen invasions. Water surrounds three of its crenellated walls, which protect a cloister and a chapel. The soil of Saint-Honorat is well suited to vines and lavender fields, while the monks' apiaries produce a sharp-tasting honey which they sell to visitors – not to speak of a liqueur distilled by them and named 'la Lérina'.

❖

The environs of Cannes, particularly the hinterland, are entrancing and sometimes spectacular. Hill towns and villages offer views of a countryside set out in a patchwork quilt of neatly planted olive trees, cypresses, roses and jasmine. Just beyond le Cannet on the way to Mougins the massive pilgrimage chapel of Notre-Dame-de-Vie, built in 1656, rises from the top of a hill. You approach it along a wide alleyway of plane trees and enter through an elegant porch. The monks of Lérins built a hermitage beside this church, and inside is a gilded wooden retable, placed here in the sixteenth century. The quaint dedication of this church refers to the belief that Our Lady could revive stillborn children here, if only for a moment, so that they might be baptised and then rest in peace. Close by is a more modern attraction, a testimony to a particular twentieth-century skill: the creation of beautiful automobiles. The Musée Automobiliste of Font-de-Currault houses 200 venerable and not-so-venerable motor cars.

Two kilometres north-west, the ancient village of Mougins, set on a 260-metre-high cone-shaped hill, is where Pablo Picasso spent the last years of his life. The name of the fifteenth-century machicolated Saracen gate (the tour Sarrasine) indicates why so many fortified hill sites such as this were occupied in the Middle Ages (and before, for Mougins was inhabited in Roman times), simply for safety's sake. Today Mougins is a gracious and prosperous town, its fountain of 1894 located in a central square of boutiques, restaurants and hotels. This hill town has preserved its eleventh-century Romanesque church of Saint-Jacques-le-Majeur, whose nave was widened in the nineteenth century. Mougins seems to possess more churches than it needs, for its town hall in the place de la Mairie occupies the former chapel of Saint-Bernardin, which was built in the sixteenth-century. West of Mougins stands an octagonal twelfth-century chapel, dedicated to Saint-Barthélemy.

From Mougins the D3 trundles its way north-east to Valbonne. The chequerboard pattern of Valbonne's streets dates from a rebuilding of 1519. They centre on the exquisite place des Arcades, with its ancient elm trees and seventeenth-century houses – a couple of them with their dates on the lintels. An extremely fine Romanesque-Gothic church, begun in 1199, has a major baroque altarpiece of sixteen panels, possibly painted by Louis Bréa. This church is by far the best preserved part of the monastery around which the village first developed. A further treat are its grapes, which are so protected by the climate of Valbonne (whose name means beautiful valley) that they can be gathered throughout the year, hence the fact that the village holds its wine festival not in September but in February.

The D3 now twists north-west and rises steeply to reach Châteauneuf-de-Grasse, passing through olive groves and olive mills on its way. Just before Châteauneuf-de-Grasse a side road to the left runs up to the minuscule village of Opio, whose excellently restored twelfth- and fifteenth-century church is set amid fig trees. It once served the Bishops of Grasse, who built a residence here in the seventeenth century, their hideaway now dwarfed by the huge nineteenth-century Château de la Bégude.

Châteauneuf-de-Grasse is equally remarkable, for in the main square of this small village with its circular, sometimes vaulted streets rises an eighteenth-century château. Next to it stands a heavily restored Romanesque church with a rustic Renaissance façade and a wrought-iron belfry. The simplicity of the exterior is deceptive, for the interior is lusciously decorated. A splendid late-eighteenth-century reredos and a baldacchino with twisting columns guard the tabernacle. From Châteauneuf-de-Grasse there are splendid views of the Mediterranean and the Estérel mountains, and just outside the village stands Notre-Dame-du-Brusc. Though its present form dates mostly from the eleventh century, the church was first built in the fifth century on the site of a miraculous spring which cured the blind and the feverish.

Becoming yet more tortuous, the D3 next reaches Gourdon, a fortress town overlooking the valley of the Loup. Like le Bar, which you can see at the other side of the valley, Gourdon was once a stronghold of the Marquises of Grasse. It derives it name, however, from a later family, the Gourdons of Lombardy, who took over the town and in the Middle Ages became powerful councillors in the parliament of Aix-en-Provence. On some of the walls of the town you can still make out their coat of arms with its three pine cones. Built on Jurassic rock, surrounded by twelfth-century walls, Gourdon is defended by a thirteenth-century château, which has managed to preserve only one of its original four towers, though others have been added and the effect is imposing. A Renaissance doorway leads into the courtyard of the château and to its vaulted halls, where you can inspect ancient furniture, guns and paintings. Nearby is the twelfth-century parish church. The citizens have lovingly restored their village of medieval streets and squares, and their shops specialize in glassware, perfumes and carved olive wood.

The limestone countryside hereabouts is fissured with streams which run underground to swell the Loup gorge, and anyone at Gourdon should not fail to explore them by taking the dizzy D12 north-west up to the plateau of Caussols. Then from Gourdon follow the D3 high above the gorges of the Loup as far as Cipières. Views back across to the Cap d'Antibes open out, before you turn off along the D603, which snakes into the village. No longer fortified, Cipières is still dominated by a château which in the fifteenth century provided shelter for Protestants. In the village itself some of the sixteenth-century houses have dates inscribed on their walls. Elm trees shade the main square. The beauty of the eighteenth-century parish church is greatly enhanced by the treasures inside (including a baroque reredos and the fifteenth-century reliquary of St Mayeul, a monk who prayed so hard in the tenth century that the Saracens fled from here of their own volition and were drowned off Saint-Tropez). Another chapel in the village, Saint-Claude, is a rare Renaissance gem housing a 'Deposition' by Rubens.

Many of these fortified villages were deliberately set within sight of each other, so that in times of danger their inhabitants could signal to their neighbours by means of smoke or fire signals. This is amply illustrated by Cipières and the next village, Gréolières. In the fifteenth century the upper part of the settlement, Haut-Gréolières, was destroyed, in spite of the twelfth-century fortress (set beside a Romanesque church) which was supposed to defend it. Basse-Gréolières, despite its name, still rises some 250 metres above the River Loup. The ancient houses along its narrow streets are often engraved over the lintel with the sign of the trade of those who once lived in them. You can make out parts of the ramparts that once surrounded everything. The ruined fifteenth-century château is huge. Saint-Pierre is a Romanesque church inside which is a fifteenth-century reredos dedicated to St Stephen. Four massive pillars separate its two naves, and in a shield over the doorway the Gothic entrance is dated 1530.

You are now high enough to ski. North of Gréolières rises a

massif whose highest peak, the Cheiron, reaches 1,777 metres. To get to the ski-resort of Gréolières-les-Neiges you must first drive westwards through the wild rocks and tunnels of the *clue* de Gréolières (*clue* being the local dialect for ravine) and then turn north-east along the spectacular mountain road (the D802). Otherwise, continue westwards along the D2 to another holiday resort, Thorenc, set among pine trees in what is, for the most part, inhospitable countryside. Its Château des Quatre-Tours was built in the sixteenth century and is still blessed with its four towers.

Thorenc is an ideal base from which to make a circuitous and dizzying tour of the ravines that slice through the jagged limestone ridges of this mountainous part of Provence. The D5 spins its way northwards up to the 1,439-metre-high col de Bleine and then joins the D10, which runs scarcely less vertiginously through the pine-covered Charamel mountain to reach the village of les Mas, with its thirteenth-century Romanesque church as well as a medieval chapel and an eighteenth-century château. You have reached the clue d'Aiglun, the deepest and – at two kilometres in length – the longest of these remarkable fissures. The cliffs on either side rise to 1,200 metres, and the route crosses a bridge seventy-five metres above the River Estéron. Aiglun appears, a tiny hillside hamlet with a seventeenth-century château. Beyond the hamlet, on the way to Sigale, you spot to the right the cascade de Vegay, a series of waterfalls that swell the Estéron.

Sigale was once a frontier town, for Roquestéron, a mere four kilometres away, from 1388 marked the beginning of the territory of the House of Savoy. In consequence, on either side of the road as you approach are two fortified cliffs, the one on the left carrying fourteenth-century ramparts, that on the right bearing the walls of a thirteenth-century château. The thirteenth-century Romanesque church of Saint-Michel at Sigale, which was enlarged in the early sixteenth century, is fronted by a fountain of 1583. If you drive on halfway towards Roquestéron you will be rewarded by seeing the chapel of Notre-Dame-de-l'Entrevignes, whose walls were frescoed in honour of its patron in 1536.

Roquestéron itself sits above the left bank of the River Estéron, and the pont de France across the river here bears a customs house, for this was the original frontier. This half of the whole complex – today for the most part an attractive eighteenth-century village with an eighteenth-century church dedicated to St Erige – became French in 1760. Sitting on the right bank of the Estéron, medieval Roquestéron (known as Roquestéron-Grasse) remained part of Savoy until 1793, its ancient houses rising up the steep rock on which is situated the Romanesque church of Sainte-Pétronille.

To the north of Roquestéron in this part of the Alpes-Maritimes are some magical, yet unsung, perched villages. By driving first of all east you reach Gilette, situated beside the River Var, which the lords of its château controlled at this point. Only at the time of the Revolution was their twelfth-century fortress ruined. A cluster of stepped streets leads up to the ruins, from which you can see almost a dozen other villages on their rocky prominences. The village sleepily strolls across the valley, sheltering under its elm trees, as far as its eighteenth-century Italianate church.

North-east (and reached most circuitously) the minuscule hamlet of Bonson rises from Mont Vial, a spot occupied before the Romans by the Ligurian tribe, then by the Gauls, then by the Romans. Its sixteenth-century church was onced owned by the Benedictines and contains a surprising number of excellent fifteenth- and sixteenth-century altarpieces, while the village itself has picturesque stepped streets. Further north, by way of the N202 which runs alongside the défile du Chaudan, and then by a winding route running alongside the River Tinée and rising up Mont Mangiarde, you are rewarded at la Tour-sur-Tinée not only by the massive, crumbling Gothic parish church, built in the sixteenth century, and by painted eighteenth-century houses, but also by a chapel of the White Penitents. Its ceiling was frescoed in 1491 with panels depicting the Passion of Jesus and a series of vivid virtues and vices (with the Devil much in evidence in the latter).

Further west along the Var valley, the N202 passes through Villars-sur-Var, once the chief home of the Grimaldi family. They have long departed, as has their château, but twenty-three huge stone columns flanking the allée des Grimaldi were once part of their garden. They lavishly patronized artists, and the Gothic church of the village has gilded altarpieces by Louis Bréa and a 1524 statue of St John the Baptist by

Mathieu d'Anvers, which was later set in a complex baroque frame.

Continue along the N202 to discover Touët-sur-Var. Above the modern village, the ancient hamlet virtually climbs up the rock face and has a church of 1609 with a nineteenth-century Lombardic belfry. Still further west lies the picturesque medieval town of Puget-Théniers. Its Romanesque church of Notre-Dame-de-l'Assomption is surrounded by delightful streets, some of them set out in chequerboard fashion. Today its population has not reached 2,000, yet as the name of the rue Gisclette indicates, Puget-Théniers once possessed a Jewish ghetto. The base of a twelfth-century keep is virtually all that remains of its fortress.

From Puget-Théniers the D221A twists and climbs and plunges its way south-east back towards Sigale. The route meets the D17 which, if you followed it, would take you high across the River Pali and through the clue de Riolan, passing by waterfalls, before reaching Sigale. If instead you turn westwards along the D221A, it brings you to Collongues. On the way appears the mountain village of Sallagriffon. The bizarre name of the village means 'the house of Griffo', for this was once a seat of Count Griffo of Nice, whose ruined château is still here. Next you glimpse across the river to the south the entrance to the deep clue de l'Aiglun.

Collongues is situated above the confluence of the Rivers Miolans and Fontane and boasts a thirteenth-century Romanesque church (though one much restored in the nineteenth century). The road now traverses pine woods to reach the fine town of Briançonnet. At the end of an alleyway of trees are the remains of an eighteenth-century château, which came to a sad end after the French Revolution. Above it lours a watchtower from the former thirteenth-century château of Briançonnet. The Roman origin of the town is revealed by the inscribed Roman stones which support the Romanesque church of Notre-Dame. Its belfry and west façade are nineteenth-century additions, and inside is Louis Bréa's painting of 'Our Lady of Mercy'.

As you leave Briançonnet look out for the fifteenth-century church of Saint-Martin. Seven kilometres further on your route turns left to cross the Estéron and tunnels through the clue de Saint-Auban. Saint-Auban itself is a village of yellow houses, with an eighteenth-century château now used as a police station. Parts of its medieval fortress and walls still stand. The nave of its fortified parish church was given a rib-vaulted ceiling in the mid-nineteenth century. Further up the hill behind it is a tiny Romanesque chapel. And from here, within seven kilometres, the D5 brings you back to the col de Bleine north of Thorenc.

The route from here back to Cannes is at times almost as spectacular as the circuit of the *clues* and the hill villages, and it is equally ravishing. Skirting Thorenc, the D5 runs south-east to cross the D2. After six kilometres the ruins of a château appear, and then the road takes you on as far as the twelfth-century Castelleras château of the Knights Templar. Further south-west is Pont du Loup. If you leave the D5 here and follow the D79 west you reach the charming, tiny village of Andon, whose church was rebuilt in 1820. This is followed some ten scenic kilometres later by the equally tiny Séranon, with its ruined château and a nineteenth-century church.

Doubling back along the wooded N85, the route rises towards the 1,169-metre-high col de Valferrière, turning right along the D2563 to meet the River Fil and run south alongside its valley to the highest village in the *département* of the Var. Mons lies 800 metres above sea-level. Much of the medieval village was ruined during the Wars of Religion, so that today the older houses mostly date from the seventeenth century or were in part rebuilt then. Most of the citizens had taken to Protestantism, and one doughty woman is reputed to have repulsed Catholic besiegers by throwing beehives over the walls at them. In the end, the citizens gave in. When the Protestant leader Henri IV retook Mons, he showed his displeasure at this capitulation by hanging twenty of them in the central square.

In the place Saint-Sébastien an orientation table indicates the panorama across the Maures and as far as the Côte d'Azur. The chapel of Saint-Sébastien, from which this square takes its name, is now the town hall of Mons, though one half has been kept as a church and houses a reredos of 1713. Even finer eighteenth-century retables are to be seen in the Romanesque parish church, which was in part rebuilt in the seventeenth century.

The road now winds down through oak trees as far as Seillans, a town of fountains, pink-walled houses, a twelfth-century church with fifteenth-century vaulting, and a town hall square enlivened with sweet balconies, all nestling around a medieval château.

East of Seillans is the town of Fayence, reached by the

D19, which passes by two enchanting chapels, Notre-Dame-del-Ormeau and Notre-Dame-des-Cyprès. The first, Our Lady of the Elm, is set amid cypresses on a spot where a statue of the Blessed Virgin Mary had been buried in the trunk of an elm to protect it from marauding heathens. Excavations have also revealed that this Romanesque church was built on the site of a pagan temple. The chapel has a fifteenth-century ceiling as well as a beautiful Renaissance reredos, carved out of walnut by an unknown Italian artist, its figures painted and gilded. Local lore has it that the artist took forty-two years to complete this retable. Notre-Dame-des-Cyprès is a Romanesque church with a sixteenth-century doorway, situated amid more cypresses along a lane to the right of the main road.

Fayence became a country seat of the Bishops of Fréjus in the thirteenth century. Their château, whose round clock tower overlooks the rest of the fortified town, dates in its present form from a hundred years later. The classical town hall, and the winding streets of the suburb of Saint-Clair, a classical church of 1740 with a handsome west façade incorporating a portico and three noble entrances, and the machicolated Saracen gateway complete the ensemble of this agricultural centre. The town seems to slide down its hillside.

A panoramic route twists eastwards to Tourrettes, whose Château de Puy dominates the surrounding countryside. Its first owner, Alexandre Fabre, had been sent by Napoleon I as ambassador to the Tsar, and his château, built around 1830 on his return, is a copy of the cadet school of St Petersburg. Less of an oddity is the seventeenth-century church at Tourrettes. Marius Alexis Aubin, explorer of ancient Mexican civilizations, is commemorated by a pseudo-Aztec plaque in this village, where he was born in 1802.

Three and a half kilometres south-east of Tourrettes the D19 joins the D562, along which you can shortly either turn left for a brief excursion to Montauroux or else drive south to one of the finest manmade lakes in this region. Montauroux is a hillside village which has lost its château but retained its ramparts. Its thirteenth-century parish church was partly rebuilt 400 years later and now boasts stucco-decorated balustrades. A Romanesque chapel, dedicated to St Barthélemy, was also considerably rebuilt in the seventeenth century and is richly painted and sculpted inside. The painting on the reredos, executed in 1748, depicts not only the patron saint but also the Annunciation. These treasures apart, Montauroux is blessed with a number of delicate old houses whose dates are inscribed on their lintels. And the village looks across a valley to the village of Callian.

Reached by a circuitous route of two kilometres, Callian is guarded by a well-restored fifteenth-century château. Its classical parish church of 1683 gleams golden in the sun. St Maxime is the patron saint of this hill village, and inside this church (among other superb classical retables) a magnificent mid-eighteenth-century reredos, with *trompe-l'oeil* paintings, enshrines his reliquary. At the heart of the village in the elm-shaded place Bourguignon is an ancient fountain fed with water brought here by the Romans.

As for the 60 million cubic metres of water that make up the Lac de Saint-Cassien, just south of the D562 by way of the D37, this artificial lake covers some 1,150 hectares. Sailors, swimmers and fisherfolk are welcome here, though some of its banks are inaccessible where the forests reach the water's edge. The road crosses the bridge that spans the lake and then runs south beside it, before crossing the A8 motorway to reach les Adrets-de-l'Estérel. Sheltered by the rocks and close to the summit of the Adrets, from which it derives its name, this pretty village is surrounded by hills and woods of magnificent pines, oaks and chestnuts. Its inn was restored in 1653 and stands today as it was then. The parish church of Saint-Marc dates from the eighteenth century.

Two kilometres south of les Adrets-de-l'Estérel you can take the N7 back to Cannes, with the red porphyry of the ancient Massif de l'Estérel rising to the south. The D237 joins the N7 north of Mont Vinaigre, at 618 metres the highest peak of the massif. As they drive into Cannes, visitors should certainly pause at two spots. Close by the airport beside the River Siagne the Romans built a temple. In the Middle Ages the land came into the possession of the monks of Lérins, who built here the monastery of Saint-Cassian. A hermitage and the seventeenth-century chapel still survive.

A little further on towards Cannes is la Bocca and the hill crowned with trees that is known as the Croix-des-Gardes. This is where in 1880 the celebrated mimosa which adds such glamour

The coast road reaches Théoule-sur-Mer, where a curious, Picassoesque and Negroid head looks over the balcony towards the blue sea. In the seventeenth century Théoule was an important enough port to be fortified by the French monarchy. Today it is a pretty harbour and seaside town. The route reveals an eighteenth-century soap factory, now transformed into a battlemented château with little towers. A second folly is discovered at Port-la-Galère, three kilometres south of la Napoule. Here in the 1970s the architect Jacques Couelle was commissioned to build a holiday resort and responded with a series of flats and villas which owe more to the plastic surrealism of the Spanish architect Antonio Gaudi than to the traditions of Provence.

The cliffside road winds high above the sea, with a hair-raising cable-car climbing yet higher. A stained-glass shop sells its trinkets. At pointe de l'Observatoire a former German block-house has been turned into a platform where you can park and relish the view of speedboats, yachts and, in the distance, larger sea-going vessels. Inevitably at all these harbours there is a customs house. In summer crickets and shrieking cicadas set up a continual screeching, and sure enough restaurants named after the latter (les Cigales) soon put in an appearance.

Rising through pinewoods, the route reveals more of the brusque red crags, the forest and the green peaks of the Estérel massif (though at Anthéor, for example, there are traces of the forest fires that so threaten this whole region of France). This spot has suffered other depredations in our century, for in August 1944 Anthéor was almost completely destroyed by allied bombers participating in the reconquest of France. Beyond Anthéor is Agay, overrun with holiday villas because of its splendid bay, and because of the railway that has been running alongside you, bringing sun-seekers from miles away.

The Romans followed this road as far as the bay of Agay, which they called the Portus Aagatonis. There their road turned right to climb into the hills, and in spite of its unhappy, touristy look Agay remains an excellent base from which to explore the massif. A notice along the avenue du Gratadis directs the motorist towards 'Estérel, Pic de l'Ours'. Of the 4,575 hectares of forests on the massif, 3,200 are a nature reserve with deer, pheasant, partridge, innumerable varieties of birdlife and a complete ban on shooting. On closer inspection the apparently inhospitable scrubland shelters orchids, asparagus, white heather and arbutus. A multiplicity of hillocks and summits contrasts with the narrow ravines. A Celtic-Ligurian people occupied the massif before the Romans came, and the huge blocks of stone that sheltered their dwellings at the top of the hills still occasionally survive. Just north of Agay are signs of even earlier inhabitancy, in the form of a couple of prehistoric menhirs, those of Are-Peyronne and Veyssières. As for Mont Vinaigre, you can drive up and park a mere 200 metres below its observation platform.

Peering out to sea at Agay, I remembered with a shiver that here on 21 July 1942 the celebrated aviator and author Antoine de Saint-Exupéry flew his plane over his sister's house and then disappeared, never to return, having presumably plunged into the waters. Then I drove along the seaside road from Agay to Saint-Raphaël. It runs by the rocky red promontory of Dramont, with its signal station, and then reveals the little golden island, the Île d'Or, whose medieval tower is really a later folly. Just before Saint-Raphaël a monument marks the spot where on 15 August 1944 French and American troops landed to begin wresting the country from the Germans. Nowadays the landing beach is surrounded by caravan sites. A nearby bar has named itself after the cicada in Provençal – lou Cacadou.

Saint-Raphaël is a bustling holiday town, many of its shops selling (it seems to me) mostly junk, its streets bedecked with palm trees. Here too are found a London 'pub' and British banks. Saint-Raphaël hosts a multitude of annual festivals, including one devoted to New Orleans jazz, another (in February) to mimosa, a summer 'Venetian' festival in the port, and a fishermen's festival on the first Sunday in August. Yet its modern aspect conceals a medieval town, which owes its origin to a priory set up here by the monks of Lérins in the eleventh century. From the promenade you reach this medieval town by way of boulevard Félix-Lepanto, on which stand numerous late-nineteenth-century villas. (Saint-Raphaël is full of them, and very fine some of them are.) Here too stands a neo-Byzantine church of 1883, curiously dedicated to Notre-Dame-de-la-Victoire-de-Lepanto (that is, the naval battle of 1571 when Spanish and Venetian galleys destroyed the Turkish fleet in the Mediterranean).

Long before the monks arrived, Roman ships had landed

here, and you can see amphorae collected from their sunken vessels in the Saint-Raphaël museum of underwater archaeology. A hundred years after the coming of the monks, the Knights Templar established an important commandery here, building themselves a fortified church. It still exists in the main square of the old town, its interior much as the Templars left it, the half-dome of the apse neatly ribbed. In front of the church you can make out signs of the former ramparts of the town. Two other chapels are worth more than a glance: the seventeenth-century Notre Dame (which has been partly modernized) and the Chapelle de la Miséricorde, distinguished for its classical eighteenth-century porch and a square belfry topped by a little tower. Napoleon's arrival here in 1799 after his victorious Egyptian campaign is marked by a pyramid; nothing commemorates his departure from Saint-Raphaël, vanquished and on his way to exile on the Isle of Elba, in May 1814.

Outside the seaside resort of Fréjus, seven kilometres west of Saint-Raphaël, is an aquatic park opposite a military airport. A safari park is another attraction, where visitors can drive among the monkeys and 600 other wild beasts. As long ago as Celtic-Ligurian times, this spot had become a market for the produce of the Argens valley. Julius Caesar, by contrast, spotted its strategic rather than commercial importance, founding a colony here to supply his troops and give them a stronghold on the march between Italy and Spain. Augustus Caesar created the port, set in a manmade lagoon and linked by a canal to the sea. After his naval victory over Cleopatra at the Battle of Actium in 31 BC, he brought 300 captured galleys and anchored them here, making Fréjus one of the three most important ports of his empire. Under Augustus Caesar the town was colonized by veterans of the 8th Legion.

When the empire fell the port gradually silted up. On its rocky plateau an episcopal town was built, initially under the guidance of the tenth-century Bishop Riculphe, protected by still-surviving ramparts. These failed to deter the troops of the Emperor Charles V who attacked the city in 1536, nor those of Prince Eugène in 1707.

Nearly half a century later one of Napoleon Bonaparte's allies, the Abbé Siéyès, was born at Fréjus. Elected deputy for Paris at the time of the Revolution, Siéyès helped to set up the National Assembly and in 1789 was a passionate supporter of the Declaration of the Rights of Man. Ten years later he and Bonaparte were plotting the Revolution of 18th Brumaire (9 November 1799, according to the Revolutionary calendar), after which, as one of the three consuls, he co-operated with his fellow consuls (Bonaparte and Roger Ducos) in partially dismantling the democratic institutions of Revolutionary France. Soon at odds with Napoleon, Siéyès resigned with a pension of 600,000 francs and the title of count. Inevitably he was exiled by the restored French monarchy, but after fifteen years in Belgium he managed to return to his own country to die in peace. At Fréjus he is commemorated by the rue Siéyès. His birthplace at no. 53 has a monumental seventeenth-century doorway whose two groaning atlantes were sculpted by Pierre Puget. It is now a wine-merchant's.

Of this stirring history Fréjus has preserved several physical mementoes, including the remains of a semicircular Roman theatre. The former Roman arena stands to the west of the town in a fine park. A complex, grey stone ellipse with red arches, it measures 114 by 82 metres and was created to seat over 10,000 spectators in the second century AD. Its gnarled stones look down on a twentieth-century version created for bullfights. In the place Agricola stands a statue of Julius Agricola, first-century governor of Aquitaine, who was born here in AD 38. Nearby, the porte des Gaules still stands from the Roman ramparts of the town. To the north of the city rise fragmentary columns, which remain from an aqueduct that once brought water from the River Siagnole to the Roman garrison. And beside the porte d'Orée have been excavated Roman baths.

But the finest ensemble at Fréjus is the cathedral, with its cloister, baptistery and episcopal palace. Begun around 1200, the cathedral of Notre-Dame is a blend of Romanesque and Provençal Gothic. Coloured tiles decorate the steeple, which peeps above the crumbling ochre-red walls of the belfry. A flamboyant Gothic entrance contrasts with the simplicity of the walls and the round apse. Inside, its ogival vaults rising from powerful square pillars date from the twelfth century, and the belfry from the thirteenth. Among the carvings on its Renaissance doors, one depicts a massacre of Saracens, the other scenes from the life of the Virgin Mary. The stalls date from the fifteenth century, and above the sacristy door is a delicate fifteenth-century painting, depicting St Margaret, by Jacques Durandi of Nice.

Beside the cathedral a double-cloister built in the twelfth century stretches around an ancient well. Its lower floor boasts pointed arches, some of whose twin columns come from the Roman theatre. The upper floor has contrasting round arches and a pine ceiling decorated in the fifteenth century with fantastic animals and grotesque apocalyptic figures. Some of the gargoyles are piquantly vulgar, and a woman is depicted with cloven hoofs. The cloister houses an important collection of Gallo-Roman remains from this region, including steles, statues, mosaics, marbles, bronzes, urns and coins.

The oldest part of this complex is the baptistery. This is in fact the oldest baptistery in France, built in the fifth century (or even the late fourth century) and still housing its original octagonal font as well as some fine choir stalls. Eight Corinthian columns from a pagan Roman building were evidently re-used in building this Christian edifice. The bishop's palace (now the town hall), built out of pink sandstone, is suitably fortified, for Fréjus was frequently under attack and the citadel that still dominates the town was scarcely enough to protect its inhabitants. If you have a taste for more impressive ecclesiastical architecture, look for the chapel of Saint-François-de-Paule at Fréjus, a sixteenth-century Gothic building that is just beginning to betray the arrival of Renaissance architecture in this part of Provence.

Roman roads dissect the city, and a ceramic on the wall of the cathedral helpfully sets them out. The cathedral square itself is pretty, dominated on one side by the classical town hall and the late Gothic porch and sculpted Renaissance doors that welcome you into the cathedral. The other side of the square has a fountain and cafés whose tables spill out of doors. The rest of the town is one of narrow shady streets, with washing hanging from upper windows.

Beyond Fréjus the scenery changes completely. Around the River Argens there are picnic areas and camp sites, with a

wide and excellent beach and an artificial cove created to
shelter water-skiers. At Saint-Aygulf, once the home of the
bishops of Fréjus, placards advertise *demi-pension* holidays in
little chalets. There are Roman remains built into the Château
de Villepey, and if you force your way past the initial debris
of an extremely popular resort, you discover shady streets. A
forest of eucalyptus, pines and mimosas sweeps down to the
shore.

Through flat countryside the route reaches Sainte-Maxime,
another holiday town whose vast beach served the allied forces
invading France on 15 August 1944. This is a rich-looking
spot, set at the foot of wooded hills, its town hall occupying
a fifteenth-century château with a sixteenth-century defensive
tower guarding its shore. This *tour carré*, built by an abbot of
le Thoronet in 1520, now houses a museum of local traditions,
and one of them lives on in the *pétanque* pitches under the
plane trees along the palm-studded promenade. Inside the parish
church of Sainte-Maxime (a nineteenth-century building refitted
in 1936) is a surprising collection of treasures, including ten
late-fifteenth-century statues and a marble altar which came
from the Carthusian monastery of la Verne. Sainte-Maxime
entertains its visitors with a casino and seven kilometres of
sheltered beaches.

Further on is Beauvallon, for the most part well-concealed amid
pine trees. A nine-hole golf course complements its camp sites and
horseback riding schools. Beyond Beauvallon lies the delightfully
successful modern seaside resort of Port Grimaud. Designed in the
1960s by the architect F. Spoerry, in the form of a Mediterranean
village fallen into a series of Venetian canals, its whitewashed
houses (2,000 of them) rise on little islands, sometimes connected
by bridges. Port Grimaud encloses five kilometres of canals, and
to visit the spot you must park your car and either walk or hire a
boat.

By now the countryside is hillier again, and the peninsula
of Saint-Tropez has appeared across the water. The sea is
almost as full of pleasure boats as the shore is overwhelmed
with cars. Men and women play *pétanque* under plane trees,
while palms decorate the villages, which are all too often
crammed with amusement arcades alongside the boutiques and
art galleries.

Before visiting Saint-Tropez a short excursion inland amid vines and woods is rewarding, first to visit the perched village of Grimaud, so-called because it once belonged to the powerful Grimaldi family. Dominating much of this region and the Alpes-Maritimes from the fourteenth to the seventeenth centuries, they were continually at war with the Counts of Savoy. The last of the line, Annibal Grimaldi, Count of Beuil, chose as his motto 'I am the Count of Beuil and I do as I please.' When the senate of Nice sentenced him to death in 1621, he insisted on being executed by two Saracens, doing as he pleased until the very end. The Grimaldis' château, which Richelieu decided to pull down, remains with its triple ramparts, an awe-inspiring ruin, deriving from the eleventh to the fifteenth centuries. Round white towers and crumbling walls add to its glamour. Since Grimaud possessed only three wells until 1886, the Grimaldis brought water to their château by means of an aqueduct, traces of which can still be seen three kilometres to the north at the pont des Fées.

The village itself is one of beautiful twisting streets, some of them, such as the rue des Templiers, arcaded. Many of its houses were built in the fifteenth and sixteenth centuries. Saint-Michel is a Romanesque parish church with a twelfth-century font. Built in the eleventh century, unusually in the form of a Latin cross, it has been supplied with modern stained glass by an artist named Jacques Gautier.

A second treat lies ten kilometres north-west of Grimaud. The village of la Garde-Freinet, set at 400 metres above sea-level in a forest of chestnut trees, is a welcome oasis amid the summer crowds of this part of the Côte d'Azur. The Saracens occupied this spot until the tenth century, regularly sallying forth to ravage the rest of Provence. In consequence the fifteenth-century château is wrongly dubbed the Château des Sarrasins. Ancient streets and houses, sometimes dug out of the rock, characterize the older part of la Garde-Freinet, while the newer part consists of wider streets and handsome nineteenth-century houses. Believers worship in the eighteenth-century church of Saint-Clément, which is flanked by a campanile of the same date and houses some treasures (such as a seventeenth-century Christ in glory attributed to Pierre Puget) from the previous church that stood here.

*

In summer the approach to Saint-Tropez is wearisome, through scrublands and usually in a traffic jam. The Ferris wheel and funfair of a 'Luna Park' operate outside the town from June to the end of September. For bathers the problem is not to find a *pied à terre* but to find enough room for a *pied dans l'eau*. Whatever else one thinks of Saint-Tropez, one must admire its public relations. Each summer French tabloids such as *Ici Paris* retail the doings of semi-celebrities in this resort.

Once genuine celebrities, such as the actress Brigitte Bardot, visited the spot and often lived here. The novelist Guy de Maupassant savoured the scent of its brine and its sardines, and described Saint-Tropez as one of the most charming and unspoiled daughters of the sea. Colette enthused over the place and was never away, persuading her friends Jean Cocteau and the actress Mistinguett to help restore the spot after the Second World War. Pierre Bonnard, André Derain, Pablo Picasso, Henri Matisse and Aristide Maillol were artists attracted by the quality of its light and its picturesque environs. Paul Signac even decided to live here permanently. Their works, and the paintings of lesser Saint-Tropez masters, hang in the Musée de l'Annonciade, which is housed in a seventeenth-century chapel in the place Grammont.

Although at the height of the season Saint-Tropez often seems to me to be filled with unprepossessing visitors vainly seeking a glimpse of long-vanished beautiful people, the more discerning seek out the many vestiges of the town's delightful past, which still peep through. The sixteenth-century citadel is well worth climbing up to, and in July and August is the venue of jazz and classical concerts. Mid-May sees the annual festival known as *la Bravade*, instituted in the thirteenth century. A town captain is elected, the statue and relics of St Tropez are carried through the old town and ancient blunderbusses are once again fired. The saint himself, incidentally, was a Roman officer named Torpes, who was beheaded during the Neronian persecutions for refusing to renounce the Christian faith. Thrown into a little boat, his corpse floated to this spot, where a Christian lady named Celerina secretly buried it. Apart from the *Bravade* in his honour, on 15 June the 'little *Bravade*' takes place to celebrate a naval victory over the Spaniards in 1637. And the beginning of September sees the wine festival of Saint-Tropez.

The old town matches this cultural heritage. Huge plane trees cover the main square, from which run semi-pedestrianized narrow streets, some of them arcaded, with five-storey shuttered houses as well as fashion and perfume shops. Many of the houses have the most enchanting sculpted doors. The parish church of Saint-Tropez was rebuilt in the eighteenth century in the Italian baroque style, whereas the thirteenth-century chapel of Sainte-Anne was rebuilt in the seventeenth-century classical style in thanks for the disappearance of a plague. Another seventeenth-century chapel is dedicated to Notre-Dame-de-la-Miséricorde.

A fish market sets itself up in the place aux Herbes, where you can also still buy vegetables, fruit and flowers. Tuesday and Saturday mornings see a market in the place des Lices. In the quartier de la Ponche you come across towers and stretches of the old ramparts. Beside the port is a pompous bewigged statue of Pierre André de Suffren de Saint-Tropez, Bailiff of the Order of Malta, Lieutenant-General of the Navy and Vice-Admiral of France. It was set up on 17 July 1929, the second centenary of his birth. The bailiff's exploits campaigning in India eclipsed for a time those of the British. He died aged sixty-six. The plump Vice-Admiral wears boots suitable for a pantomime baron.

For those who wish to escape the sight of tourists crowding to have their portraits sketched by mini-Picassos, and who yearn to explore other peaceful aspects of Saint-Tropez and its environs, the local tourist office in the place Jean-Jaurès has maps and plans for hikes or strolls, some of them around the peninsula. Two villages south of Saint-Tropez are especially delightful, both of them perched on hills. Gassin was founded by the Knights Templar on the site of the Saracen citadel. From its belvedere the whole region is revealed – vast forests, half-hidden farms and particularly the vineyards, which produce a *VDQS Côtes de Provence* – while the tortuous streets of the village and the machicolated remains of its thirteenth-century ramparts run concentrically at the foot of the medieval fortress. The twelfth-century parish church, dedicated to the Nativité-de-Notre-Dame, is itself a mini-fortress.

Ramatuelle lies further south-east amid vineyards, again a village of serpentine streets and ancient houses. Pliny the Elder called it 'Regio Camatullicorum', after the Camatullici tribe who were living here in the first century AD. A fortified gateway 'des Sarrasins' speaks of the invaders who occupied the village throughout most of the eighth century. The sixteenth-century parish church was given its belfry in the seventeenth century. Both Gassin and Ramatuelle have decent hotels and camp sites, and sponsor a host of festivals throughout the holiday season. Ramatuelle also attracts pilgrims to the tomb of the actor and film star Gérard Philipe, who was buried in its cypress-shaded cemetery in 1959.

The main route south from Saint-Tropez runs through la Croix-Valmer (a name deriving from a vision of the cross said to have been vouchsafed on this spot to the Emperor Constantine) to reach the long sandy beach of Cavalaire-sur-Mer, long a favourite for French family holidays. Rows of pleasure boats and yachts shelter in an artificial port. Overlooking the port here are the remains of a château destroyed in 1646.

The route now runs beside the cornice of the Maures massif, with some fine sea-views (especially from le Rayol), reaching le Lavandou. Apart form its long beach, le Lavandou is not particularly enticing, save for its white and rosé wines, the numerous walks into the Maures mountains and the chance to sail out to the islands of Port-Cros and le Levant. Since 1963 the former has been designated a natural park, with the aim of protecting a delicate balance of marine ecology and some 114 resident birds, as well as many migrants – an aim undoubtedly endangered by some 100,000 tourists who visit each year. The old château on the island dates from the sixteenth century. A well laid-out botanical path is matched in fascination by the possibility of swimming underwater with goggles and breathing equipment to explore the formation of the sea-bed with its calcified algae. Le Levant is different, a haven for nude bathers who sun themselves at the village of Héliopolis.

Five kilometres further west from le Lavandou lies one of the prettiest villages of the whole coastal road, Bormes-les-Mimosas. Known as Bormes centuries before it acquired its well-deserved suffix, the town was continually sacked throughout the Middle Ages and into modern times – by Saracens, Corsairs, Moors, Genoese (under the celebrated Admiral Andrea Dorea) and finally during the Wars of Religion.

Its well-restored spick-and-span houses, its maze of streets and ginnels, gardens, steps and arcades, its churches and its craftsmen's shops, everything climbing to the ruined thirteenth-century château with its superb panorama, are particularly charming when not invaded by battalions of visitors. The citizens cram cacti and flowers into every available cranny, as well as into wheelbarrows and pots. Their huge parish church of Saint-Trophime was built in 1783 and is filled with paintings and statues, including some gilded eighteenth-century reliquaries. Its sundial declares *ab hora diei ad horam Dei* ('from the hour of the day to the hour of God') and happens to be wrong by one hour fourteen minutes. Bormes-les-Mimosas is prouder of another religious building, a sixteenth-century chapel dedicated to Saint-François-de-Paule, patron saint of the town ever since he rescued it from a plague in 1482. The church square offers a delicious view across old Bormes, and at its far corner is an ancient tower that was once a windmill.

Your aim is to reach Hyères (from which you can also sail to the islands of Port-Cros and le Levant) and finally Toulon. A far more enticing route from Saint-Tropez than the coast road is to travel south-west through the southernmost part of the Massif des Maures. The name of this massif, incidentally, does not derive from the Moors or Saracens, who so frequently threatened the region, but from the Greek word *amauros*, which means dark or sombre, a reference to the gloom underneath the pines and oak trees that clothe the hillside. Today these ancient trees have been infiltrated by newer varieties – orange, mimosa, eucalyptus, lemon – introduced during the last century.

Three and a half kilometres west of Saint-Tropez take the N98. The vegetation is lush, with ranges of hills on either side. Stallholders sell melons and tomatoes at the roadside, while vineyards nestle amid the woods. Over to the right just off the main road at the confluence of the Môle and the Giscle lies Cogolin, which was still called Cogollinus when it was given the rights of a city in 1079. The Saracens had been driven out from here by Count Guillaume I of Provence in 972. Later the town became a fief of the monks of Saint-Victor, Marseille, and then in the fifteenth century an autonomous town. In that century the Knights of Malta fortified Cogolin.

Arcaded streets, ancient alleyways, the clock tower that rises on a gateway remaining from the fortifications which were dismantled in the sixteenth century, and a ruined château make a visit irresistible. A further delight is the eleventh-century Romanesque church of the Transfiguration, which was extended in the sixteenth century, so that its ancient nave and transepts are complemented by a Gothic side-aisle. The church houses some of the tapestries for which Cogolin is noted, seventeenth-century statues and a polychrome marble high altar created in the eighteenth century. Seek out the triptych of St Anthony between two bishops, painted by André Carton in 1540. Cogolin has become celebrated for its carpets, a skill brought here in 1922 by Armenian refugees.

Passing a little airstrip with monoplanes, the D98 reaches la Môle, a little village on the edge of the Dom forest and at the confluence of the Rivers Môle and Verne. Equally as ancient as Cogolin, la Môle likewise gained its city rights in the eleventh century. Its château dates back to the same era, though it has been constantly rebuilt, its two pepperpot towers guarding a massive terrace. An even older part of la Môle once stood two kilometres away in the little corner known as la Madeleine, but only ruins now remain. In the present town the parish church was rebuilt in 1870, but the priory of Saint-Marie-Madeleine is perhaps old enough to have been built in the tenth century. Once again vineyards are sheltered from the winds by woods, by now chestnuts adding their weight to cork oaks and pines. On either side of your route the vintners will sell you wine from their properties, all of them offering *appellation contrôlée Côtes de Provence*.

For a physically invigorating and spiritually refreshing outing from la Môle you can drive off the N98 north-east and then north-westwards, abandoning your car and taking the marked path to the ruined Carthusian abbey of la Verne. The abbey is open to the public daily from 10.00 to 19.00 (except on Tuesdays from the beginning of October to the end of May). Founded in the late twelfth century by Bishop Pierre Iznard of Fréjus and Bishop Prédol d'Anduze of Toulon and several times rebuilt, it was finally abandoned at the Revolution, though recently parts have been restored by its secular friends. Today a new religious community, the Order of Bethlehem, inhabits la Verne. Protected by an army of chestnut trees, their monastery stands on a little eminence beside a spring. The contrast between the yellow and green-tinted stones is particularly fetching. You pass through its monumental, machicolated gateway (part of the earliest abbey) to visit its oil press, its sixteenth-century bakery and its large kitchen. There are substantial remains from its Romanesque chapel and from a later seventeenth-century church, as well as from the cloister.

Returning to la Môle, take the N98 south-west through olive groves, with the locals offering you *pain à l'olive*. The scents of the forest are succulent. A winding road takes you past a forester's house with a placard declaring that between October 1940 and January 1942 this spot hid the first clandestine printing press of the anti-Nazi resistance in the Maures forest. Alas, just beyond this house, the last time I was here, a forest fire had left behind vast areas of blackened trees, only the road itself acting as a fire-break.

Near here a less strenuous way to reach the Chartreuse de la Verne is to drive north-west through the Maures and then east along the D14 to the quiet village of Collobrières, whose local delicacy is a chestnut purée. Fewer than 1,500 villagers are blessed by the Gothic parish church of Saint-Guillaume, which looks down on antique houses and a town hall square with a fountain. Continuing along the D14 and then forking right, and driving for six kilometres along the gravel road, will bring you to the abbey.

On its way to Hyères the N98 makes a slightly perilous snaking descent, with more vineyards among the trees, before flattening out and running through vineyards producing still more classy wines. I have never visited the tropical bird garden which is signposted as being four kilometres to the right of the road, knowing that I will almost certainly be delayed by a traffic jam as Hyères draws nearer. Sheltered by the foliated *mas* of the Maurettes mountains, the town sits amid market gardens and outcrops of palm trees.

Hyères is the oldest fashionable bathing place on the Côte d'Azur, deliberately setting out from the 1820s to attract tourists and visitors of the eminence of the historian Jules Michelet (who died here in 1874), the composer Charles Gounod (though he wrote his *Romeo and Juliet* at Saint-Raphaël) and the poet Alphonse de Lamartine. Mistral dubbed the place the garden of the Hesperides. British visitors included Queen Victoria and Robert Louis Stevenson – one of the many who came here in the hope of curing his tuberculosis amid the oranges and olives of this sheltered spot.

Its earlier history is equally fascinating. Founded by the Greeks and then colonized by the Romans, Hyères became a quasi-independent state in the thirteenth century as well as an important staging post for crusaders on their way to the Holy Land. Cistercian and Augustinian monks settled in monasteries here, followed by the Counts of Provence and then the Angevins. (Charles d'Anjou is honoured with a statue in the jardins Alphonse Denis.) Finally King François I of France laid claim to the spot. Because of its strategic position, Hyères was much fought over during the Wars of Religion. The Catholic League established troops in the château, until they were driven out in 1589 by the Duke of Guise, who then partially destroyed their stronghold. In the next century King Louis XIII's minister Richelieu greatly reduced Hyères, dismantling many of its defences, with the result that her naval hegemony passed to Toulon.

Thenceforth Hyères remained dutifully Catholic, one of her sons, Jean-Baptiste Massillon (1663–1742), becoming Bishop of Clermont and one of the most eloquent and noted preachers of his age. Louis XIV once declared that 'Each time I hear him, I become discontented with myself.' This feeling clearly made little difference to his dissolute life. Though Massillon was born at no. 7 rue Rabatan, the town has honoured him with a statue in the place de la République.

As well as an excellent beach, Hyères has preserved many evocative reminders of this sometimes turbulent past. Still partially fortified, the town is defended by a group of aggressive-looking towers and gateways built in the thirteenth and fourteenth centuries. The towers of the former château poke their stubby fingers up and around a hillock. Among the picturesque streets of the old village (which sits five kilometres inland) are the rue Saint-Blaise, the rue du Portalet, the rue de la Barnacane and the delightfully named rue Paradis. Dating from the fifteenth to the seventeenth centuries, their houses boast windows with little columns and Renaissance lintels. In the rue Paradis is found one of the rare Romanesque secular houses still surviving in France, its windows again divided by columnettes. The market place is dominated by the tour Saint-Blaise, in fact the apse of a former Templars' church, whose commandery was founded here in the twelfth century. Today the tower houses the local history museum. Gaudy parasols shade the squares.

As for religious buildings, the sixteenth-century collegiate church of Saint-Paul has retained a Romanesque belfry and a Renaissance doorway outmatched by a splendid neighbouring Renaissance house. The church of Saint-Louis dates from the thirteenth century. Dedicated to Louis IX of France, who landed at Hyères in 1254 on his way back from crusading in the Holy Land (where he had been defeated, captured and forced to pay a ransom of 100,000 marks), its ogival vaults rise from a basically Romanesque building. One notable secular building is universally given a religious nickname by the Hyèrois. The cubist Villa de Noailles, built in 1924 by the architect Robert Mallet-Stevens, is known as the Château Saint-Bernard, since it occupies the former site of a Bernardine convent abandoned at the Revolution and allowed to fall into ruins.

From Hyères-Plage a boat trip of one and a quarter hours takes you alongside the Giens peninsula, with its ruined Château de Pontevs, to the often windy island of Porquerolles. The peninsula is connected to the mainland by the narrowest strips of land. Some eight kilometres long and two kilometres wide, Porquerolles boasts magnificent pine-sheltered beaches on its northern coast and permanently supports only 250 inhabitants. Fortresses that once defended the island now add to its quaintness, and in one of them, the Fort de Sainte-Agathe which was built in 1531 during the reign of François I, there is now a museum devoted to the history of the Île de Porquerolles. Fort du Langoustier dates from the early seventeenth century. Richelieu had a third fortress built to defend this island, the Fort du Petit-Langoustier, set on an outcrop of rock in the sea at the western end of the island. As for the lighthouse, it ranks second only to that of Marseille in size and guards the plunging cliffs on the southern side of the island.

Due west of Hyères is la Valette-du-Var, a modern town reached through a countryside of limestone peaks. Five kilometres north rises the old town of la Valette, whose keep survives in inadequate health and whose parish church of Saint-Jean-devant-la-Porte-Latine is half-Romanesque, half-Gothic. Its pride is its main doorway, sculpted with scenes from the Apocalypse either by Puget or one of his pupils. The local farmers grow strawberries, violets, olives and vines.

From here drive south-west along an imperial road (today the N98) laid out from Hyères by Napoleon Bonaparte at the request of his sister Pauline Borghese, in order to reach the walled, naval town of Toulon. Although its surprisingly classical porte de l'Italie (which you come across as you drive into the city) still preserves its drawbridge, Toulon is a large and modern city, some of whose thoroughfares have an Oxford Street look about them, their buildings rising for eight or so storeys. Its shipyards and their cranes are there to make money, not to attract holidaymakers, though they shelter a three-masted galleon named *le Neptune*.

Historically the city suffered the usual vicissitudes of this part of France, including the devastation of the 1720 plague, which carried off 17,000 of its 26,000 inhabitants. During the Second World War, as France's first military port, Toulon was bombarded eight times. The rebuilt residential quarters occupy Super-Toulon, with its views out to the sea no doubt reminding some of the 40,000 shipyard workers of their daily toil. This is not to suggest that the modern town is devoid of interest. The museum of art and archaeology, in particular, is housed in a former hospital built in the seventeenth century.

What remains of old Toulon is a group of mainly seventeenth- and eighteenth-century buildings: the tour Carré, topped by a campanile; the eighteenth-century naval museum, a bazaar of model sailing ships and proudly carved prows; the former naval hospital; the Fort de la Grosse Tour, built under Louis XII in the early sixteenth century to command the smaller harbour; the seventeenth-century Fort Saint-Louis, built to command the main harbour. The cathedral of Sainte-Marie-de-la-Seds lies at the centre of the old city. Contrary to the customary Christian tradition, its altar lies at the north end, not the east, for in the mid-seventeenth century a new Gothic building was erected using the former Romanesque cathedral (which faces the right way) as its transept. The classical south façade of 1696 is the work of the Marseille sculptor Albert Duparc. The massive belfry with its wrought-iron campanile dates from 1738. A baroque altar attributed to Pierre Puget swirls with excess. As for the baroque church of Saint-François-de-Paule, built in the 1740s (though its belfry was added only in 1873), it served during the Revolution as the Jacobins' club. Toulon also boasts another notable church, the classical Saint-Louis, built in the 1780s.

Head for the beaches, passing by Fort Saint-Louis, begun in 1602 and now the home of a private sailing club. Could this squat white fortress once have protected the port? Shady pine trees and well-watered lawns lead down to the sea and to the pebble beaches, rendered safe by artificial breakwaters. As Emma-Jane and I lay in the sun on our straw mattresses, children hurtled into the water down a twisting slide, while a beach boy staggered past us carrying twenty beach mats and a dozen stacked chairs at one and the same time.

Menton to Nice: a coast and its hinterland

Menton is but thirty-eight kilometres from Nice, yet the Azure Coast between them includes such redolent spots as Monaco, Monte-Carlo and Saint-Jean-Cap-Ferrat, while the hinterland encompasses an awe-inspiringly beautiful natural park whose central zone of 68,500 hectares is surrounded by a secondary natural park of another staggering 140,000 hectares.

The speediest way of reaching Menton is by taking the A8 motorway, which burrows through the foothills of the Alps and stalks on huge, reinforced concrete feet towards Italy. Turn off at the Menton sign or else you will find yourself at the Italian town of Ventimiglia. Behind you, as you leave the motorway for Menton, rises the hill village of Gorbio. Its houses, many of them entered by rustic flights of steps, line vaulted streets and medieval porticos. Its main square is shaded by a huge elm tree planted in 1713 and watered by a fountain. The baroque parish church of Saint-Barthélemy dates from 1683, while Gorbio's ruined château was built in the twelfth century, and a seventeenth-century chapel dedicated to St Roch speaks of the plague years, when the citizens of this minuscule village would implore the saint to save them from death.

Menton has some justification for claiming to be the 'pearl of France'. Ruled by the princes of Monaco from the mid-fourteenth century to 1848, the citizens then declared that they wished to become Sardinian. The princes demurred, but when Menton voted overwhelmingly to join France in 1860, they graciously sold the town to Napoleon III.

It then blossomed by attracting countless consumptives, some 5,000 of them British. Since many of them died here, the citadel was transformed into a multinational cemetery. Fittingly, it is the first spot you reach as you drive down into Menton from the motorway. Offering superb views over the bay and as far as the blue mountains that plunge into the sea, the cemetery divides its illustrious inmates by nationality. In Russian Orthodox tombs lie, for example, Prince Pierre Troubetzkoy (1822–92) and the Archpriest Nicolas Akvilonnof, who died in June 1929. Of the British dead, the tomb of Edward Benson Tawney, MA, of Trinity College, Cambridge, is inscribed:

> The winter is past,
> The rain is over and gone.

The tomb of the historian John Richard Green struck an echo in my heart, so I sat on another tomb and meditated on his career. An Anglican clergyman, a passionate Oxford high churchman like myself, he had been expelled from Magdalen College School at the age of fourteen for writing an essay which concluded that Oliver Cromwell was right and Charles I wrong. Becoming a scholar of Jesus College, he led a solitary life as an undergraduate, disliking the moribund views of his mentors. Ordained in 1860, he fervently promoted the well-being of his impoverished parishioners, carefully prepared his sermons, yet preached them extempore. His spare time was spent studying in the library of the British Museum and writing vigorously about the Middle Ages. J.R.Green, said his biographer, could 'read history in every landscape'. By 1869, however, he had developed a disease of the lungs and had to abandon his clerical work to sojourn in Lambeth Palace as its librarian. His *Short History of the English People* was twice revised before its publication in 1874. It was that rare achievement – an instant popular and intellectual success. Green set about transforming this study into a larger four-volume history.

In 1877 he felt strong enough in health to marry the daughter of the Archdeacon of Meath. Alas, he and Alice, who threw herself

wholeheartedly into the historian's researches, had but six years
of married joy. After a trip to Egypt in 1881 he fell sick again, and
finishing his new book, *The Making of England*, proved arduous.
Alice and J.R.Green reached Menton the following autumn in a
desperate search for improved health. The historian was fighting
to conclude his *Conquest of England*, aimed at tracing the history
of his native land as far back as the arrival of the Normans.
Toiling steadfastly at the book, he passed away on 7 March
1883. (Mrs Green finished the book on his behalf before the
end of the year.) As the inscription on his tomb at Menton
declares, 'He died learning.' Some of the metal letters have fallen
off.

Emma-Jane and I walked down towards the town, reaching
the church of the Immaculate Conception, which has a *trompe-
l'oeil* painting above the high altar and larger-than-life statues
of St Jerome and St Theresa. Its façade dates from 1765, again
decorated with statues, each of which has a symbolic meaning. In
the centre of the façade is a statue of the patroness. Beside her St
Isidore and St Elm stand sculpted in niches, the former the patron
saint of farmers, the latter of sailors. On top of the pediment sits
a statue of Faith, with Charity on her right and Hope on her
left. The statue above them is that of St Charles Bororomeo,
much loved by the White Penitents for whom this chapel was
first built. Nearby in the square a pompous archway celebrates
the life of Antony, first Lord of Menton and Monaco. Dated
MDCCII–MDCCXXI, it leads into an attractively irregular square
in which rises the church of Saint-Michel.

Saint-Michel was built in 1620 in the early baroque style, and
then continually enriched. The 53-metre-high belfry was added in
1701. Over the church porch St Michael slays Lucifer. He does
so three more times inside the church, each depiction of the saint
and his victim quite different. (In one the saint seems to be aged
six and is smiling serenely.) Ancient damask curtains hang inside
this church, given by Prince Honoré II of Monaco when he was
married here in 1757. He and his bride would have stood in the
choir created by Antoine Manchello in 1565.

Menton's town hall is pink, low-lying, classical and be-flagged.
The resort is filled with sumptuous *belle-époque* palaces: the
Orient Hotel is suitably topped with onion domes; the Palais de
l'Europe grandly scintillates. The equally lavish Kursaal, where

those such as J.R.Green often failed to be cured, stands in the jardin Biovès. Prince Antony I of Monaco is remembered by the early eighteenth-century Palais Carnolès, which was his summer residence and is now the municipal museum. Its collection ranges from the primitives of the Nice genius Louis Bréa through members of the so-called Paris school (Raoul Dufy, Maurice de Vlaminck and their contemporaries) to modern painters, among which I particularly admire the chubby pictures of Marcel Gromaire.

English-speaking visitors of a literary turn of mind will want to see Villa Isola Bella in a street named after another consumptive, the rue Katherine-Mansfield. The villa is inscribed with some words she wrote to her husband John Middleton Murry in 1920: 'You will find Isola Bella engraved on my heart.'

Though she died not here but at Fontainebleau in 1923, in a short story called 'Miss Brill', Katherine Mansfield perfectly captured the atmosphere of the Côte d'Azur during the mid-war years. Old men in velvet coats leaning on carved walking-sticks, and an Englishman wearing a large panama hat while his wife walks around in button boots, are among the crowds thronging the parks.

To and fro, in front of the flower beds and the band rotunda, the couples and groups paraded, stopped to talk, to greet, to buy a handful of flowers from the old beggar who had his tray fixed to the railings. Little children ran among them, swooping and laughing; little boys with big white silk bows under their chins, little girls, little French dolls, dressed up in velvet and lace.

Young girls in red join up with a couple of soldiers in blue. Straw-hatted peasant women gravely lead smoke-coloured donkeys. A cold, pale nun hurries by. And beyond the rotunda Miss Brill sees slender trees whose yellow leaves are starting to droop, and beyond them a line of sea stretching to the blue sky with gold-veined clouds. And the band blows 'Tum-tum-tum tiddle-um! tum tiddley-um tum ta!'

The bands still play at Menton, though these days they include celebrated jazz groups and the chamber orchestras that perform annually in the square of Saint-Michel. And the elderly (for one-third of Menton's population consists of retired people) still wisely sun themselves or sit in the shade of palm trees, usually on the appropriately named promenade du Soleil.

From Menton drive to Roquebrune-Cap-Martin. Inland from the modern town, the tunnelled streets of this ancient perched village can be entered only on foot. It sits 300 metres above sea-level on a platform created by a seventh-century landslide. According to legend the sirens, who longed to lure sailors to watery graves, had caused great boulders to tumble down the mountainside in the hope of destroying the village.

For centuries the rulers of Ventimiglia disputed possession of Roquebrune with the Counts of Provence. The Monégasques claimed it in the fourteenth century, and then − no doubt exasperated by the pretensions of such princelings as the Grimaldi − in the revolutionary year of 1848 Roquebrune proclaimed herself a free republic, reverting to France in 1860. The Grimaldi family is to be thanked for restoring the eleventh-century fortress of this hill town in the nineteenth century. In consequence a couple of square towers and a keep, a mighty kitchen and machicolated walls still guard the twisting arcaded streets of Roquebrune, while its spiritual needs are cared for by the eighteenth-century church of Sainte-Marguerite, which has retained a distinct aspect of its Romanesque predecessor. The governor of this little commune lived in an eighteenth-century Italian residence which still stands in the town.

South of Roquebrune the wooded promontory of Cap-Martin is planted with sumptuous villas, as well as being dotted with the oldest palaeolithic remains in Europe. On this headland the garden of Villa Lumone contains the remains of a Roman mausoleum. Monaco, too, in its observatory cavern in the exotic garden displays remains tracing back 200,000 years to the Lower Palaeolithic age.

In 1215 the Genoese were the first to build a fortress on the rock that dominates Monaco. On 8 January 1297 a Guelph named Francesco Grimaldi (but, not surprisingly, nicknamed the 'malicious one') disguised himself as a monk, gained admittance to the fortress, opened the gates to his troops and took over. Henceforth the coat of arms of the Grimaldi family was to be flanked by a couple of monks wielding swords. Francesco's successors gained the title of princes from the Spaniards in 1633, and then proceeded eleven years later to enlist the help of the

French in expelling the Spanish garrison. Honoré II, the ruling prince who accomplished this, was also a man of taste, and he set about transforming the fortress of Monaco into the present superb palace. Fortunately ramps and towers have survived to evoke the old stronghold. The white marble staircase in the principal courtyard and the balustrade to which it rises are only a hint of the sumptuousness of the rest.

The road which snakes vertiginously down to Monaco makes one fear for one's life, especially as drivers who ought to be negotiating hairpin bends are continually distracted by the fantastic views out to sea. As an independent principality, Monaco has its own petty rules, such as the one which declares that no male should bare his chest. (Should such a rule apply to the twentieth-century princesses of Monaco the world of the tabloid press would be the poorer.)

As you descend the hill, look for the scrupulously ordered parking and the lift that ascends to the magnificent exotic garden, first laid out in 1859 by the prince's head gardener, Augustin Gartaud. Huge cacti, enormous ferns, multicoloured flowers, azaleas and tropical plants are set beside winding paths, where those fearful of heights can hang on to concrete bridges and fences. In a grotto you can visit cascading underground streams. Be warned that there is no lift to take you back to your car park.

A cleverly designed one-way system takes visitors through tunnels and around Monaco. Fountains, wrought-iron balconies, art nouveau lanterns, swaggering domes, bare-breasted caryatids characterize the architecture of Monaco, while roses, begonias, orchids and tropical trees festoon its streets.

Outside the half-Byzantine, half-Gothic cathedral of Saint-Charles is a statue of Cardinal Seduto, sculpted by the Italian Giacomo Manzù in 1982. Normally I warm to the work of Manzù, but here he seems to have intended to portray the cardinal in prayer, but depicted him asleep (admittedly one of my own frequent lapses when worshipping). The white marble cathedral was designed by Charles Lenormand and consecrated in 1884. On the left-hand side of its choir is the tomb of Grace Kelly, the American film actress who married Prince Rainier III of Monaco in 1956 and was killed in a car accident in 1982.

Inseparable from Monaco is Monte-Carlo, which grew up around the casino at the end of the nineteenth century. Gambling is legally impossible in France, and when Menton and Roquebrune seceded from this principality in 1848, the wife of the ruling prince (Florestan I) suggested that she capitalize on this by inviting Frenchmen to come and cast their dice here. After the comparative failure of the first two casinos, Florestan's successor, Charles III, successfully established a new one on the Spélugues plateau. The spot was renamed after the prince and became Monte-Carlo.

The architect of the Paris Opéra, Charles Garnier, was called on to design the casino in 1879, and ten years later the turrets that are its most exotic feature were added. Princes and kings, bankers and adventurers of both sexes, flocked to play here. Dominating the Salle blanche is a painting entitled 'Les Grâces Florentines'. It depicts, *déshabillées*, three noted courtesans. In the centre is Caroline Otéra, flanked by her rivals, Liane de Pougy and Cléo de Mérode. Caroline was as passionate a gambler as lover. In her later years she was supported by small monthly pensions from the casinos of Monte-Carlo and Juan-les-Pins, as well as by another pension paid by the municipality of Nice. We have already seen her, yet more startlingly depicted, at Cannes.

Among the hotels that grew up around this casino, the bizarrely luxurious Hermitage of 1900 is frescoed with *belle-époque* excess, its green copper roofs, arches and balustrades bespeaking the genius of an impoverished prince who decided to become rich on the recklessness of gamblers. Today Rolls-Royces glide towards the casino, where valets in maroon shirts take over the driver's seat to park the opulent cars, and even the police wear white gloves.

From Monaco you climb towards Nice and discover at a T-junction a signpost directing you towards the Trophée des Alpes. At the sign for la Turbie take a sharp right and, five kilometres later, by way of a singularly panoramic and slightly scary route you reach the spot. On an ancient house in la Turbie are inscribed three lines from Dante's *Purgatorio*:

> *Tra Lerici e Turbìa – la più Diserta,*
> *La più rotta ruina è una scala,*
> *Verso di Quella – agevole e aperta.*

In Dante's time Lerice and secluded Turbia stood at either end of the republic of Genoa, and the poet is lamenting the difficulty (impossibility even) of climbing one of the mountains of purgatory, insisting that 'the widest, least trodden path in all the land between Lerice and Turbia would have been easier of access'.

Dante was right. To reach la Turbie today is no mean feat even in the best maintained of motor cars. Once arrived, Emma-Jane and I walked through the twisting, vine-clad and arcaded streets of the ancient village to reach the massive Roman monument on what was once the Via Julia. This Trophée was built by the senate of Rome to honour Augustus Caesar's brilliant conquest of the forty-four hostile Gaullish tribes still refusing to accept the rule of Rome after the death of Julius Caesar. The monument dominates the whole region, including Italy to the east.

This magnificent example of Roman triumphalist architecture was almost lost, its stones used to build walls and gates around la Turbie. Invading tribes demolished it still further. Christians were opposed to the monument as a symbol of paganism, until in the fifteenth century a scholarly Franciscan monk took a different attitude and set about retrieving its history and stones. Only in our own day has sufficient money been gathered (much given by an American named Edward Tuck) for a thoroughgoing restoration. Even so, not every stone cannibalized from the Trophée can be recovered. Some are incorporated in a surviving town gate. In 1777 other stones helped to build the baroque church of Saint-Michel at la Turbie (which houses a sixteenth-century *pietà* done in the style of Louis Bréa). Though the Trophée as it stands is tremendous, to envisage the monument in its integrity you must study the model in the nearby museum.

La Turbie is an ensemble of delightful old houses and narrow streets. My daughter and I also discovered that Napoleon Bonaparte had been there before us, staying at la Turbie – according to a plaque on a wall – on 2 April 1796. Thence we repaired to the Bar La Trophée, where we ate first the extremely satisfying *soupe au pistou*, which is created in Provence from *haricots verts, blancs* and *rouges*, courgettes, potatoes, tomatoes without their pips, garlic, basil and olive oil. I relished this meal and remember it well. After the soup Emma-Jane took a *salade niçoise*, while I ate my rabbit stew (*lapin en gibelotte garni*), a dish sautéd in red wine and flavoured with onions, mushrooms, bacon and herbs. Since we were in Italianate France, our dishes were served with *capillettis*, that is stuffed, round ravioli. The *patronne* of the restaurant was wearing Roman-style boots.

From la Turbie to the col d'Èze you drive along a mountainous region that was once the natural forest of the Grande Corniche. 'Where are the trees?' asked Emma-Jane, answering her own question a moment later when a placard told us that they had been ravaged by a fire of 1986 and were now being replanted.

As for Èze itself, its cobbled streets cling around its ruined château and the early fourteenth-century chapel of the White Penitents, as if afraid of the sheer drop down from the crest on which she perches. Èze has a classical eighteenth-century church built in 1764. Its medieval fortifications and fourteenth-century gate today defend boutiques and restaurants.

The sumptuous *belle-époque* villas of Beaulieu-sur-Mer await you on your way to Nice. As the days of the fashionable beau monde of Beaulieu receded, the town consciously set itself out simply to be an excellent seaside resort, while still exploiting tastefully enough the remains of that golden age. These include in particular the casino, and Villa Kerylos, a villa built in the first decade of this century for an archaeologist named Théodore Reinach, who decreed that it should resemble an ancient Greek villa. A visit is worthwhile not only for the authentic Greek remains on show here, but also to savour the praiseworthy craziness of Reinach's folly. At the heart of this villa (classed officially as an ancient monument) is a massive, octagonal Naiad bathroom.

Due south of Beaulieu-sur-Mer is Saint-Jean-Cap-Ferrat and the promontory and marina of Cap-Ferrat itself. Saint-Jean-Cap-Ferrat is now the site of a zoological park created in 1950. In an expanse of tropical vegetation that once belonged to King Leopold of Belgium, lions lick their cubs into shape, while kangaroos, flamingos, gazelles, monkeys and the rest seem perfectly at home. Another treat at Saint-Jean-Cap-Ferrat is a visit to the Villa Île-de-France, which was built in the Italian Renaissance style at the same time as the Villa Kerylos, this time for the Baroness Ephrussi de Rothschild. A vast array of furnishings bought up from churches and other noble villas is on display inside the villa, alongside paintings by such masters as Monet and Boucher, Fragonard, Sisley and Renoir. The superb gardens and lake are in part set out in the form of a ship, for the Île-de-France was the name of the baroness's own seagoing vessel.

Villefranche (which gained its name, 'free city', in 1297) is all that remains before Nice. A sheltered harbour, ancient streets, some of them tunnelling through passages, a sixteenth-century citadel and the baroque church of Saint-Michel enhance this little medieval town. Towers, ramparts and a keep remain from its fortifications. I confess I do not like the frescos, which Jean Cocteau painted in 1957 in the church of Saint-Pierre, a sometime Romanesque building by the port.

And since we have just visited a zoological park, Nice is the ideal spot to take off for a visit to one of the stupendous natural parks of France. Motor cars, dogs, campers and rifles are banned in most of the Parc national du Mercantour. Horses, fishers, skiers and canoers are welcome. From the information centre at no. 23 rue d'Italie, Nice, you can obtain detailed routes for hikes and treks. You learn that you can sometimes drive in certain parts of the park, as for example in summer along the circuit of the col de la Bonette, which at 2,802 metres becomes the highest motor road in France.

Other such centres are to be found in the national park itself. One is at the beautifully preserved medieval village of Saint-Martin-Vésubie. A second is found at the mountain village of Saint-Dalmas-de-Tende, and a third at Entraunes (whose graceful churches and chapels contrast with its desolate, romantically savage situation). You find another at Saint-Sauveur-sur-Tinée, a village of severe houses, whose thirteenth-century church of Saint-Sauveur has a Renaissance façade and a late-Romanesque belfry dated 1333.

The beasts, birds and flora of the Mercantour national park are among the rarest and most valuable in France. The animals wander amid Alpine sites and by lakes (including the Lac d'Allos, where there is another information centre). The vallée des Merveilles is a delicate survival of Bronze Age art.

But my own favourite suggestion is that you take the railway train which runs from Nice by way of Sospel to Saorge and Tende. Situated at the confluence of the Merlanson and the Bévéra, Sospel was a bishopric in the fifth century, and its present cathedral is a massive seventeenth-century baroque masterpiece. The whole city hides ancient streets and noble buildings, some of them with Romanesque and Renaissance windows. A ruined château, a square keep and the remains of late-fourteenth-century ramparts keep watch over the city.

Saorge (whose name derives from St George) is equally entrancing, its tall fifteenth-, sixteenth- and seventeenth-century houses rising above the valley of the torrential Roya. Narrow, cobbled streets of ochre and blue houses rise up to chapels and churches. Some are baroque (such as the seventeenth-century Franciscan convent whose church is decidedly Italianate and whose cloisters bear fragmentary frescos of the life of St Francis). Others are half-Gothic, half-classical (such as the parish church of Saint-Sauveur). A kilometre east of the village is the very early Romanesque chapel of the Madone-del-Poggio. In the sixteenth century it gained an elegant belfry. Its late-fifteenth-century wall-paintings, depicting the Annunciation and the coronation of the Virgin Mary, are by Jean Baleison.

The little medieval village of Tende is perhaps the finest-situated of the three, with craggy mountains rising beyond its own slopes. The chief treasure of its twisting ancient streets is the Renaissance church of Notre-Dame-de-l'Assomption. Its Lombardic belfry dominates the whole village. Some of the houses have Gothic or Renaissance porches, their roofs are of green slate and nearly all of them have charming balconies.

These exquisite spots flank the easternmost part of the Mercantour national park. And I should add that another entrancing railway line takes you from Nice a distance of 151 kilometres as far as Digne-les-Bains, passing by way of some of the most spectacular of the territory and towns discussed elsewhere in this book, including Touët-sur-Var, Entrevaux and the Verdon gorges. The trains run five times a day in summer and four times a day in winter.

As for Nice itself, sitting by a fountain at our table outside the restaurant la Claire Fontaine in the place Rossetti and tucking into a couple of superb pizzas, Emma-Jane and I could have been forgiven for thinking we were in Italy. Quite apart from the food, our hard-pressed waiter had just cried, 'Mamma mia, aide-moi!' As dusk fell, not only was the square softly illuminated but the fountain as well. Young lovers held hands at the tables, as if summoned by some central casting to add to the ambience of the spot. A jazz band made up of visiting Americans played for us, closing down only when the lights of the fountain turned themselves off at 10 p.m.

The suspicion that Nice is part of Italy is strengthened by the massive statue (usually with a pigeon or two on its head) of the Italian patriot Giuseppe Garibaldi in the arcaded place Garibaldi, save that the plinth gives his Christian name as Joseph. Born in Nice in 1807, Garibaldi was the son of a Genoese coastal sailor. But for his French nationality, Joseph would probably have been executed in 1834 for taking part in an abortive attempt by Mazzini's 'Young Italy' movement to seize Genoa. Happily, he managed to escape back to Nice and then to Marseille. Being French, he also served as a deputy for the Seine, the Côte d'Or and the Alpes-Maritimes. And the last military adventure of his life was a hopeless defence of the French republic in 1871. His Nice statue was created by Etex and Gustave Deloye in 1891.

As for the square itself, it was laid out in the early 1780s not for a Frenchman but for Victor Amadeus III, King of Sardinia from 1773 to 1796, the then ruler of Nice. He commissioned a triumphal arch through which visitors from Turin would enter Nice. Alas, the Turin gate was demolished in 1847, but what still stands in the square is the chapel of the Saint-Sépulcre, a classical building raised in 1782 and sheltering a couple of late-sixteenth-century polychrome statues, one of the Virgin Mary, the other of St Sebastian, who was reputedly vigilant at protecting the citizens from the plagues which had almost finished off their city in the Middle Ages. Its architect was a Swiss-Italian named Antonio Spinelli.

Nothing is quite what one expects in Nice. This applies supremely to the food. Even *salade niçoise* varies with the season, its base of tomatoes, cucumber and basil enriched variously with hard-boiled eggs, tuna fish, raw artichokes, anchovies and red peppers. A variant use of these ingredients creates *pan bagnat*, in which a piece of round white bread is sliced in two and then liberally dosed in olive oil, followed by vinegar, salt and pepper. These halves come together in a sandwich filled with anchovies, onions, green peppers, black olives and tuna fish. When you also spot that favoured vegetables include zucchini, and that ravioli is usually on offer spiced with beef cooked in a wine sauce, once more the Italian connection intrudes.

Yet Nice, though Sardinian, was never Italian. A part of Provence since Roman times, the city sought the protection of the Counts of Savoy only in 1338. The region became the *comté* of Nice. When Duke Victor Amadeus of Savoy was crowned King of Sicily in 1713, Nice became, in a sense, Sicilian. When Victor Amadeus was forced to exchange the kingdom of Sicily for that of Sardinia, Nice became Sardinian. The French annexed Nice in 1792, and with the fall of Napoleon twenty-two years later she became Sardinian again. But when the kingdom of Italy was finally created in 1860, Nice opted to become part of the French empire.

By then the settlement was some 400,000 years old, for prehistoric men and women have left their traces here (some of which you can see in the Terra Amata Museum at no. 25 boulevard Carnot, near the Lympia harbour). Named after Nikaia, the Greek goddess of victory, the city itself was founded around 350 BC by Greeks from Marseille, evidently attracted by the existence of a defensible port and the possibility of building on a hilltop. Then the Romans built a camp at Cimiez, north of the present city, calling it Cemelenum. Cemelenum became the capital of the Roman province of the Alpes-Maritimes. Here too you can explore Roman remains: the arena; the baths of Cemelenum; and what has been excavated and is on display in the archaeological museum. Both settlements existed side by side until the Roman one was abandoned in the fifth century AD.

Only in the thirteenth century did the Niçois start building at the foot of the hill, shortly before internal dissension forced the Counts of Provence to cede the city to the Dukes of Savoy. Their rule left a permanent Italian imprint on its life, food and architecture. Italian became the official language of Nice, though the citizens insisted on speaking *nissart*, a patois closely linked to the *langue d'oc*. In consequence this part of Provence offers an entrancing synthesis of southern France, Piedmont, Liguria and the culture of the Alps.

In the eighteenth century Nice became a health resort, a prelude to its present role as capital of the Côte d'Azur. In spite of the plagues that frequently beset the city in the seventeenth century, in 1763 it was characterized by the naval doctor Tobias Smollett as a haven of pure air for consumptives like himself. Within a decade some 120 foreign families were living at Nice, solaced by a casino, a theatre and a foreign newspaper. Smollett happened to be wrong about the curative effects of the climate, and countless sick persons must subsequently have suffered even more by taking his advice and convalescing here. (Some reparation was paid to these invalids when a vaccine against tuberculosis was developed by Albert Calmette, who was born at Nice in 1863.) Smollett was also wrong in describing the women of Nice as pot-bellied and superstitious – though of course they may have been in his day. As more and more tourists and convalescents arrived, the city spread westwards across the River Paillon.

By 1820 no more than 20,000 people lived in Nice. Today it is the fifth largest city in France, its hotels alone employing 60,000 staff. Yet to my mind Nice remains comfortable, its old quarters ravishing, its museums (hardly any of which charge for admission) succulent honeypots attracting thousands of delighted visitors who would never normally step inside an art gallery, its churches remarkable, its gastronomy unique and its narrow streets devoted to a perpetual carnival.

Today the heart of the city is the place Masséna, named after Napoleon's marshal André Masséna, who was born here in 1758. The northern side of the place Masséna is bounded by an arcaded ensemble of buildings inspired by the rue de Rivoli, Paris, the whole created by the architect Joseph Vernier in 1836 (though not finished until 1850). Around 1880 the river was covered over, doubling the size of this handsome square. The place Masséna was once bounded to the east by the Nice casino, built in 1884 by the architect Omer Lazard, but in 1979 the casino was pulled down so as to enlarge the square yet further and enable the city authorities to lay out the clipped lawns and superb fountains that now adorn it. No one can deny that this is a gorgeous example of urban parkland, but I should like to have seen Omer Lazard's casino.

Still, it is agreeable to sit beside the nineteenth-century band-stand in the jardin Albert I and listen to the Harmonie Municipale playing light music by Bizet, Offenbach, Strauss and Meyerbeer, the musicians dressed in plum-coloured jackets and either grey jackets or black skirts (the ladies, that is, in skirts). I always want to applaud at the end of a piece, as we do for instance by the bandstand in Regent's Park in London, but this is not the custom in Nice. People do applaud during the annual international folk dancing festivals hosted by the city and held in the place Masséna. One evening I watched the Bolivians, the girls decked out in yellow dresses and long plaits, the men in straw hats and scarlet shirts, as they skipped to the music of a band whose musicians were barefoot and wore black trilbies and silk scarves. Then Spaniards danced a version of *la Farandole*, followed by twirling Filipinos and finally Russians. Russian girls with ribbons in their hair, their sleeves red, green, yellow and puffed out, clapped castanets, while accordionists played *Kalinka* and extraordinarily agile men in boots spun round and round while crouching close to the ground.

The greenery and fountains run eastwards into the espace Masséna and on to square Leclerc, which is adorned by a statue of Masséna himself. Sculpted by Albert Carrier-Bressin in 1869, its base depicts the victories of Napoleon's finest marshal, who defeated the Russian general Suvorov in 1799, destroyed the army of the Archduke Charles in Italy and brilliantly conducted much of the campaign against Austria in 1809. When he saved the lives of his soldiers by a masterly retreat in the face of forces commanded by the Duke of Wellington, Napoleon insulted Masséna as a coward − an error, for the marshal refused to join his former leader when Napoleon escaped from Elba in 1815.

Yet more spaciousness is created to the south of the place Masséna by the palm trees and exotic plants that blossom in the Albert I garden (named after the Belgian king who loved the Côte d'Azur). Ornamented with statues of Apollo and Mercury, the gardens are watered by an eighteenth-century fountain.

Across the boulevard Jean-Jaurès from the espace Masséna, the rue de la Préfecture runs towards the Palais de Justice and the *vieille ville*, passing the Del Rio Café, which was so expensive that Emma-Jane and I declined its drinks, politely asking the waiter why he was charging so much. He said that the price had been doubled because of some Mexican musicians (who were not even performing at that moment) and added, for good measure, that opposite the café were beautiful gardens. Beautiful they are, *mais quand même*!

The Palais de Justice at Nice is the usual classical affair of major French cities, enlivened by a fountain in its square. Built in the seventeenth century as the palace of the Kings of Sardinia, it took on its classical aspect after Nice became French in 1860. At the corner of the square a plaque declares that on 28 August 1944 the Resistance fighter Jean Bobichon (known as 'Boby') was executed here by the Nazis. Nearly every building around the square dates from the eighteenth century. No. 5 in particular, with its rococo doorway and wrought-iron balcony, is worth a lingering glance.

More opulent doorways grace nos 15, 18 and 23 of the rue de la Préfecture, and a plaque on the last building tells you that here in 1840, staying with his friend the Comte de Cessole, died Niccolò Paganini – yet another Italian connection, for the violinist and composer was born the son of a Genoese porter in 1782. Well aware of his reputation for being in league with the Devil, Paganini had taken to annoying his neighbours by imitating on his violin the wailing of cats. In consequence the Bishop of Nice refused him a Christian burial. Some wanted to throw his corpse into the River Paillon, but the count managed to spirit Paganini's corpse away to Villefranche and then the Isles of Lérins. After a temporary burial in Geneva, Paganini's bones reached their final resting place at Parma only in 1896.

As the swags, ornamental balconies and frequent appearances of lusciously carved ladies holding them up reveal, much of the *vieille ville* was rebuilt in the baroque style in the seventeenth and eighteenth centuries. No. 18 rue de la République is a medieval palace. And this corner of the *vieille ville* has become pedestrianized. Running from the northern corner of the square, the traffic-free rue du Marché and rue de la Boucherie are crammed not just with food shops but with antique vendors, crafts and clothes shops. To the south of the square, cours Saleya is lined with mid-eighteenth-century houses and with shops and restaurants selling all manner of seafood. Its daily flower market thrives on the sub-tropical climate of Nice, and is overlooked by a curious seashell museum, the Musée de la Malacogie, housed in a seventeenth-century convent. The flea market that also animates cours Saleya sells a remarkable variety of junk and spills over into the place Pierre Gautier. And the eastern end of the cours opens out into the place Charles-Félix (named after an early nineteenth-century King of Sardinia), where, as a plaque declares, the painter Henri Matisse lived from 1921 to 1938.

A few paces further east rises the chapel of the Holy Shroud (le

Saint-Suaire), which once was eighteenth-century baroque, was restored in the nineteenth century and now belongs to the Red Penitents of Nice. These Red Penitents are one of four surviving confraternities of laymen who from the fourteenth century have accepted responsibility for caring for the poor, orphans, pilgrims and invalids, as well as for burying the dead. Depending on the colour of their pointed hoods and capes, they are known as Black, White, Grey and Red Penitents. (The Blue Penitents, who I think have disappeared, once owned the church of Saint-Sépulcre in the place Garibaldi.) Saint-Suaire houses a painting of the Holy Shroud done by the Nice artist Gaspard Baldoino in 1660, and next to the church stands the Palais Ribotti-Caïs, built in the seventeenth century, though a little too much transformed in the nineteenth.

We are wandering too far, for rising to the east of the place Pierre Gautier is one of the gems of Nice baroque, the chapel de la Miséricorde-des-Pénitents-Noirs. Guarino Guarini began building the church in 1675, but it was the Turin architect Bernardo Antonio Vittone who, between 1740 and 1785, really created this chapel of the Black Penitents, the swags and curves of its façade tempting one inside. To get inside you must either arrange for a guided tour at the Palais Lascaris (see p. 167) or else worship here on a Sunday morning, for otherwise the chapel is locked. Its nave bulges in a baroque ellipse, gilded stucco and false marble columns swirling, the vaults giddily rising from pendentives. Six elliptical chapels surmounted by a gallery add to the architectural wildness of this building. Of the two paintings of Our Lady of Mercy (*la Miséricorde*) inside the church, one is by Louis Bréa, who arrived from Liguria in the early fifteenth century. The other is portrayed on an altarpiece painted around 1425 and signed by Jean Miralhet. Miralhet's triptych is deceptively complex. The Virgin in a green robe shelters bishops, kings and layfolk under her mantle. Below her three panels depict Jesus dead, the empty tomb, and the risen Jesus appearing to St Mary Magdalene. Above the Virgin's head Jesus is painted, rising from death but still suffering, his head bowed and crowned with thorns, his hands crossed and pierced with wounds.

Further east runs the rue Barillerie, which is named after the barrels in which fish was salted. It abuts on to the old fishmongers' street, rue de la Poissonnerie, which is blessed by a late-seventeenth-century baroque church once dedicated to St James the Less, today dedicated to St Rita of Cascia, and therefore known as Saint-Giaume-Sainte-Rita. Though she died in 1477, Rita of Cascia was not canonized until 1900, when she swiped this church from St James the Less. Her uncorrupted body lies in an art deco shrine at Cascia in Umbria, with a Latin inscription over the entrance declaring that from the thorns of her Saviour she was reborn as a beautiful rose. Roses are much in evidence inside her richly decorated church at Nice, especially filling her chapel (the first on the right).

Since Saint-Giaume-Sainte-Rita was in part restored in the nineteenth century, seek out inside it the two chapels that best preserve the baroque of the 1680s, namely the ones dedicated to St Peter and St Julien. Paintings on the former by Abraham-Louis Van Loo (done in 1699) depict the deliverance of St Peter and St John the Divine on the island of Patmos. Since Sainte-Erasme's chapel (the first on the left) is dedicated to one of the patron saints of seamen, it incorporates an early eighteenth-century maritime scene. A lovely statue of the Virgin Mary in the chapel of Mont Carmel was carved around 1730.

Beside the church is a sixteenth-century loggia which is filled with roses on St Rita's feast day (22 May), brought here by the faithful for a blessing. A more secular monument in the rue de la Poissonnerie is a bas-relief of 1584 on the wall of no. 8. It depicts a half-naked man and woman, about to beat each other over the head with clubs.

The *vieille ville* of Nice is sheltered to the east by a rocky hillock which rises ninety-two metres above the port. Once this hillock was crowned by a château built by the Dukes of Savoy, after a siege of 1543 by King François I and his Turkish allies. Legend has it that the besiegers would have won, had not a heroine named Catherine Ségurane seized the Turkish standard from a startled soldier and thrown it to the ground, before fighting the assailants away by showing them her bottom.

Louis XIV ordered the destruction of Nice's symbol of independence in 1706, yet the mound is still known as *le château*. It offers a splendid panorama of Nice, though to enjoy it, instead of climbing to the summit, I confess that I prefer to take the lift from the rue des Plonchettes near the place du 8 Mai 1945. This is where the early nineteenth-century tour Bellanda houses Nice's naval museum. In 1844 it housed the composer Hector Berlioz.

If you prefer to walk instead of taking the lift, the rue Place Vieille climbs to the right of the rue de la Poissonnerie, followed by the steps of the rue du Château and then of the montée du Château. These terraced streets lead up to the hillock, which offers a view stretching from the Estérel to the Italian riviera. The top of the hill has been transformed into a park (with some imaginative mosaic pavements), and here also you can explore the excavations of the former eleventh-century cathedral of Sainte-Marie.

Here too is the Jewish cemetery of Nice, many Jews having been attracted to the city by its tolerant traditions. (Only in 1723 did the reactionary King of Sardinia insist that the Jews live in a ghetto and wear the yellow star of David.) In a neighbouring cemetery is buried the Republican Léon-Michel Gambetta – the politician who ruled France for five months after the fall of Napoleon III in 1870 and died, probably by suicide, in 1882 – as well as the Russian nihilist Alexander Herzen. I am not much in favour of segregating the dead religiously, but why is Gambetta lying here, for he was Jewish?

If, instead of climbing to the château, you turn left from the rue Place Vieille along the rue Droite, you will reach first the church of the Gésu and then the Palais Lascaris. Rue Droite ('a street called straight') was once the main thoroughfare of Nice, running between two gates of the old city, and is now (like many of its narrow neighbours) filled with tiny Arab bars and butchers, along with Algerian, Armenian, Tunisian and Vietnamese restaurants. Shops spill out into these streets, selling fruit, vegetables and above all black olives. The Niçois buy from open-air stalls chunks of hot *socca*, a base made out of chick-pea flour and then seasoned with these black olives, with red peppers, onions, tomatoes, basil, salt and pepper, eating them with their fingers, which they then proceed to lick with gusto.

For a second time at Nice a church spurns an apostle named James. Officially the church you are looking for is really dedicated to St James the Great, yet everyone dubs it the Gésu. Built by the Jesuits in the seventeenth century, it received its baroque façade only in 1825. Although its tower seems mild and unpushy, inside excess rules – retables sporting baroque clouds, marble columns and foliage, cherubs and stucco-work adding their ornate lushness to the building. The Gothic tabernacle of 1525, though lovely, seems out of place, and I wish the nineteenth-century stained glass did not cast an air of gloom over the riotous baroque.

Palais Lascaris is another baroque treasure, well-restored and opened to the public in 1969. In 1648 Jean-Baptiste Lascaris de Peille, who was nephew of the grand master of the Knights of Malta, bought four houses in the rue Droite, demolished them and commissioned this lavish palace. The entrance hall and staircase hall, as well as parts of the second storey, teeter from baroque into rococo. The Genoese artist Giovanni Battista Carlone frescoed most of the rooms. A *trompe-l'oeil* version of the Lascaris family's coat of arms with its two-headed eagle is painted in the vault of the entrance hall, incorporating their motto *Nec me fulgaris* ('Not even lightning strikes me'). For some reason an eighteenth-century pharmacy from Victor Hugo's birthplace at Besançon now occupies one of the ground-floor rooms. Statues of Mars and Venus, stucco columns and niches and more *trompe-l'oeil* decoration ornament the staircase and the state apartments. On the ceilings Genoan painters depicted the fall of Phaeton and a scene of Mercury introducing Psyche to Olympus, both again interpreted in *trompe-l'oeil*. Above a four-poster bed Daphne is shown transforming herself into a laurel tree to escape from an amorous Apollo. The third storey of the palais is occupied by a local history museum.

The rue Droite crosses the rue de la Loge and eventually becomes the rue Saint-François. A daily fish market appears early each morning in the place Saint-François, near the late-sixteenth-century town hall (now the city's labour exchange) and the surviving tower of the eighteenth-century Franciscan church. The labour exchange has been considerably enhanced since 1580, first with a seventeenth-century baroque portal and then with an eighteenth-century classical façade added by the Turin architect Gio-Pietro. The dolphin fountain in the square is a chubby work of 1938 by François Aragon.

Across the square is the rue Parolière, the street of the copper-smiths, from which you can climb up to the steps that lead to another baroque church. Saint-Martin was built for Augustinian monks in the seventeenth century, and their eighteenth-century convent, next door, is now a barracks. Saint-Martin's oval nave is flanked by baroque chapels, and the chancel houses a splendid marble altar as well as two magnificent painted panels. One, a *pietà*, is by Louis Bréa; the other, Saint Anthony of Padua, was painted by Louis's nephew François. Fixed to the wall of this church is one of the many cannonballs fired by the Turks when they assaulted Nice in 1543.

Follow the rue de la Providence south from here, walking alongside a former convent to reach yet another baroque church, Saint-François-de-Sales, built in the 1670s and enlarged in the eighteenth century. Opposite this church, on the corner of the rue de la Providence and the rue François-Zanin, is a vine-covered building that seems unusually familiar – la Treille, immortalized in the paintings of Raoul Dufy. Walk west along the rue Sainte-Claire to turn left down the rue de la Croix and you reach the seventeenth-century chapel of the White Penitents, Sainte-Croix, which was restored after the Second World War. Over the sacristy door the lintel depicts two hooded penitents kneeling before their crucified Lord. Inside is a little museum of the White Penitents, housing their banners and torches. Yet another Italian connection is provided in this church by a painting of the discovery of the True Cross, which was brought here from Rome in the 1680s.

As you walk from Sainte-Croix westwards along the rue de la Loge you discover at the corner of the rue Droite another of the cannonballs that fell on Nice in 1543. A few paces further west the rue de la Loge reaches the place Centrale and the rue Mascoinat (which means 'street of the greasy spoon'), its narrow five-storey houses typical of this whole area. By following the street of the greasy spoon you reach the ravishing place Rossetti, with its obelisk fountain. In this square rises the cathedral of Sainte-Réparate.

A Nice architect named Jean-André Ghiberti created the cathedral between 1650 and 1680 on the site of a chapel built by Benedictine monks in the eleventh century. Ghiberti was military engineer to the Duke of Savoy and perhaps not so skilled as he should have been at church architecture, for halfway through the construction the vault collapsed, killing the Bishop of Palletis. None the less, what he has left us is impressive, a church whose three naves and dome are obviously modelled on St Peter's, Rome.

The white stones of the separate Italianate campanile date only from the eighteenth century, while the classical façade of the cathedral was added in 1825. Four saints adorn this façade, their names inscribed over their statues, but I confess I know nothing about any of them. Inside, the influence of St Peter's is instantly obvious in a baldacchino patterned on Bernini's Roman masterpiece. The cathedral reeks of incense. Cherubs hold up the roof. Luscious baroque detail enriches the side chapels – particularly that of the Blessed Sacrament – while a painting of the beheading of St John the Baptist is set against a background of the *vieille ville* of Nice, the River Paillon, the hillock of the château and the Bay of Angels. This bay is where, if legend can be trusted, the mortal remains of the third-century martyr St Reparata arrived, in an unmanned boat which had sailed under the guidance of a dove from the Holy Land.

Make your way back to the flower market in order to rejoin the modern city by way of the rue Saint-François-de-Paule. Its eighteenth-century buildings include a palace at no. 2, built in 1772 and bearing a plaque stating that Napoleon Bonaparte stayed here in 1796. Just before the church of Saint-François-de-Paule rises the Opéra, built in 1884 by a Nice architect named François Aune, who was clearly inspired by the heady, glamorous vulgarity of the opera houses of Monte-Carlo and Paris, which were designed by Charles Garnier. The interior of the church, which was built in 1736, was redecorated in the nineteenth century but still undulates in a satisfyingly baroque fashion – though I find it the most austere of the baroque churches of Nice.

Along the next street to the right stands the Hôtel de Ville. Built as a seminary in the mid-eighteenth century, the town hall was considerably enlarged in the 1930s and 1970s without its sober beauty being too much destroyed. A little further along the rue Saint-François-de-Paule you reach the rue de l'Opéra, which takes you to the fountain of the planets at the south side of the place Masséna. You are now back in *belle-époque* Nice, a city of palaces and villas, whose naked, full-breasted caryatids hold up exuberant balconies.

Beside the place Masséna and along the seafront west of the jardin Albert I, the promenade des Anglais stretches for five kilometres as far as the arenas and the Nice-Côte d'Azur airport. It owes its origin to the savage winter of 1820, which threw many men out of work and reduced families to poverty. A charitable

English clergyman, the Revd Lewis Way, raised enough money to set the unemployed to work on a two-kilometre stretch of coastal road, which was dubbed the 'Camin dai Anglès'. The municipality extended it further in the 1840s, renaming it the promenade des Anglais. By 1930 it had been planted with gardens and pine trees and had reached as far as the boulevard Gambetta. Finally, in 1965 it was extended as far as the airport.

Nice is a city of festivals, in particular the Mardi Gras carnival and the flower parades when thirty or so floats parade the streets. The festival committee is installed in the first of the exotic buildings along the promenade des Anglais from the *vieille ville*, an art deco confection at no. 5. The next major building of this sunny and glamorous thoroughfare is the Palais de la Méditerranée, an opulent casino built by the architect Charles Delmas in 1929, its art deco sculptures by Maubert and Sartorio. Next appear the sumptuous hotels of this promenade, the Royal of 1908, the elaborate balconies and façade of the Westminster-Concorde, built by Louis Castel in 1880, the West-End, originally built in 1855, and the Negresco, which Edouard Niermans designed in 1912.

The West-End gleams white, its overhanging balconies decorated with swags and friezes. The doormen of the Negresco are obliged to dress up in Edwardian costume, to match the bulbous dome, the thick pilasters, the mansard-roof and dormers, and the bull's-eye windows of the *belle-époque* monstrosity.

Beyond the Negresco stands the Palais Masséna, built between 1898 and 1901 for Marshal Masséna's grandson, Victor Masséna. Incongruously, its garden of palm trees and exotic plants also shelters statues of twentieth-century French military men. Its elegant semi-circular terrace looks out over palm trees and the blue sea. Its wrought-iron gates are voluptuous. Its overripe, First Empire furniture was designed by Jacob Desmalter, the four candelabra are by Thomire and the murals were painted by Paul Grolleron. Today the Palais serves as the city's art and history museum. Religious art mingles with European primitives, with French and German armour from the fifteenth to the eighteenth centuries. The Palais also houses a library of rare books and regional manuscripts.

Nice is a hive of superb art galleries, nearly all of them admitting the public free of charge. The Musée Jules Chéret at

no. 33 avenue des Baumettes is discovered by continuing along
the promenade des Anglais, and turning right three streets past
the boulevard Gambetta and then following the signposts. This
is Nice's gallery of Fine Arts, displayed in a palatial ochre and
white classical villa built in 1876 for Princess Kotschoubey of
the Ukraine. Massive white statues of women, naked save for
huge pots of fruit on their heads, greet you in the entrance
hall. In the same hall stands Rodin's 1877 bronze, the 'Age of
Airan', this time a naked man. The frothy, art nouveau works
of Jules Chéret (1836–1931) on display here are matched by the
more decadent paintings of Fauve artist Kees Van Dongen. The
museum possesses over fifty sculptures, paintings and drawings
by Jean-Baptiste Carpeaux, as well as an equally large series
of paintings by Dufy, and rows and rows of fine Impressionist
paintings.

Still further south-west along the promenade des Anglais you
turn right along the avenue Fabron, passing an ornate Italianate
villa built in the 1870s by Sébastien Biasani, to find at Château
Sainte-Hélèn, on the avenue du Val-Marie, the Anatole Jakovsky
international collection of naïve art, this time housed in a late-
nineteenth-century villa built for François Blanc, the founder and
first director of the casino of Monte-Carlo.

Three more unmissable art galleries are situated in the suburb
of Cimiez. In the second half of the nineteenth century this
suburb became the favoured winter haunt of Europe's élite.
Here stood Queen Victoria's favourite hotel, the Régina, built
by Sébastien-Marcel Biasani in 1897 and now transformed into
apartments without destroying its superb façade. This was where
Matisse spent the last years of his life. (Like Raoul Dufy, he is
buried in the Cimiez cemetery.) Victoria's statue still fronts the
building. Other grandiose, even mad nineteenth-century buildings
grace the suburb: the neo-Renaissance Château Valrose, now the
university faculty of science; the Moorish Hôtel Alhambra, with
its twin minarets; the so-called Winter Palace.

Here on the corner of the boulevard du Cimiez and the avenue
du Docteur-Ménard stands the national Marc Chagall Biblical
Message gallery. Chagall planned seventeen Biblical canvases for
a chapel in Vence, decided they were too large and was persuaded
by his friend André Malraux to give them to the state, which built
this gallery for them in 1971. The artist then presented another

205 preparatory sketches, 105 engravings, thirty-nine gouaches, 215 lithographs, three stained-glass windows and an enormous mosaic. This is the one gallery in Nice that I remember having to pay to visit.

The Henri Matisse gallery is a seventeenth-century Genoese villa, pink, three-storeyed, frescoed with *trompe-l'oeil* paintings and set in the Cimiez park at no. 164 avenue des Arènes de Cimiez. Matisse died at Nice in 1954, and his wife donated a large collection of his paintings and drawings to the city. Subsequently Jean Matisse, the artist's son, added to the collection versions of virtually every one of his father's sculptures. Here too are displayed all the books to which the artist contributed illustrations. Close by (at no. 160 avenue des Arènes) is the modern archaeology museum, designed by Vladimir Mitrofanoff in the 1980s and standing at the western boundary of the third-century Roman baths and the fifth-century episcopal palace. Its collections date from the Bronze Age to the Middle Ages, and in a rotunda on the ground floor a model suggests what the Roman community of Cemelenum might have looked like. Appropriately the lower level of the museum is devoted to burial rites.

The third museum of the Cimiez suburb is as delightful for its home as for its contents. The Franciscan museum is situated in a frescoed seventeenth-century convent with a Gothic church and cloisters. Its exhibits include three retables by the Bréa family.

The latest of Nice's art galleries opened in June 1990. Situated on the promenade des Arts, this totally modern architectural ensemble designed by Yves Bayard and Henri Vidal consists of four towers clad in Carrara marble, joined by transparent footbridges. It comprises a theatre as well as the gallery. Its curious grey tiles seem to rustle like the sea. I find its contents the most entrancing of all the superb Nice collections. Massive metal mobiles by Alexander Calder swing outside the building. Two striking yellow, blue and red works by Roy Lichtenstein are matched in bizarreness by 'Shrimps on a fork', which Claes Oldenburg created in 1985 out of paint, plastic, polystyrene and wood. Ben Vautier contributes what he calls his museum, in which an electric motor spins a model Ben around, while a tape recording of his voice groans in misery. A little blue heart on a portrait of a girl by Martial Raysse lights up. Naked blue torsos by Yves Klein burst from the walls. I wish I could have made Jean Tinguely's complex 'Homage to Schmela' work, but it was not plugged into the electricity. A smashed-up motor car, created by César in 1959, which created a scandal when it was first exhibited, seems perfectly at home here today.

Happily, on our visit to Nice Emma-Jane and I were staying in the Hotel Westminster-Concorde. Apart from the Imperial in Vienna, this is the grandest hotel in which I have ever lodged. Sole among the great hotels in Nice, in spite of necessary modernization (for guests today like sound-proof, air-conditioned rooms and swift, silent lifts), the Westminster-Concorde, with its huge staircases and its ebullient façade, represents the Côte d'Azur that entranced royalty and the rich, late-nineteenth-century beau monde. Its only fellow is the Hermitage in Monte-Carlo, for even the Hôtel de Paris in Monte-Carlo was completely rebuilt in 1906 in a different style.

The walls of a grand hotel conceal secrets but also, in their very architecture, evoke bygone days. Commissioned by the great-grandmother of the present owner, the architect of the Westminster-Concorde united a couple of 1860 villas and added a fifth floor. At the beginning of the twentieth century the hotel was further enlarged by the building of a lobby and the construction of two large rooms now used for conferences and for breakfast, all delicately frescoed in the fanciful style of the era. Guests breakfasted (and still do) amid coffered ceilings, chandeliers, stuccoed swags and garlanded busts. The windows of the conference room are filled with yet more entrancing stained glass. Delicately blown roses, pale peaches, apples and pomegranates mingle in art nouveau langour, and the windows are signed by the leading French glass-maker of the time: 'Ch. Champigneuille, 40 rue Denfert Rochereau, Paris, 1902'.

The director-general of the Westminster-Concorde, M. Pierre Gouriand – who with his ally, M. Claude Suard, has made this hotel his home since 1968 – delights in expounding the social significance of all this.

'The larger of these two rooms had a small balcony for musicians, because it used to be the *table d'hôte* of the restaurant,' he explained to us. 'It was a real *table d'hôte* at that time, with a bell that you would ring at noon and seven, and a large table presided over by the host – the owner of the hotel – where everybody would sit and eat the fixed menu.' As for the smaller

room, which is more sumptuously decorated ('shall we say, full
of gauze?' suggests M. Gouriand), it was designed for service *à la
carte* at small tables. 'Today,' he adds, 'although you still see the
information that service will be by the *petite table*, no one knows
what it means. As opposed to the large table of the host, the *petite
table* existed for individual service.'

M. Gouriand was also enlightening on why the British homed
in on Nice. First they began to come at the end of the eighteenth
century because Dr Tobias Smollett had declared the region
good for curing tuberculosis. 'Now we have discovered that the
climate is very bad for TB,' added M. Gouriand. 'The good Dr
Smollett must have killed many, many Englishmen – but that's
another story.' Second, during and after the French Revolution
and during the Napoleonic Wars the British refused to holiday
in France, but of course Nice then belonged to the Kingdom of
Sardinia, and was not French.

As for the Russians, when Russia lost the Crimean War in
1857, the fleet of the Tsarina was in Mediterranean waters.
The Dardanelle Straits were blocked. So the Tsarina made an
arrangement with the King of Sardinia whereby she rented the
bay of Villefranche so that her fleet could hibernate. She then
visited Nice, followed by most of the Russian aristocracy. Nice,
like Cannes, boasts a Russian Orthodox church, an onion-
domed, spiky and colourful building designed by the architect
Preobrazhensky between 1903 and 1912. Inside it is a gilded
bronze iconostasis, one of many testimonies to the wealth and
piety of Tsar Nicholas II and the long-gone Russian aristocracy
who sojourned here. Here also hang numerous icons, some of
them exceedingly ancient.

M. Gouriand also tells a good tale about Queen Victoria.
'Between 1895 and 1899, when she used to stay at the Hotel
Régina, she would go around Nice in a little carriage pulled
by a donkey called Jacko, preceded by a servant who would
cry, "La reine passe." Just one person with Queen Victoria!
The most powerful sovereign in the world! Extraordinary!' He
slyly adds, 'And you should see our heads of state now.' As a
bonne-bouche M. Gouriand pointed out that Victoria was not
the only reigning sovereign to spend the winter season in Nice.
'Here were the Kings of Portugal, of Denmark, and several East
European ruling princes as well. As all the power in the world

was concentrated in Europe and all the wealth of the world too, you could say that global politics were determined in Nice during those four months of the winter season.'

We had already eaten in the open air at a restaurant along the pedestrianized rue de France, before walking on to listen to a raucous jazz band entertaining the crowd in the place Magenta. Thus regaled by M. Gouriand, my daughter and I took a bottle of the local red *appellation d'origine Bellet* (for though I am given to the white, she prefers red and I am the weaker of the family), and sat on our balcony overlooking the Bay of Angels until the sun went down.

Nice to Antibes
and the route Napoléon

The prolongation of the promenade des Anglais, Nice, becomes the N98, running along the littoral and shortly reaching Villeneuve-Loubet. In 1934 the luxury hotels, exquisite villages and sparkling blue waters of this coastline seemed to the American novelist F. Scott Fitzgerald the perfect setting for his *Tender is the Night*, a novel in which wealth and incest corrupt human ideals. The region is undoubtedly sybaritic. Palms cool the flushed façade of Fitzgerald's 'large, proud, rose-coloured hotel', which stands before a dazzling beach. 'The hotel and its bright tan prayer rug of a beach were one,' wrote Fitzgerald. 'In the early morning the distant image of Cannes, the pink and cream of old fortifications, the purple Alps that bounded Italy, were cast across the water and lay quivering in the ripples and rings sent up by sea-plants through the clear shallows.' These are among the quintessential images of the Côte d'Azur.

The lure remains, and not solely for the rich and corruptible. Just occasionally mass tourism has cast a shadow over the natural beauty of the land and its villages. At Villeneuve-Loubet, for instance, do not be put off by the long stretch of beach, with its sometimes tatty restaurants and its seemingly endless camp sites and motels, for the ancient town with its fountains and stepped streets lies some three kilometres inland. On the left bank of the River Loup the village of Villeneuve-Loubet occupies a hilltop site protected by a château that has stood here since the twelfth century. Though the best-preserved fortress in the *département* of the Alpes-Maritimes, its present aspect dates from the fifteenth and the nineteenth centuries.

The celebrated chef Auguste Escoffier was born at Villeneuve-Loubet in 1847. Having worked for a Russian grand-duke, he profited from the Franco-Prussian War by becoming head chef of the general staff of the Rhine Army. His subsequent glittering career included stints as chef of the Grand Hotel, Monte-Carlo, a sojourn at the Savoy in London and, the climax of his career, fame as the chef of the Carlton. The man who invented *pêche melba* richly deserved the *légion d'honneur* awarded to him in 1920. Today his birthplace at Villeneuve-Loubet is a museum of culinary art (including some surviving examples of the fragile art of flowers made out of sugar, these by Escoffier himself). The military museum in the centre of the village bored me, though for those fascinated by countless uniforms it no doubt has its charms.

As a holiday resort Villeneuve-Loubet is equipped with seven golf links, numerous camp sites for caravans and tents, and a pebble beach. More immediately evident on the coastline here is a sinuous modern seaside development, the holiday complex of Marina-Baie-des-Anges, where the notion of individual chalets and high-rise flats has been transformed into a work of architectural genius verging on delirium. Initially derided as architectural monstrosities, these immense pyramids were conceived by the architect André Minangoy at the beginning of the 1970s. They are increasingly appreciated by tourists and architects alike.

Rising inland you can see le Haut-de-Cagnes, reached by taking a little flyover and following the signs towards Grasse and Vence. Leaving the coast, you are about to embark on a tour enhanced by the hills and crests of the valleys of the Var and the Loup, and scented by the olives and orange trees growing on their slopes. Le Haut-de-Cagnes is the ancient part of Cagnes-sur-Mer, overlooking the new town from a height of seventy-seven metres. You must penetrate the village on foot.

From 1309 to the Revolution the town belonged to the Grimaldi family, though it was never secure from attacks by the armies of the Holy Roman Emperor, the Piedmontese and the Dutch. Rainier de Grimaldi, admiral-of-the-fleet to King Philip the Fair, built a château here. Crenellated and machicolated, its ancient walls rising above the crumbling white stone houses of le Haut-de-Cagnes conceal an interior which was transformed into a Renaissance palace in the seventeenth century. Today it is a museum, well worth visiting for its collection of modern paintings (among them works by the Hungarian Victor Vasarély, by Van Dongen and by Marc Chagall), for its ancient mill and for its museum dedicated to the olive tree. But the greatest treat is the Renaissance château itself, especially the so-called *salon Carlone*. Apart from a monumental baroque fireplace, the ceiling was painted in the most astonishing *trompe-l'oeil* fashion by the Genoese G.B.Carlone and by Giolio Benso, its supposed Corinthian columns dizzily supporting a painting of the fall of Phaeton. The wildly flailing legs of his leading stallion seem to be hurtling to the ground. Since 1969, from July to September the château has also housed an annual international festival of painting, attracting the finest contemporary artists by offering prestigious prizes.

Cagnes is fond of firework displays, supposedly to evoke the many colours of Renoir's paintings. The town also panders to the vain, its shops devoted to selling contact lenses and slimming recipes. The route climbs up the higgledy-piggledy village, which centres on a fourteenth-century oratory whose medieval frescos were rediscovered only in 1936. A battlemented château, flags flying, dominates the spot. Stone lions guard the staircases up to this château and its art gallery. Visiting any gallery one should, I believe, choose one favourite work of art which, if a choice were offered, would be accepted as a gift. In the Musée du Château of Cagnes my undoubted choice would be a Cubist portrait of Suzy Solidor by Tamara de Lempicka, who lived from 1898 to 1980. Suzy, with vivid red lips and painted fingernails, languidly displays a cone-like breast against a background of oddly sloping city apartments. Who was she? The portrait was painted in 1933, just as Adolf Hitler was about to become dictator of Germany.

I have never visited the alleyways and arcades of Cagnes when anyone seemed awake here, save for women selling fresh gladioli and the proprietors of the tiny restaurants. Maybe I was fortunate at arriving during the time of the siesta, when even the dogs were asleep. Flowery houses, vine-clad walls and cobbled, sometimes vaulted streets add to the charm of this village. Women also sell gladioli in the street that rises from the oratory to the château, and on a wall a plaque declares that the Hungarian poet Attila József (1905–37) spent the summer of 1927 here. This was not the last major event to effect Cagnes, for in 1936 some early sixteenth-century frescos depicting scenes from the life of the Virgin Mary were discovered in its fourteenth-century oratory of Notre-Dame-de-Protection.

The parish church of Saint-Pierre is an early Gothic building enlarged in the sixteenth century and given a new belfry and campanile in the eighteenth. In an olive grove just outside the modern town of Cagnes-Ville is les Colettes, the house where Auguste Renoir stayed from 1895. Today it is a museum devoted to his memory, with a reproduction of his studio, his old wheelchair, his easel, and even some of his clothing – though, alas, few of his paintings.

A steep and awkward drive from Cagnes reaches Saint-Paul-de-Vence, with stunning views of the hill town appearing before you reach it. You are welcomed into the town by a cannon, a double gateway with a portcullis and more cobbled streets. Amateur painters gather round a magnificent fountain in which a massive urn seems to leak the water. Commercialism is more rife here, I think, than at Cagnes, with boutiques selling T-shirts stamped with Gauguin prints as well as jewellery, pottery, paintings and perfumes. Tourists pack its narrow streets. Even so, the arches of the town satisfactorily crumble, and crumbling retired Frenchmen play *pétanque* under the plane trees of the place du Général-de-Gaulle. In 1988 I heard some Germans here indulging in the perennial argument of whether one lives to work or works to live. Heedless, an Alsatian sheepdog slept in the shade of a well beside the ramparts, with their enticing view of distant peaks.

King François I ordered the fortifying of Saint-Paul-de-Vence, but in spite of these and a thirteenth-century defensive tower the spot scarcely seems a fortress. Beginning with a fountain, the narrow and pedestrianized Grand'Rue, flanked by seventeenth- and eighteenth-century façades, rises from the porte Royale and then descends to the porte Sud. Other stepped streets have such cheeky names as the montée du Casse-Cou. The montée de l'Église rises from a junction known as les Quatre Coins, the only spot in the town where four streets converge.

Walk up the montée de l'Église to find a Romanesque-Gothic

parish church dating from the thirteenth century, whose belfry
and vaulted nave were rebuilt in 1740. Sumptuous seventeenth-
century woodwork and paintings grace the interior. One of the
richest crannies of the church is the chapel of St Clement, paid
for by Bishop Pierre-Jean de Bernardi around 1685. A canon of
St Peter's, Rome, as well as Bishop of Saint-Paul-de-Vence, he had
his chapel decorated with a copy of the 'Virgin between St Charles
and St Ignatius', which Carlo Maratta had recently painted for the
church of Santa Maria in Vallicella, Rome. The subtle difference
is that the bishop substituted for the portrait of St Ignatius that
of his own patron, St John.

Beyond the parish church stands the chapel of the White Penitents, nowadays serving as an art gallery. Saint-Paul-de-Vence is
also the home of a celebrated modern arts centre, the Maeght
Foundation, created in 1964 by the Catalan architect José Louis
Sert for Aimé and Marguerite Maeght. Sert's work and the
materials he used respect the environment of this foundation,
which houses an extensive library of books on modern art as
well as work by Braque, Kandinsky, Bonnard, Giacometti and
their contemporaries.

From here the forest road climbs higher and higher to the
modern outskirts of Vence, which soon give way to an ancient
gateway, fortifications and bustling medieval streets filled with
tourist shops as well as Renaissance and classical fountains. The
town rises oval-shaped from its walls. A modern statue of the lady
of Vence by Ritchie stands in the place Clemenceau opposite the
town hall (and is an insult to womankind, said my daughter).
Trees grow out of the cathedral tower, and its yellow and green
eighteenth-century doorway admits you to admire a mosaic of
1979 by Marc Chagall depicting Moses in the bulrushes. Inside
too are a Roman sarcophagus and an eighteenth-century vestment
chest. Under the seats of the fifteenth-century choir stalls, carved
by Jacques Bellot of Grasse, are some pleasing Gothic miseri-
cords. As I stood inside this partly Romanesque cathedral its
bells began to jangle, so I retreated into the town, which has
a satisfying number of eating places shaded by awnings in little
squares.

Vence is where a weary D.H.Lawrence – another victim of
tuberculosis – died in March 1930, two years after com-
pleting *Lady Chatterley's Lover*. After his death his ally Richard

Aldington found among his literary remains one of his very last, fragmentary poems, part of which runs:

> My soul has had a long, hard day
> she is tired,
> she is seeking her oblivion!

The poem was to be called 'The Ship of Death', and Aldington commented, 'He was too weary, he could not find strength to build his ship of death and at the same time to build the whole song of it.'

Lawrence's 'Ship of Death' begins:

> Now it is autumn and the falling fruit
> and the long journey towards oblivion.

He could have been describing the luscious autumns of Provence, 'The apples falling like great drops of dew to bruise themselves and exit from themselves.' Distressed not solely by sickness but also by the prosecution for obscenity of his paintings and *Lady Chatterley's Lover*, and in these last days having, as he put it, 'been defeated and dragged down by pain and worsted by the evil world-soul', Lawrence also insisted in one of these poems:

> But still I know that life is for delight
> and for bliss
> as now when the tiny wavelets of the sea
> tip the morning light on edge, and spill it with delight . . .

Is this a reference to the littoral near which he spent his final days? At Vence a similar life-enhancing delight is to be discovered in the Dominican Chapel of the Rosary on the route de Saint-Jeannet. Henri Matisse spent the last years of his own life here, near the villa 'Claude-Bourdet' of his friend Marc Chagall, and when this simple chapel was built in 1947 he began to decorate it with fluid lines representing the Virgin and child and St Dominic himself. Sunlight through stained glass warms the delicate designs. The chapel was consecrated by the Bishop of Nice in 1951, and three years later Matisse was dead.

Five kilometres west from Vence along the D2210 is Tourrette-sur-Loup, *en route* to which you pass a château-museum of perfumes and liqueurs. Attracted by the placard that announces a *restaurant des arômes* attached to the château-museum, I paid it a visit. Set up in a former abbey, it courteously labels its exhibits in English, French, Italian and German. The history of perfume from Biblical Frankincense to eau-de-Cologne and Miss Dior – a complete genealogy of artificial scents – is related. Ancient stills, flower presses and cauldrons mingle with exhibitions of plum tree roots, sage rose, jasmines and the various soaps of yesteryear, this whole farrago of human vanity exhibited in the cellars of long-dead monks, who once were dedicated to the suppression of self-love. The monastery has been, I must add, extremely well restored, decorated in the late 1980s by sharply defined blue, red and yellow stained glass by Maurice Lavoillote. Fake icons are on sale, a genuine font of 1578 on display; and my delight in the terraced gardens with their ornamental trees, fountains and statuettes almost made me feel guilty about not having bought any perfume. The washrooms of the *restaurant des arômes* proffer different kinds of soap, apparently related to the signs of the zodiac, and since I was born under the sign of Pisces, with Pisces soap I washed my hands.

Tourrette-sur-Loup, rising on a rocky spur in an amphitheatre of hills and in a region famed for its violets, is clearly a town devoted to *pétanque*, the pitches properly laid out under double rows of trees, walled, sanded and provided with benches for the spectators. Set among pink-walled houses with white shutters, its church is frescoed with the life of St Felicity and her seven children. Refusing to make sacrifices to idols, this exemplary Christian begged her children to follow her example. They did. Denounced before judges, all were sentenced to death. Felicity was doubly tortured by having to watch her children killed first. Her skull is on view here, surrounded by reliquary busts. A triptych inside this church was certainly painted at Nice in the fifteenth century, perhaps by Louis Bréa himself.

The town derives its name from three medieval towers that still survive from its fortifications. Today grey-walled houses have replaced the ramparts, some of these homes peering over a sheer drop into the valley. Through the medieval gateways under the towers you walk along a tracery of equally ancient, cobbled streets, with workshops and panoramic views of terraced hillsides. Beams and lintels hold up walls set with ivy, fuchsias and vines. Where steps rise to the doorways, they bear pots of begonias. The town possesses but one church, the sixteenth-century Saint-Grégoire-le-Grand, behind whose high altar are the remains of an altar dating from the first century AD and deriving from a temple to Mercury. The town hall is a fifteenth-century château, considerably altered in the eighteenth century. Since it is also the home of an arts and crafts museum, you easily gain access to its fifteenth-century staircase and Louis XIII banisters.

Twisting its way panoramically to the hamlet of Pont-sur-Loup, the D2210 here turns south and reaches the perched village of le Bar-sur-Loup. Le Bar is set on a conical hill among orange groves, and I find it hard to believe that this village was once an important stronghold in the fiefdom of the Marquises of Grasse. Yet its site dominates the chief pass on the way to the plain. A huge thirteenth-century tower is topped by a church set at the summit of the rocky peak, down which the houses of le Bar tumble. Then a fourteenth-century château was built at le Bar, its round corner towers still defensive, though within a couple of centuries it became celebrated for the *savants* who revelled here.

Pillaged at the time of the Revolution, and then sold as national property, the château has now been rescued from dereliction. In front of it stands the Gothic parish church of Saint-Jacques-le-Majeur, which contains a lavish fifteenth-century reredos painted by Louis Bréa. The doorways were sculpted by the same Jacques Bellot who carved the stalls in the cathedral of Vence. Look out too for the 'Danse Macabre', where dancing men and women are depicted carrying devils on their heads, while skeleton archers transfix them with their arrows. Other demons dip the damned into the jaws of a fearsome dragon. A text accompanies the dance, but being in Provençal I failed to understand it all.

Wind further south to find the white walls and red pantiles of Magagnosc, with its hotels and restaurants. Four hundred metres above sea-level, Magagnosc has an eighteenth-century church, built by Italians and dedicated to St Laurent. Surrounding the church, the twisting streets of the medieval quarter are dotted with ancient houses, and opposite the church stands a sixteenth-century Penitents' chapel. Turn east at the village and the road will take you through wooded hills dotted by superb properties by way of Roquefort-les-Pins back to Villeneuve-Loubet.

Ten kilometres separate Villeneuve-Loubet-Plage from Antibes. On the way you should turn right at la Brague to make a short diversion north-west and visit the hill town of Biot, whose name, for some reason, the people of Provence pronounce hitting the final 't'. Roman and medieval ramparts, incorporating two powerful sixteenth-century gateways (the porte des Tines and the porte du Migrainier) still guard the sloping streets and flaking walls of the town. The clays of the limestone peak on which it stands have generated a thriving modern ceramics industry, which in turn has attracted glassmakers along with other artists and craftsmen.

In the fourteenth century the Black Death decimated the population of Biot, and the villagers that survived were no match for the bandits, who in 1387 drove them out of their homes. Only in 1460 was Biot repopulated, when the Bishop of Grasse brought four dozen families from Genoa to the village. Roi René favoured Biot, ordering the Knights of Malta to protect its citizens, and a couple of Maltese crosses still figure prominently in the seventeenth-century mosaics of the courtyard fronting the church of Sainte-Marie-Madeleine.

This fifteenth-century church, with a west porch dated 1536 and closed by seventeenth-century doors, stands on the site of an earlier Romanesque building and rises beside an arcaded square, some of whose arches date as far back as the twelfth century. Over the doorway a terracotta statue of Mary Magdalene dates from 1638. Inside the church is a painting by Jean Canavesio depicting Jesus being viciously mocked, and a more homely painting, the Virgin Mary with the rosary, by Louis Bréa. The pillars of the apse are almost certainly Roman.

Four kilometres away, built on the side of a pine-covered hill, is a museum designed in 1959 by a Nice architect named André Svetchnine and devoted to the works of the Cubist painter Fernand Léger. At the end of his life Léger planned to make Biot his home. In 1955 he bought a property here, and died fifteen days later. His widow Nadia gave the gallery no fewer than 347 of his works, insisting that Svetchnine incorporate in the gallery a vast mosaic created by her husband for the Olympic stadium in Hanover and an almost equally monumental stained-glass window, made in Lausanne to his designs. Inside the museum you can trace Léger's evolution from his earliest drawings of 1904 to the 'Birds against a yellow background' on which he was working at the time of his death.

If you are sated with art, try Biot's eighteen-hole golf course, or else visit Marineland four kilometres north of Antibes, where acrobatic dolphins are the star attraction of Europe's most important marine park. Friendly penguins, appealing seals, the sea-lions and the massive sea-elephants seem happy enough, and in any case the youngsters visiting Marineland soon tire of them and instead plunge down the aqua-splash into their own swimming pools.

Like Villeneuve-Loubet, Antibes – whose strenuous holiday-makers paraglide on the pebble beach, which merges into sand – seems initially slightly repelling. Its promenade is disfigured by flashy clothes shops and redeemed only by the sight of Vauban's fortress, whose white stones contrast with clipped grass, gay flowers and parasol pines. Closer inspection of the modern town reveals some luxurious *belle-époque* villas and luxuriant gardens. Yet, save for the delights of its beaches and the gentle surf of the sea, the inland city is far more rewarding.

Greeks lived here six centuries before the birth of Jesus, dubbing the spot Antipolis. Barbarian invasions ruined the settlement, and Antibes began to revive only with the establishment of a bishopric. When the bishops took the wrong side during the Avignon schism, Pope Clement VII confiscated their benefices and goods in 1385, handing the city over to the Grimaldi family. The Grimaldis ceded Antibes to King Henri IV in 1608.

As a frontier town between France and Savoy, *vieil* Antibes was once defended merely by a square tower, built in 1575 on the orders of Henri II. Exactly a hundred years later Vauban transformed this tower into one of his customary star-shaped fortresses, though he respected a twelfth-century bastion enough to retain the venerable pile. There is much else to see here. Part of this bastion, Fort Saint-André, is a Greek, Roman and Etruscan archaeological museum. And there is yet more to see dating from antiquity at Antibes. Remnants of Roman walls and gateways once surrounded the city, though these were partly destroyed in 1894 as Antibes expanded, and the old city now spills outside those that remain.

The fortified, crenellated château, built as a stronghold by the Grimaldi family and later rebuilt to include a magnificent eighteenth-century staircase, is now a Picasso museum. In 1928 the citizens of Antibes had transformed their château into a local history museum; in 1946 the Mayor of Antibes was wise enough to lend part of the place to Pablo Picasso. Picasso worked here from July to December and in gratitude left the city a rich collection of his works (175 in all), many of them created during that period. Also on display here are paintings by the Russian abstract painter Nicholas de Staël. In the avenue Amiral-de-Grasse you can see the house from whose window he leapt to commit suicide in 1955. The terrace of the château has been set out as a garden of modern sculptures.

Close by the château the former cathedral of the Immaculée-Conception, built on the site of a pagan temple to Diana, has a Romanesque transept, a classical façade with splendidly carved doorways of 1710, and a retable of the Madonna with a rosary, painted by Louis Bréa in 1515. Each July it houses a festival of sacred art, while the rest of the town is celebrating a jazz festival and the ancient fortress is the venue of a festival of theatre.

Not to be missed is the city's flower market, for Antibes is the centre of France's rose industry and also cultivates gladioli, tulips and carnations. A daily Provençal market is installed in the cours Masséna, just west of the château and the former cathedral, with a bric-à-brac market on Thursdays and Saturdays in the neighbouring place Audiberti. The daily market spills out along the rue Georges-Clemenceau, where you discover the white façade of the classical town hall of 1828.

To the south of Antibes the cap d'Antibes pokes its finger into the Mediterranean to provide shelter for the golfe de Juan, with its popular bathing beaches, little shops, palms and plane trees. Two particular delights of this peninsula are the 103-metre-high lighthouse, built in 1837, which is open to visitors, and the remarkable collection of Australian, South African and tropical plants of the Thuret garden. The lido is sandy, and parking by the beach outside Juan-les-Pins is free. In the warm, early-evening sun, pigeons flutter by the bathers and sunbathers, the birds tame and searching for food. We lay in the sun near two mischievous boys and their mother. When she went to sleep, the boys built a mound, shaped like one of them. He hid, his brother woke their *maman* and, imagining that one of her sons was buried in the sand, cried, 'Où est ton frère?', desperately burrowing down to where his head might be.

Just before the lido beach at Golfe-Juan, on the avénue de la Gare off the promenade, a notice proclaims, 'Ici commence la route Napoléon.' On Sunday, 26 February 1815, Bonaparte had sailed from exile in Elba, making sure that his valet Marchand had packed a tricolour cockade with which to replace the Elban emblem on his black beaver hat. By the afternoon of the following Tuesday the crew of his ship *Inconstant* had caught sight of the snow-covered peaks of the Alpes-Maritimes. On Wednesday morning Napoleon ordered his men to run up the tricolour flag. Troops disembarked to secure Antibes (an attempt which failed, for the governor imprisoned a detachment of soldiers and closed the town gates). Shortly after four o'clock in the afternoon Napoleon himself was rowed ashore, walking up the beach to bivouac with his troops in an olive grove. He was nearly 1,000 kilometres from Paris.

Napoleon planned to march his men fifty kilometres a day. (It is, of course, easier to drive, and the *route Napoléon* passes through some of the most delightful towns in Provence.) Once the moon had risen, the Emperor led his men towards Cannes, joining an advance guard that was bivouacking there on the beach in front of the church of Notre-Dame-de-Bon-Voyage. Then they marched north-west through le Cannet towards Grasse.

Since you are not planning to reach Paris, I suggest before driving through le Cannet a 2-kilometre diversion north of Golfe-Juan to Vallauris. Vallauris means 'golden valley', and the first settlement here was a thirteenth-century priory founded by the monks of Lérins. They built a fortress to protect their priory, and Raymond of Turenne razed it in 1568. A new town was laid out in a grid pattern in the sixteenth century for Italian immigrants, who spotted that the local clay was ideal for making pottery. Today 200 or so artisans have come together to make Vallauris an international centre for pottery and ceramics, and the village has a museum of ceramics and contemporary art. Here too is the national Pablo Picasso museum, for the artist himself had spent two years making pottery here. I think Picasso's repulsive statue of a man carrying a sheep, which stands in the place Paul-Isnard at Vallauris, is almost enough to deter anyone from visiting his museum, which is housed not far away in part of the Romanesque priory of 1227. Next to the priory rises Vallauris's town hall, which was built in 1867. In the same square as Picasso's shepherd rises the baroque church of Saint-Martin, with a square Romanesque tower.

From le Cannet the route to Grasse passes Mougins, another exquisite village haunted by Picasso, who died here in 1973. His spirit lives on in the exhibition of his photographs permanently on display in the photographic museum of Mougins. In the middle of the town hall square is a 100-year-old elm tree and a late-nineteenth-century fountain, on which stands a bronze lady. Picturesque old streets radiate from the centre of the town, surrounded by remains of the fortifications and a couple of defensive gateways. Beyond them are several sumptuous modern secondary homes, set among fields of roses and olives. Once Romanesque, the church of Saint-Jacques-le-Majeur was restored in the fifteenth century and a new aisle was added in the nineteenth.

The mighty seventeenth-century chapel of Notre-Dame-de-Vie rises on a hill to the south-east of Mougins, not far from Picasso's last home, where, seduced by the olives and cypresses, the view of Mougins and the surrounding countryside, his widow Jacqueline continued to live in the same farmhouse until her own death in 1986. The chapel itself, set on an esplanade of cypresses and entered by an arcaded porch, is yet another in Provence to which stillborn babies would be brought, under the illusion that for a brief moment they could be restored to life for baptism – a practice forbidden by the Bishop of Grasse in 1730. The environs of Mougins are also enlivened by an automobile museum, set up in 1984 with some 200 classic vehicles.

Through a rolling countryside of olive groves, market gardens and fields of jasmine and roses, the N85 runs north-west from Mougins by way of Mouans-Sartoux to Grasse. The holiday village of Mouans has a classical church in the form of a Latin cross and a nineteenth-century château – a fierce restoration of a triangular bastion built in the sixteenth century. Its narrow streets, with houses dating from the seventeenth to the eighteenth centuries, are set out in a chequerboard pattern.

Tumbling down a mountain, Grasse overlooks a fertile countryside and was inevitably coveted by numerous would-be overlords. The citizens managed to survive as an independent republic from the twelfth century, enclosing their city within walls in 1323 and further fortifying its boundaries half a century later. Skins imported from the Levant fostered its tanners, who treated them with substances derived from the myrtle trees growing abundantly around the town. Perceiving that the Medici had inaugurated the foppish habit of wearing perfumed gloves, the tanners of Grasse set about supplying them, thus inaugurating the perfume trade that made the city famous and prosperous.

As Grasse's population grew, the medieval houses in its narrow streets rose in the seventeenth and eighteenth centuries by six and seven storeys. From the eighteenth century the bourgeoisie built themselves luxurious country residences outside and inside the town. The museum of the art and history of Provence at no. 2 rue Mirabeau is housed in one of these bourgeois homes, the former Hôtel de Clapiers-Cabris of 1774. As nineteenth-century Grasse became the world's capital of perfume, the town exploded outside its walls and soon was making yet more money as a fashionable health resort. Today Grasse is a centre for winter sports, and all year round it entertains holidaymakers with an aeroclub, hunting, a sports stadium and some extrememly well set-out camp sites.

Galimard, Molinard and Fragonard are the three world-renowned perfumeries of Grasse. The last is named, of course, after the painter Jean-Honoré Fragonard, who was born here in 1732, studied under François Boucher and gained renown as a delicate and flattering recorder of the recreations of the French court and aristocracy. He painted a bucolic countryside of eighteenth-century elegance. A plaque at no. 23 rue Tracastel notes his birthplace, and Emma-Jane and I parked just above a square adorned with his periwigged statue. A seventeenth-century villa with a sculpted doorway in the boulevard Fragonard, though dubbed the Musée Fragonard, contains but one early self-portrait by the artist. This was his cousin's home, and reproductions of three panels on the theme of the pursuit of love (the originals now in the Frick Collection, New York) hang on its walls. Mme du Barry had commissioned them in 1770, but rejected the finished works as too playfully rococo, so Fragonard brought them back home. The villa's staircase is delicately decorated with *trompe-l'oeil* wall-paintings by the artist's son.

We walked down to square le Clavecin, where following a

Revolutionary tribunal of 1794–5 thirty citizens of Grasse were guillotined. Grasse had become the seat of the Revolutionary tribunal of the Var in 1793, contrary, it seems, to the wishes of most of its citizens. When some of the town's treasures were sold, instead of being demolished as happened elsewhere, they were kept intact by the ordinary folk, who simply waited for the terror to end.

Nearby at no. 8 place du Cours is the town's museum of perfume, housed in a shocking-pink, eighteenth-century balconied villa. Although I would not describe the admission charge as exorbitant (for after all the collection does illustrate 4,000 years of perfume), I none the less prefer the Fragonard perfumery at no. 20 boulevard Fragonard, where the trip around the factory is free. You need to visit such a museum with a companion, so as to spray on each other's arms or behind each other's ears the various scents on offer. Mimosa pleased us most, with carnation running a close second. In 1990 the museum began mounting occasional exhibitions of contemporary art, the first one dedicated to the theme of flowers – a motif intimately connected with the perfume industry.

Columns and fountains, narrow streets, alleyways, courtyards, trees and pots of flowers, homely shops, sculpted doorways, a sixteenth-century clock tower, arcaded squares and the occasional waterfall help to make Grasse one of the finest urban ensembles of the Côte d'Azur. A daily market is held in the arcaded place des Aires. The first time I visited the town the simple, strong Romanesque cathedral of Notre-Dame-du-Puy added more magic to the day by blessing a couple of weddings. One bride worked in the tourist information office, so I had already met the bridesmaids and retainers when I had called the previous day to seek their help. Inside the cathedral jewelled vestments and ecclesiastical treasures are on display. The massive pitted pillars are held together with iron bands, and from them rise thick groined vaults. (The scorching on these pillars dates from a fire of 1795.)

A Rubens crucifixion belonging to the cathedral was once matched by two others executed by the same masterly hand, one a 'Deposition', the other depicting Christ crowned with thorns. Today the 'Deposition' hanging here is a copy, for the original was allowed to deteriorate so scandalously as to become unrecognizable. All three originals were painted in 1602, when the 80-year-old artist was working in Rome. They were bought by a citizen of Grasse in 1827. The cathedral also shelters a Gothic-framed altarpiece of St Honorat by Louis Bréa, a classical chapel with *trompe-l'oeil* paintings, and in the chapel of the Holy Sacrament a rare religious painting by Fragonard, the 'Washing of the Disciples' Feet'.

If you leave the cathedral by its thirteenth-century north doorway you discover the former episcopal palace, built in the eleventh and twelfth centuries and now the town hall (where, according to French law, marriages must be celebrated before the bride, groom and merrymakers move to the cathedral next door). More merrymaking centres around the annual rose festival, which takes place in May, and the August jasmine festival, which is marked by decorated floral floats gliding down the streets and the election of an annual jasmine queen.

For a taste of medieval Grasse, take the narrow rue Mougins-Roquefort north-west from the cathedral and town hall, turn right into the winding rue Rêpitrel and then left again along the equally picturesque rue Rêve-Vieille. To the left across the rue Marcel Journet you discover the rue de l'Oratoire, along which rises the 1662 church of l'Oratoire. A piquant Gothic element was added to this classical building during the nineteenth-century restorations, when the architects added a fourteenth-century doorway and window brought from a former Cordeliers convent.

Rue de l'Oratoire continues to meet the rue des Quatre-Coins, where a left turn will bring you to the exquisite place aux Aires, home of Grasse's flower market. Laid out in the fifteenth century, the arcades of this square are some 200 years younger. The clock dates from 1802, and the fountain was created here in 1821.

By 1815 the medieval spirit of independence had waned in Grasse. The mayor was no republican and therefore not inclined to welcome Napoleon Bonaparte, but since there were only five muskets in the town, he offered no opposition to the approaching force of 4,000 men and speedily made his escape, hoping in vain to find an army from Antibes pursuing the emperor. Napoleon and his men rested from eight in the morning till noon on the plateau of Roquevignon outside the town.

In 1809 Napoleon had ordered a new road to be constructed between Grasse and Sisteron. To his dismay he discovered in

1815 that it had never been built. The available route could take neither his cannons nor Pauline's carriage, which had to be abandoned while the troops traversed a mountain track on foot, with mules carrying their baggage. Today the N85 crosses the 782-metre-high col de Pilon, which he and his men negotiated by a narrow, snow-covered track, and then drops down eighty metres into Saint-Vallier-de-Thiey. There under an elm tree Napoleon allowed his men to rest, a spot marked by a flamboyant Corinthian column topped with a bust of the emperor. Overlooking the Siagne gorge, Saint-Vallier-de-Thiey centres around its complex parish church, with a humble round apse, a twelfth-century Lombardic belfry, a second nave added in 1555 and a classical seventeenth-century façade. You enter some of its houses here through rare Romanesque doorways. This medieval village is surrounded by a series of rich prehistoric sites, including sepulchres, tumuli and caves.

Circuitously crossing the pas de la Faye (where today you can park and survey a vast panorama), by five o'clock in the afternoon the column led by Napoleon had wound its way to the village of Escragnolles, where the men were allowed a third halt. Here the emperor paused to take by the hand Mme Mireur, the mother of one of his generals who had perished in the Egyptian campaign. Escragnolles has preserved in their original condition some five kilometres of the *route Napoléon*. Even more remarkably, it is still buttressed by prehistoric retaining walls. Once a Roman colony, the village supports two churches, one built in the sixteenth century, the other set beside it, built in the eighteenth century and now the *mairie*. Napoleon's route took him not by the present main road but alongside the early Romanesque chapel of Saint-Martin, which I regret to report has been allowed to fall into ruins.

It was dark by the time Napoleon and his men had climbed through forests of pine and fir trees and over the col de Valferrière to push on across the plain and reach the village of Séranon, which lies 1,060 metres above sea-level. One of the column's mules had drowned in a gully, losing a considerable part of Napoleon's treasure. But at least the troops were fifty kilometres from Cannes at the end of their first day's march. The emperor decided to spend the night at Séranon, he himself sleeping in the Château de Brondet, the home of the Marquis of Gourdon.

Today the old village with its crumbled château and walls rises on a rocky cliff, surrounding a ruined fifteenth-century chapel. Modern Séranon is served by an unloved nineteenth-century church.

Napoleon rose early, and the column set off again. Pausing at le Logis-de-Pin for a bowl of hot soup, Napoleon led his men on through the hamlet of la Garde (today retaining vestiges of a medieval fortress and a Romanesque chapel) to Castellane. His soldiers must have gazed in awe at the gigantic 184-metre-high crag, which rises above the village and bears the early eighteenth-century pilgrimage chapel of Notre-Dame-du-Roc (a chapel originally founded in the ninth century). In 1815 the village was so remote from the rest of the world that when his emissaries arrived and demanded 5,000 rations of meat, bread and wine, no one in Castellane had heard of Napoleon's escape.

Bonaparte himself took lunch at the sub-prefecture, a meal commemorated by an inscription over its lintel. Today the village is as picturesque as it was in 1815 and infinitely livelier, the centre of a tourist industry that includes hiking, fishing, horseback riding and canoeing. Castellane has equipped herself with swimming pools and tennis courts. A fifteenth-century bridge spans the river, while older medieval ramparts, towers and a couple of gateways guard the village. Its parish church of Saint-Victor dates from the late twelfth century and is partly Romanesque, partly Gothic. Undoubtedly the church's finest masterpiece of religious art is a retable of 1724 on the altar of the Blessed Virgin. Another priory survives from the twelfth century.

Castellane is also a major centre for exploring the breathtaking gorges de Verdon, twenty-one kilometres of crevice scooped by the River Verdon out of the limestone plateau. These canyons are even more impressive than the gorges du Tarn and are reckoned by many to be the finest in Europe. The D952 will wind you south-west from here to the spectacular pointe Sublime. From here by dark tunnels you can climb down a footpath to the canyon itself.

For Napoleon's men the terrain was not a delight but a burden. Having secured its provisions at Castellane, the little force marched on for twenty-five kilometres through snow-covered fields and summits by way of Senez to the village of Barrême.

At Senez no one paused to explore the twelfth-century cathedral of Notre-Dame-de-l'Assomption or its Gothic porch. Its majestic nave stretches for thirty-two metres and rises fourteen and a half metres. Hanging on its walls are seven late-seventeenth-century Aubusson tapestries depicting scenes from the Old Testament. An eighth, from Flanders, dates from the end of the sixteenth century. The choir stalls were carved in the seventeenth century.

Passing the seventeenth-century episcopal palace and crossing the seventeenth-century bridge, the force arrived at Barrême by 8 p.m. Bonaparte was content to have accomplished his second leg of fifty kilometres. He slept on a sofa which, in his anxiety (so I have read), he repeatedly slashed with his pocket knife. Today you can speedily reach this summer holiday resort from Nice by means of a railway. Little remains of the village founded before the Romans reached Provence. The parish church was built in 1875, but a twelfth-century chapel dedicated to Notre-Dame-de-la-Miséricorde guards the entrance to Barrême.

At seven o'clock in the morning Napoleon's column set off again to reach Digne-les-Bains. Here the royalist General Loverdo had been ordered to defend the bridge over the River Bléone, but since some of his soldiers were already shouting Bonapartist slogans, he discreetly withdrew to the hills. This town had long been a health resort and spa, with no fewer than eight springs, seven of them hot ones. Its dusky-coloured thirteenth-century cathedral of Notre-Dame-du-Bourg was to inspire the opening chapters of Victor Hugo's *Les Misérables* (and the celebrated tale of the bishop's candlesticks, stolen by Jean Valjean, who was graciously forgiven by the holy prelate). A three-apsed choir and a single nave bespeak the typical Romanesque style of this region, a style modified by the Gothic rose window of the west façade. Inside the cathedral is a Merovingian altar, and you can make out traces of thirteenth-century frescos. Tortuous streets, sixteenth- and seventeenth-century houses and a sixteenth-century clock tower add to its charms.

Since Digne is in effect two towns joined together, the *vieille ville* houses another cathedral, dedicated to St Jerome. Founded in 1490, it was extensively rebuilt in the nineteenth century. In 1979 a geological reserve was created around the town. A couple of swimming pools announce the energetic pursuits offered to tourists at Digne: tennis, hunting, riding, mountaineering, cycling and canoeing among them. The less strenuous fish. As for the abundant lavender grown here, the citizens give thanks for it on the first Sunday of August by holding an annual festival in which flower-bedecked floats traverse the streets.

At Digne-les-Bains Napoleon lunched at the Hôtel du Petit-Paris in the rue du Jeu-de-Paume, taking a couple of hours over his meal before setting out again south-west for Malijaï. Today the hotel is a clinic, readily identified by the inscription commemorating Napoleon's lunch. Reaching Malijaï beside the River Bléone, the emperor spent the night in the eighteenth-century château, sending ahead an officer with forty men to seize the river crossing at Sisteron. He need not have worried. General Loverdo had considered blowing up the bridge over the Durance and prudently changed his mind.

I have never eaten duck with olives at Volonne (on the D4 and the right bank of the Durance), but the following day Napoleon did at the Auberge du Poisson d'Or. Today the inn is a pharmacist's, but it is identified by a Provençal inscription: *ichi lou 5 mars 1815, Napoleon Ier P et P*, the last three initials meaning *passa et pissa*. Volonne's church of Saint-Martin is eleventh-century Romanesque (though restored in 1604 after a fire), and its late-seventeenth-century and splendidly decorated château now serves as the town hall. Another church, Notre-Dame-des-Salles, with a Gothic nave and a Romanesque apse, was built as the chapel of an Augustinian abbey.

No doubt contented with the food of Volonne, the emperor arrived at Sisteron in time to dine at the Hôtel du Bras d'Or in the rue Saunerie. The *route Napoléon* continues from here as far as Paris, which the emperor reached on the Monday of Holy Week, but for us it stops at Sisteron, the gateway from the Dauphiné into Provence. A royalist town, Sisteron did not rally to the emperor, which made little difference to his plans.

Here the Rivers Durance and Buëch slice through the Alpine limestone. The town itself lies on the west bank of the Durance on an outrageously picturesque site at the foot of a massively folded cliff. On top of the cliff rises the splendidly preserved thirteenth-century citadel whose fortifications were strengthened by Vauban in order to command the Durance.

Almost as splendid are the ramparts, with their three fourteenth-century towers and three contemporary gateways.

A maze of stepped and arcaded streets (which are known here as *andrônes*) leads into little squares. The avenue Paul-Arène (named after the writer who collaborated with Alphonse Daudet on the *Lettres de mon moulin* and was then forgotten) tunnels under the citadel and then runs beside the gleaming white, Lombardic cathedral of Notre-Dame-des-Pommiers, built in the twelfth century. On the other side of the Durance stands the former convent of Saint-Dominique. Created by Béatrix of Savoy in 1248, it has preserved its Romanesque belfry. In Sisteron itself a twelfth-century chapel of Saint-Jacques vies in antiquity with the cathedral, and the lavender honey sold on the Wednesday and Saturday markets vies with both in sweetness.

La Provençale
and a few late mimosas

La Provençale is a motorway, officially the A8. Except in cases of urgent necessity, travel writers and leisurely travellers generally steer clear of motorways. *La Provençale* is one of the few exceptions, for several reasons. First, it runs through stupendous countryside, the multicoloured and convoluted rocks of Provence rising on either side. Second, the authorities have taken advantage of the climate of the region to fill its central divide with exotic flowers, camellias, mimosas and roses, so that in summer especially it is set alight with colour.

Finally, on either side of this motorway are conveniently placed treasures of Provence. Many of them have already been described in this book, especially where *la Provençale* runs south-west from Menton to enter the sparse trees, the attractive hillocks and the red and yellow soil of the Estérel massif just before Fayence and Fréjus. A few minutes beyond them, to the left of the motorway, are two spots worth a pause, Puget-sur-Argens and, on the other side of the river, Roquebrune-sur-Argens.

In 990 Puget-sur-Argens was described as the villa on a balcony ('Villa Pogito') and today the town, surrounded by vineyards, still gently rises above the river valley. By the nineteenth century the place was expanding largely because of the silk industry, but its medieval heart, though no longer fortified, is still threaded with narrow, climbing streets whose medieval houses enclose a square splashed by a fountain. The humble Romanesque chapel of Saint-Barthélemy is charming, but no match for the parish church of Saint-Jacques-le-Majeur. Of its triple apse, the centre sanctuary dates from an earlier, fifteenth-century church. Inside Saint-Jacques-le-Majeur is a Roman milestone, for the town lies on what was once the Aurelian Way. The Christians transformed the milestone into a font. An eighteenth-century vaulted gateway, topped by a belfry, is the sole remains of the former walls of the town.

The terrain has changed since Fréjus. On either side there are mountain ranges, though the countryside is flatter and peopled with parasol pines. Take the N7 north-west and then the D7 south to discover Roquebrune-sur-Argens poking stubby fingers into the air. The rocks nearby are gnarled and curled like an old man's hand, and the mighty peaks of le rocher de Roquebrune burst forth out of the undergrowth. Their red-brown colour has given Roquebrune its name. The richly cultivated valleys are watered not only by the Argens but also by its tributaries, the Mourette, the Valette, the Fournel and the gorges of the Blavet. As at Puget-sur-Argens, this is excellent camping country. Roquebrune-sur-Argens is a much bigger town, but it derives from the old village which grew up on a rocky perch after the Saracens had been expelled in 973. Most of its ramparts were destroyed in 1582 during the Wars of Religion, but one tower and a few other vestiges still stand. Tunnelled passageways, arcades, Renaissance houses (and one that belonged to the Knights Templar in 1249) are watched over by a seventeenth-century château.

Again, as at Puget-sur-Argens, you can trace the successive extensions of the parish church, here dedicated to Notre-Dame-et-Saint-Pierre-et-St-Paul. The first chapel on the left was once all that stood here, a simple twelfth-century Romanesque building. A late Gothic church swallowed it up in the sixteenth century. Sixteenth- and seventeenth-century reredoses fill the chapels and the sanctuary, and the crossings are ogivally vaulted.

The Christian religion seems to have taken a strong hold on Roquebrune-sur-Argens and its environs. In the seventeenth century the chapel of Notre-Dame-de-Pitié, built in 1649 on a hillock amid pines and eucalyptus trees, became a centre of pilgrimage. It is one of countless churches of the same dedication that sprang up throughout France after King Louis XIII had dedicated the country to the Virgin of Sorrows in 1638. South-east of the town along the D7 stands the Romanesque chapel of Saint-Pierre, while north-east at Palayson are the ruins of the eleventh-century monastery of St Victor. To the west, set on a tree-shaded slope, is the massive seventeenth-century chapel of Notre-Dame-de-la-Roquette.

Rejoin *la Provenç*ale and drive on west. Soon le Muy is signposted to the right, a town whose name in the *langue d'oc* means marshy. Once again you are in well-watered countryside, this time with the Rivers Nartuby and Endre emptying themselves into the Argens. The fertile soil supports chrysanthemums as well as plums, olives and vines. Le Muy has seen stirring times, especially in 1536 when two of its citizens decided to ambush the Emperor Charles V, planning to hang him. By error they caught and hanged a poet named Garcilaso de la Vega instead, and the emperor made his escape. He grimly promised pardon to the town if it surrendered, then broke his word and hanged his two would-be executioners.

The sole remaining tower from the fortifications that were razed by Henri IV is today called after Charles V, its machicolations as stern as he was in 1536. The parish church of Notre-Dame is equally stern, built in the Gothic style in 1500 and fortified during the troubles of the following century. Although le Muy is a modern town (of some 6,500 inhabitants) and few of its streets are medieval, the ones that have survived are picturesque. Profiting from its stunning position, le Muy has developed as a centre for hiking and horse-riding. It also possesses several well-appointed camp sites.

Instead of returning to the motorway, take the N7 south-west so as to turn right at the D55 and reach les Arcs. A Roman settlement, the spot was the meeting place of Mark Antony and Marcus Aemilius Lepidus, which became a turning point in the career of the former. Antony had been defeated in 43 BC and driven out of Italy into Gaul. Lepidus had a considerable force at his command, and Mark Antony set about gaining his confidence, before taking command of the troops and returning to Rome with seventeen legions and a force of cavalry. The result was that he, Octavian and Lepidus declared themselves triumvirs of the Roman empire, entering into an orgy of plunder and murder. Lepidus eventually became ruler of Africa.

Apart from vestiges of a Roman bridge over the Argens, the chief Roman legacy at les Arcs serves today as an oil mill and is known as the Columbarium. The rest of the old village crams itself on to a rocky perch, dominating the modern village, the whole overseen by a twelfth-century keep and surrounded by the ruins of its medieval château and double rampart. Though broken, the remains of these ramparts are impressive, especially its fortified gateways. Overhanging houses twist around its ancient streets. The mid-nineteenth-century church of Saint-Jean-Baptiste should not put off the visitor. It houses a gilded reredos by Louis Bréa and a fifteenth-century polyptych (with sixteen panels) attributed to Jean de Troyes.

The Château of Sainte-Roseline three and a half kilometres north of les Arcs was once a Carthusian monastery, named after a saint who died in 1325. Her bones lie in a reliquary in the Romanesque monastery chapel which, like the fourteenth-century cloister, has been beautifully restored. Its high altar is sheltered by a gilded early seventeenth-century retable, which enshrines a 'Deposition' painted in 1493. The pulpit and the choir stalls date from 1693. This monastery was deconsecrated at the Revolution and bought as private property, hence its transformation into a château, surrounded by a superb eighteenth-century park with an alleyway of plane trees.

You are now in a region of flatlands, punctuated by occasional rocky hills, with distant ridges far away in the haze to the south. Vidauban lies on the N7 seven kilometres south-west of les Arcs. Its name may well refer to the white vines that grow hereabouts. The spot is well guarded to the north, by the magnificent nineteenth-century Château d'Astros (with an equally magnificent terraced park) and at Astros-le-Vieux by the Bastide de Trois, a thirteenth-century commandery of the Knights Templar rebuilt in the sixteenth century. Vidauban itself has a nineteenth-century parish church and is surrounded by a couple of seventeenth-century chapels.

None of them can vie in evocative splendour with your next stop, the abbey of le Thoronet. Alongside the D17 stand long, powerfully built farmhouses, as the road runs for seven kilometres directly north-west through woodlands to le Thoronet from the

N7 and A8. The pines seem to have come out of Italian paintings. In between the woods are vineyards, with the fields protected by dry-stone walls.

The monastery lies beyond the tumbledown village with its multi-coloured shutters and its seventeenth- and nineteenth-century parish church. The trees begin to assume a curious scarlet-red colour, like the earth itself, the devastating effect of nearby bauxite quarries. These have also despoiled the walls of the monastery itself, one of the three great Cistercian abbeys of Provence. Even this desecration, however, cannot destroy the splendour of this place (though it might well damage the stones irrevocably).

You descend into a simple, barrel-vaulted church with two aisles, a round apse and fantastic acoustics. Not surprisingly, the abbey has been the scene of an August music festival since 1987. Crumbling wall-paintings are bathed in an ethereal low light from the semicircular windows above the altar. Over the vault of the nave rises a little square belfry.

Founded in 1146, the abbey surrounds a Romanesque cloister. Today the abbey belongs to the state, and restoration of this cloister was still in progress when Emma-Jane and I descended into it from the church. An exhibition of the history of monasticism is complemented by another displaying the process of restoration. Monastic cellars house vats and wine presses. I heartily approve of the bilingual notices setting out where you are and the significance of the buildings. I greatly dislike the occasional rumblings from the bauxite quarry as you walk around this holy spot.

The church at the abbey of le Thoronet was built between 1175 and 1230. Beginning in 1210 the monks started building their sacristy and library, which were finished at the same time as the church. So were the chapter house, the monks' warming room and the entrance to the monastery. You are therefore looking at an example of Cistercian architecture which, all of a piece, exemplifies the utter simplicity enjoined on his followers by St Bernard of Cîteaux. Only the cloister garden of 1250 to 1300 and the refectory, built between 1420 and 1425, break this unity. To the south of the complex a tithe-barn houses an oil mill.

Bernard's attacks on luxury were matched only by his invective against those Christians who wished to persecute the Jews.

Austere in every habit, he lived chiefly on coarse bread softened in water. So indifferent was he to drink that one of his companions spotted him imbibing oil instead of water, without noticing the difference. As for womenfolk, he once looked on the face of a beauty and (says the hagiographer Alban Butler) 'immediately reflecting that this was a temptation, ran to a pond, and leaped up to the neck into the water, which was then as cold as ice, to punish himself, and to vanquish the enemy'. One matter he was scrupulous about was personal cleanliness, since in his view dirtiness involved the sin of sloth. But he used to say that, 'Our fathers built their monasteries in damp, unwholesome places, so that the monks might have the uncertainties of life more sensibly before their eyes.' Maybe, therefore, he would not have minded the bauxite disfiguring the Cistercian monastery at le Thoronet; but I do.

La Provençale continues west, towards le Vieux Cannet, which rises ahead on its hill, its medieval (and occasionally Romanesque) houses surrounding a small Romanesque church. Just south of the motorway is le Cannet-des-Maures, whose Romanesque parish church of Saint-Michel dates from the thirteenth century, save for the seventeenth-century belfry. Some ten kilometres south-west is Gonfaron, with a little, tree-shaded central square. Climb its antique streets to the chapel of Saint-Quinis, which was rebuilt in the nineteenth century but seems equally antique.

Around le Cannet-des-Maures are the vast vineyards of the Var, but as you travel further west, trees start taking over the countryside, which begins once more to undulate. Then vineyards become even more frequent, and the road descends into a thickly wooded valley. Exit 4 takes you to Brignoles, its old town fortified, its sixteenth-century Palais des Comptes de Provence (now a regional museum) incorporating a thirteenth-century château. Charles V sacked the town in 1539, after which the hospice of Saint-Jean, with its powerful caryatids, was built in 1542. The parish church of Saint-Sauveur was rebuilt in the same century, preserving its fifteenth-century nave. Both survived a ferocious attack by Huguenots in 1563. In the rue Poissonerie a plaque recalls the massacres of several citizens by these Protestants. The rue des Boucheries is the site of the former ghetto, and a relief depicting the sacrifice of Abraham identifies the former house of the rabbi.

The modern town is well served with equestrian stations, camp sites, gymnasia and sports stadium. Further west from Brignoles the peaks become wilder, almost mountainous. To the south rises the 839-metre-high peak of the mountain of la Loube. You drive on past it towards the impressive sight of the basilica of Sainte-Marie-Madeleine at Saint-Maximin-la-Sainte-Baume. The best has been saved to the last on this tour.

Although the town has lost its ramparts, it remains substantially that built by Charles II of Anjou in the late-thirteenth century. To him we also owe the magnificent basilica, surely the finest Gothic building in Provence. He rebuilt it in 1295 for Dominican monks, and by the time it was finished in 1536 Sainte-Marie-Madeleine had reached a height of nearly 29 metres, was 72.6 metres long and 37.2 metres wide. In its Gallo-Roman crypt repose the bones of Maximin, the first Bishop of Aix-en-Provence, who lived here in the fourth century. Here too is a reliquary said to contain the skull of St Mary Magdalene, hence the basilica's dedication.

Over the centuries this relic ensured that the basilica became one of the major centres of European pilgrimage, attracting to Saint-Maximin-la-Sainte-Baume princes both of the realm and of the Church. In consequence the baroque furnishings of the basilica are astonishingly rich, including ironwork by Peironi, and ninety-four sculpted choir stalls. Their twenty-two medallions, carved by Vincent Funel in 1691, glorify St Dominic and the Dominican order in general. (It comes as no surprise to learn that Funel was a Dominican himself.) Other treasures include a superb classical organ of 1773 designed by Brother Jean-Esprit Isnard, and a retable of 1517 by the Venetian painter Francesco Ronzen. Isnard's organ of 2,981 pipes remains in its original state, unspoiled by later builders. And among the panels of Ronzen's retable is one containing the oldest surviving painting of the papal palace at Avignon.

The Dominicans' cloister and lodgings (including a chapter house and two refectories, one for the monks and one for pilgrims) stand beside the town hall, another former conventual building, which was intended as a hostelry when first conceived in the eighteenth century. Saint-Maximin-la-Sainte-Baume also rejoices in medieval streets, which encompass a fourteenth-century Jewish ghetto (centred on the arcaded houses of the place des Arcades), and a couple of eighteenth-century fountains to match several eighteenth-century houses. Frédéric Mistral's bust is located on the obelisk fountain among the cafés of the place Mirabeau. In the place Martin-Bidouré a seventeenth-century belfry carries a bell cast in 1476. The whole town is a tourists' paradise, and has set itself out to welcome holidaymakers with every possible sporting recreation, as well as with concerts, conferences and exhibitions. It also hosts a daily market.

From here *la Provençale* takes you by way of towns and cities you have already enjoyed, such as Gardanne and Aix-en-Provence. Though its central reservation ceases to be a flame of colours, the scenery remains breathtaking, as the motorway runs beside red cliffs before tunnelling through white rocks and running beside pine-covered crags. This is the countryside of Cézanne. At the hamlet of Coudoux, twenty-three kilometres beyond Aix-en-Provence, is an eighteenth-century church. And here *la Provençale* becomes the *autoroute du Soleil*, which runs north-west towards Salon-de-Provence, Avignon, Orange and Bollène. Its only fault is that at Bollène you leave Provence.

Bibliography

Alpes-de-Haute-Provence, Richesses de France no. 106, J.Delmas & Co., Paris, 1975.

Alpes-Maritimes. Riviera-Côte d'Azur – Principauté de Monaco, Richesses de France no. 91, J.Delmas & Co., Paris, 1972.

Jean-Jacques Antier, *La Côte d'Azur, ombres et lumières*, Éditions France-Empire, Paris, 1972.

Jean Arrouye, *La Provence de Cézanne*, Edisud, Aix-en-Provence, 1982.

Honoré de Balzac, *Mémoires de deux jeunes mariées* in *Oeuvres complètes*, Louis Conard, Paris, 1912.

Pierre Borel, *Côte d'Azur*, Arthaud, Paris, 1968.

Henri Bosco, *Le Mas Théotime*, Alger and Corbeil, Paris, 1946.

——*Le Sanglier*, Nouvelle Revue française, Paris, 1932.

Cyril Connolly, *The Rock Pool*, Obelisk Press, Paris, 1936; Oxford University Press, Oxford, 1981.

J.-P.Coste and P.Coste, *Nous partons pour la Provence*, Presses Universitaires de France, Paris, 1977.

Alphonse Daudet, *Lettres de mon moulin* in *Oeuvres complètes*, Librairie de France, Paris, 1929–31; John Murray, London, 1979.

J.-M.Delettrez, *Le Rhône de Genève à la Méditerranée*, Arthaud, Paris, 1974.

F. Scott Fitzgerald, *Tender is the Night*, Scribners, New York, 1934; Penguin Books, Harmondsworth, 1986.

John Flower, *Provence*, George Philip, London, 1987.

Norman Mackenzie, *The Escape from Elba. The Fall and Flight of Napoleon 1814–1815*, Oxford University Press, Oxford, 1982.

Katherine Mansfield, *The Garden Party and Other Stories*, Constable, London, 1922; Penguin Books, Harmondsworth, 1971.

Merveilleuses Provence Côte d'Azur, Éditions Princesse, Paris, 1987.

Frédéric Mistral, *Mirèio. Pouèmo Prouvençau*, J.Roumanille, Avignon, 1859.

——*Le Poème du Rhône*, Alphonse Lemerre, Paris, 1897.

Marcel Pagnol, *Le Château de ma mère*, Éditions Pastorelly, Monte-Carlo, 1958; John Murray, London, 1973.

——*La Gloire de mon père*, Éditions Pastorelly, Monte-Carlo, 1957; Thomas Nelson, Walton-on-Thames, 1985.

——*Le Temps des secrets*, Éditions Pastorelly, Monte-Carlo, 1960.

David Sweetman, *The Love of Many Things: A Life of Vincent Van Gogh*, John Curtis/Hodder & Stoughton, London, 1990.

Le Vaucluse, Richesses de France no. 56, J.Delmas & Co., Paris, 1963.

Constant Vautravers, *Provence*, Arthaud, Paris, 1974.

Index